Table of Contents

W9-AHB-697

Introduction

Basic Math Skills is based on current NCTM standards and is designed to support any math curriculum that you may be using in your classroom. The standard strands (Number and Operations, Algebra, Geometry, Measurement, and Data Analysis and Probability) and skills within the strand are listed on the overview page for each section of the book. The skill is also shown at the bottom of each reproducible page.

Opportunities to practice the process standards (Problem Solving, Reasoning and Proof, Communication, Connections, and Representations) are also provided as students complete the various types of activities in this resource book.

Basic Math Skills is to be used as a resource providing practice of skills already introduced to students. Any page may be used with an individual child, as homework, with a small group, or by the whole class.

Skill Practice

Each skill is covered in a set of six reproducible pages that include the following:

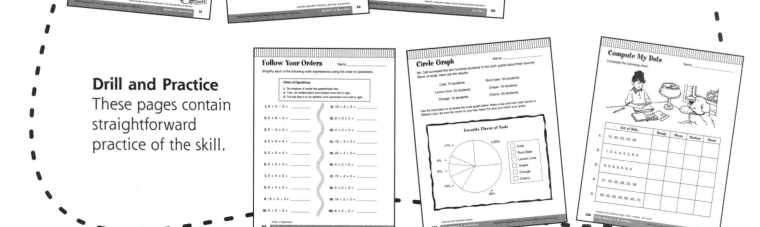

"Fun" Activities
Skills are practiced as students complete riddles, mazes, codes, and other game-oriented activities.

Drill and Practice
These pages contain straightforward practice of the skill.

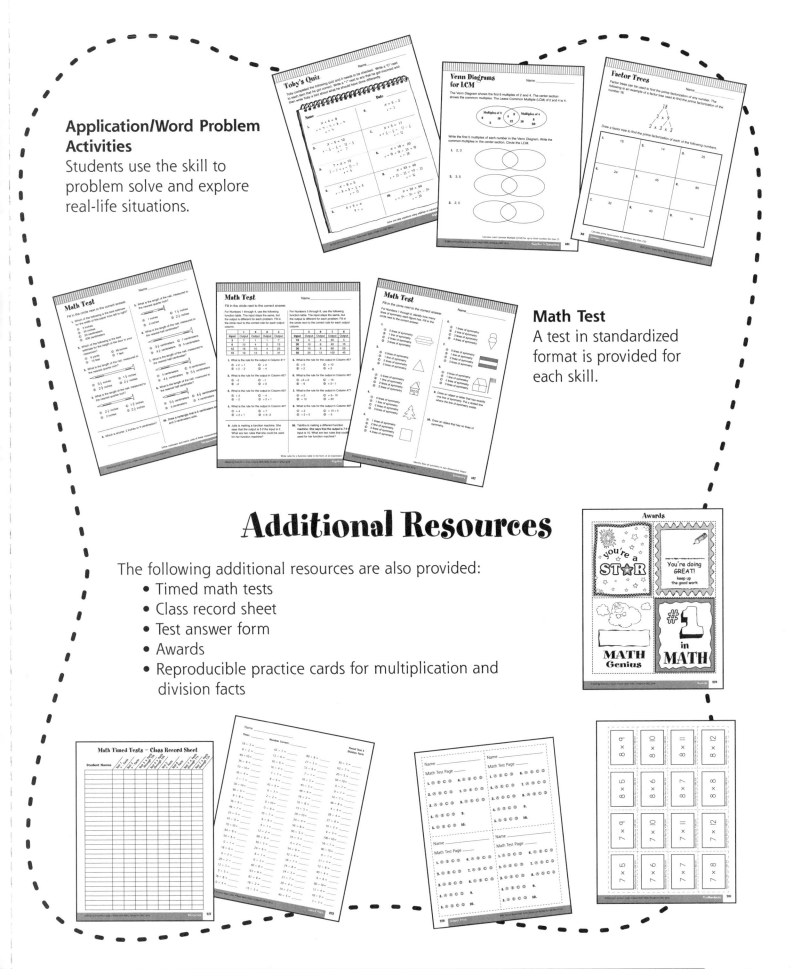

Application/Word Problem Activities

Students use the skill to problem solve and explore real-life situations.

Math Test

A test in standardized format is provided for each skill.

Additional Resources

The following additional resources are also provided:
- Timed math tests
- Class record sheet
- Test answer form
- Awards
- Reproducible practice cards for multiplication and division facts

Number and Operations

Computation with whole numbers

Computation with fractions

Computation with decimals

Percents and their equivalencies

Number theory

EMC 3019 • Basic Math Skills, Grade 6 • ©2003 by Evan-Moor Corp.

Tongue Twister #1

Name _____

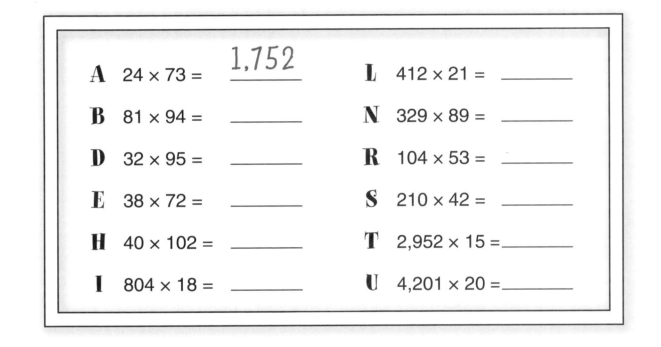

Complete each multiplication problem. Write the corresponding letter on the line above the answer. The letters will spell out a tongue twister. Try to say it quickly three times.

A 24 × 73 = *1,752*

B 81 × 94 = _____

D 32 × 95 = _____

E 38 × 72 = _____

H 40 × 102 = _____

I 804 × 18 = _____

L 412 × 21 = _____

N 329 × 89 = _____

R 104 × 53 = _____

S 210 × 42 = _____

T 2,952 × 15 = _____

U 4,201 × 20 = _____

____   ____   ____   ____   ____   ____   ____   ____   ____
7,614 8,652 84,020 2,736 7,614 14,472 5,512 3,040 8,820

        ____   ____   ____   ____   ____   ____
       14,472 29,281   7,614 8,652 84,020 2,736
                                    A

____   ____   ____   ____   ____   ____   ____   ____   ____
7,614 14,472 5,512 3,040 7,614 1,752 44,280 4,080 8,820

Demonstrate multiplication of whole numbers up to a four-digit number multiplied by a two-digit number

Number & Operations

Riddle

What do you get if you cross a rug with a banana?

To solve the riddle, complete each multiplication problem below. Then write the corresponding letter above each product. The letters will spell out the solution to the riddle.

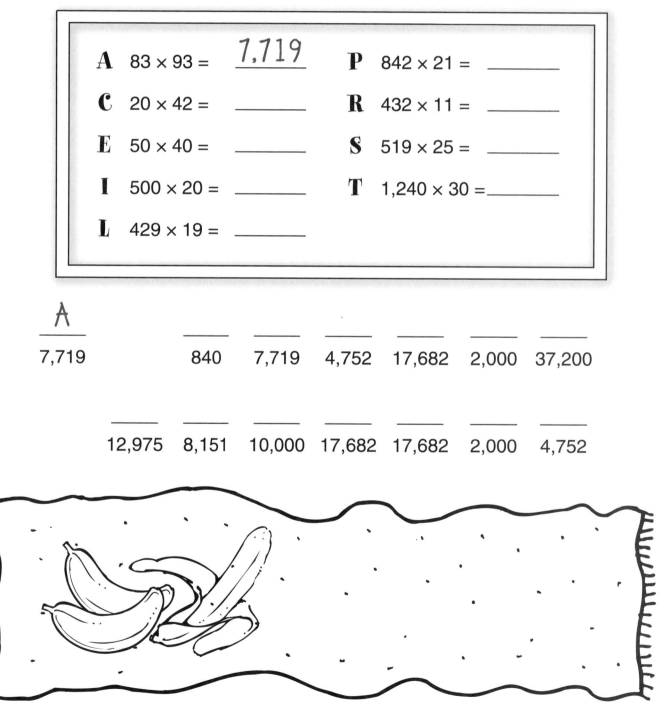

A $83 \times 93 =$ ___7,719___ **P** $842 \times 21 =$ _____

C $20 \times 42 =$ _____ **R** $432 \times 11 =$ _____

E $50 \times 40 =$ _____ **S** $519 \times 25 =$ _____

I $500 \times 20 =$ _____ **T** $1,240 \times 30 =$ _____

L $429 \times 19 =$ _____

A
‾‾‾‾‾
7,719   840   7,719   4,752   17,682   2,000   37,200

12,975   8,151   10,000   17,682   17,682   2,000   4,752

Demonstrate multiplication of whole numbers up to a four-digit number multiplied by a two-digit number

EMC 3019 • Basic Math Skills, Grade 6 • ©2003 by Evan-Moor Corp.

What's the Product?

Name_____

Find the product of each of the following.

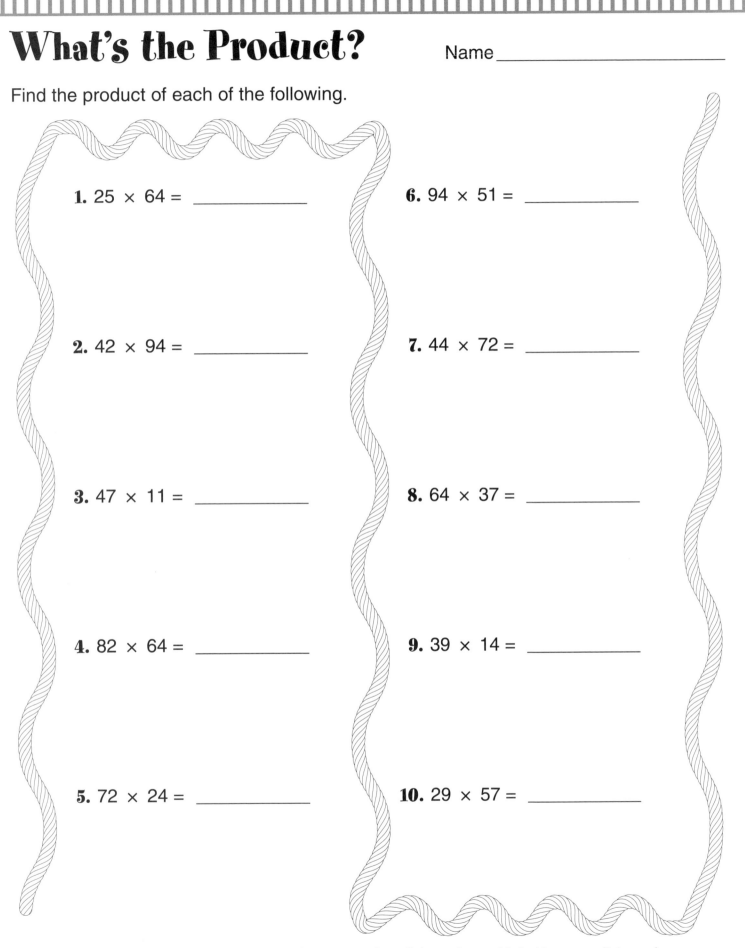

1. 25 × 64 = _____

2. 42 × 94 = _____

3. 47 × 11 = _____

4. 82 × 64 = _____

5. 72 × 24 = _____

6. 94 × 51 = _____

7. 44 × 72 = _____

8. 64 × 37 = _____

9. 39 × 14 = _____

10. 29 × 57 = _____

Demonstrate multiplication of whole numbers up to a four-digit number multiplied by a two-digit number

What's the Product II?

Name _____

Find the product of each of the following.

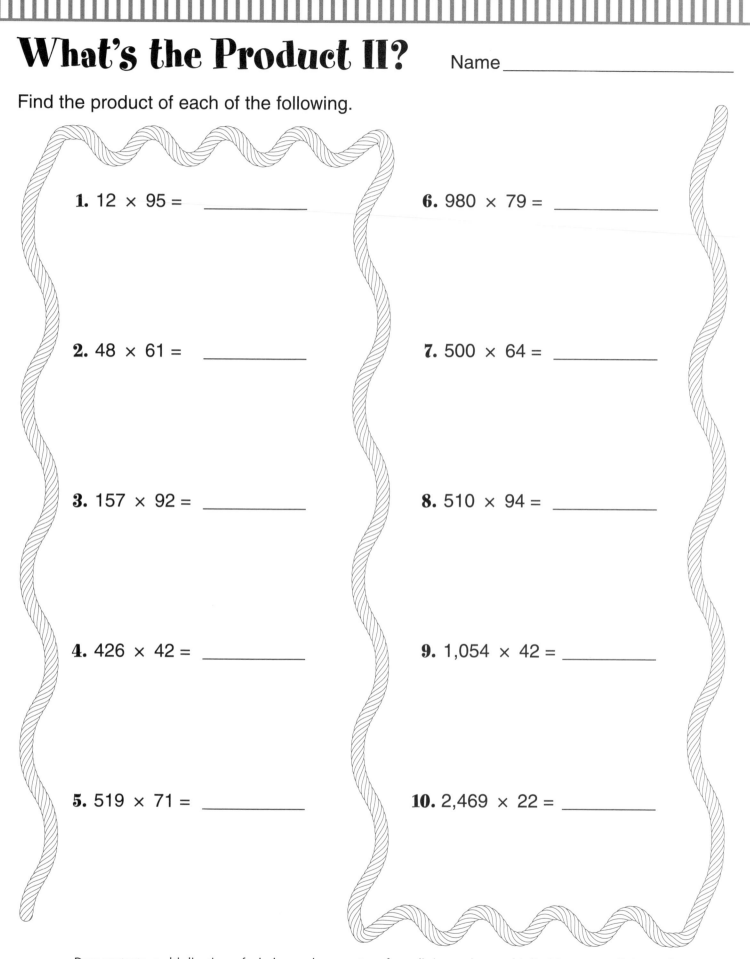

1. 12 × 95 = _____

2. 48 × 61 = _____

3. 157 × 92 = _____

4. 426 × 42 = _____

5. 519 × 71 = _____

6. 980 × 79 = _____

7. 500 × 64 = _____

8. 510 × 94 = _____

9. 1,054 × 42 = _____

10. 2,469 × 22 = _____

Demonstrate multiplication of whole numbers up to a four-digit number multiplied by a two-digit number

EMC 3019 • Basic Math Skills, Grade 6 • ©2003 by Evan-Moor Corp.

Jackson Middle School

Name_____

Solve each problem.

1. At Jackson Middle School, there are 24 classrooms. Each classroom has 35 chairs. How many chairs are in the school?

   _____

2. The school is purchasing new chairs for all its classrooms. If each chair costs $19, what will be the total of the new chairs?

   _____

3. There are 32 teachers at Jackson Middle School. The average teacher has been teaching for 12 years. About how many years have all the teachers been teaching in all?

   _____

4. At Jackson Middle School, there are 22 homeroom classes. In each homeroom class, there are about 27 students. How many students attend Jackson Middle School?

   _____

5. Each of the students bought a school T-shirt for $7.00. How much money was collected for the T-shirts?

   _____

Demonstrate multiplication of whole numbers up to a four-digit number multiplied by a two-digit number

Snack Shop

Name_____

Solve each problem.

1. The students are counting the snacks at the Snack Shop. Tim counts 32 cases of soda. If there are 24 sodas in each case, how many sodas are there?

   _____

2. Shirley counted 30 packages of cupcakes. Each package has one dozen cupcakes. How many cupcakes are there?

   _____

3. Julie counted 15 bags of candy. Each bag has 108 pieces of candy. How many pieces of candy are there?

   _____

4. Ian counted 2 large bags of paper cups and 1 large bag of paper plates. Each large bag has 280 cups or plates. How many cups and plates are there in all?

   _____

5. Of the four students listed above, who counted the largest number of items?

   _____

Demonstrate multiplication of whole numbers up to a four-digit number multiplied by a two-digit number

Math Test

Fill in the circle next to the correct answer.

1. 28 × 19 = _____
   - Ⓐ 280
   - Ⓒ 300
   - Ⓑ 530
   - Ⓓ 532

2. 72 × 40 = _____
   - Ⓐ 288
   - Ⓒ 2,800
   - Ⓑ 2,880
   - Ⓓ 298

3. 16 × 27 = _____
   - Ⓐ 171
   - Ⓒ 432
   - Ⓑ 423
   - Ⓓ 189

4. 942 × 51 = _____
   - Ⓐ 48,042
   - Ⓒ 4,320
   - Ⓑ 5,652
   - Ⓓ 765

5. 754 × 82 = _____
   - Ⓐ 61,828
   - Ⓒ 7,540
   - Ⓑ 61,808
   - Ⓓ 7,828

6. 264 × 41 = _____
   - Ⓐ 1,320
   - Ⓒ 10,824
   - Ⓑ 492
   - Ⓓ 10,560

7. 4,634 × 52 = _____
   - Ⓐ 240,968
   - Ⓒ 230,170
   - Ⓑ 9,268
   - Ⓓ 23,170

8. 1,690 × 80 = _____
   - Ⓐ 13,520
   - Ⓒ 13,500
   - Ⓑ 1,352
   - Ⓓ 135,200

9. Jared stacked 16 boxes of pens. There are 144 pens in each box. How many pens did Jared stack?

   _____

   _____

   _____

10. Write a story problem that would require the student to multiply 12 × 26 to solve the problem.

    _____

    _____

    _____

Demonstrate multiplication of whole numbers up to a four-digit number multiplied by a two-digit number

Tongue Twister #2

Name_____

Complete each division problem. Write the corresponding letter on the line above the answer. The letters will spell out a tongue twister. Try to say it quickly three times.

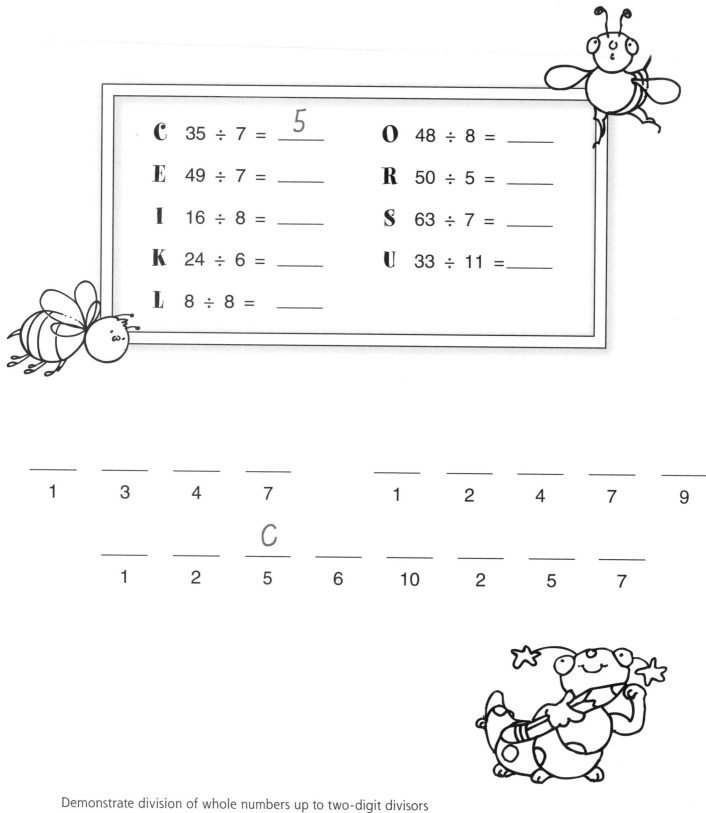

C 35 ÷ 7 = _5_

E 49 ÷ 7 = ____

I 16 ÷ 8 = ____

K 24 ÷ 6 = ____

L 8 ÷ 8 = ____

O 48 ÷ 8 = ____

R 50 ÷ 5 = ____

S 63 ÷ 7 = ____

U 33 ÷ 11 = ____

| __ | __ | __ | __ | | __ | __ | __ | __ | __ |
| 1 | 3 | 4 | 7 | | 1 | 2 | 4 | 7 | 9 |

| __ | __ | _C_ | __ | __ | __ | __ | __ |
| 1 | 2 | 5 | 6 | 10 | 2 | 5 | 7 |

Demonstrate division of whole numbers up to two-digit divisors

Number & Operations   EMC 3019 • Basic Math Skills, Grade 6 • ©2003 by Evan-Moor Corp.

How Do Pigs Say Good-bye?

Name_____

To answer the riddle, draw a straight line between each division problem on the left and its answer on the right. Each line will go through at least one number. Write the corresponding letter on the line above each number. The letters will spell out the solution to the riddle.

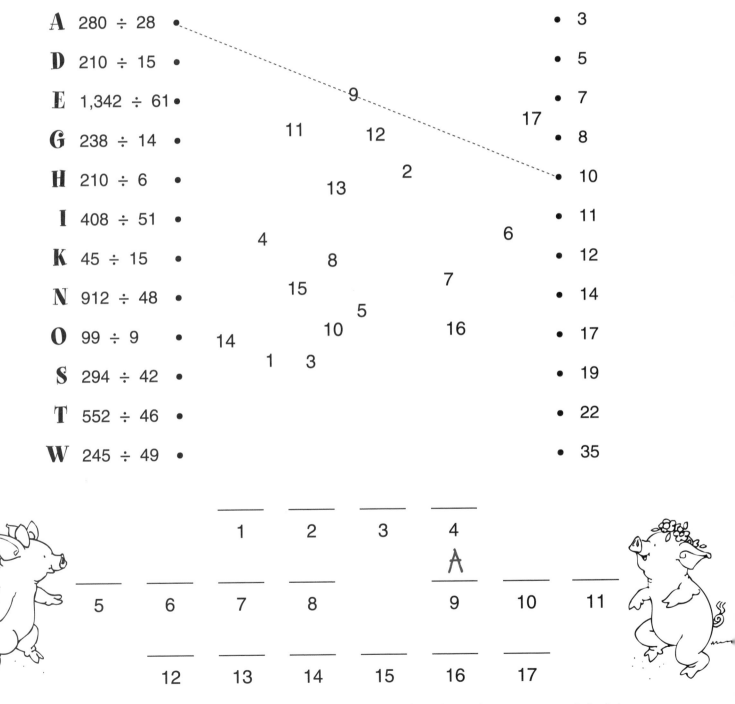

A   280 ÷ 28 •

D   210 ÷ 15 •

E   1,342 ÷ 61 •

G   238 ÷ 14 •

H   210 ÷ 6 •

I   408 ÷ 51 •

K   45 ÷ 15 •

N   912 ÷ 48 •

O   99 ÷ 9 •

S   294 ÷ 42 •

T   552 ÷ 46 •

W   245 ÷ 49 •

• 3
• 5
• 7
• 8
• 10
• 11
• 12
• 14
• 17
• 19
• 22
• 35

9   11   12   17   2   13   4   8   15   7   5   10   16   6   14   1   3

___ ___ ___ ___
 1   2   3   4
              A
___ ___ ___ ___ ___ ___ ___
 5   6   7   8   9   10 11

___ ___ ___ ___ ___ ___
 12 13 14 15 16 17

Demonstrate division of whole numbers up to two-digit divisors

Let's Divide

Name_____

Complete each of the following division problems.

1. 1,575 ÷ 63 = _____

2. 832 ÷ 52 = _____

3. 658 ÷ 14 = _____

4. 798 ÷ 19 = _____

5. 3,528 ÷ 49 = _____

6. 2,952 ÷ 72 = _____

7. 7,200 ÷ 9 = _____

8. 1,104 ÷ 23 = _____

9. 3,220 ÷ 46 = _____

10. 78,182 ÷ 97 = _____

Demonstrate division of whole numbers up to two-digit divisors

EMC 3019 • Basic Math Skills, Grade 6 • ©2003 by Evan-Moor Corp.

Divide and Conquer

Name _____

Complete each of the following division problems.

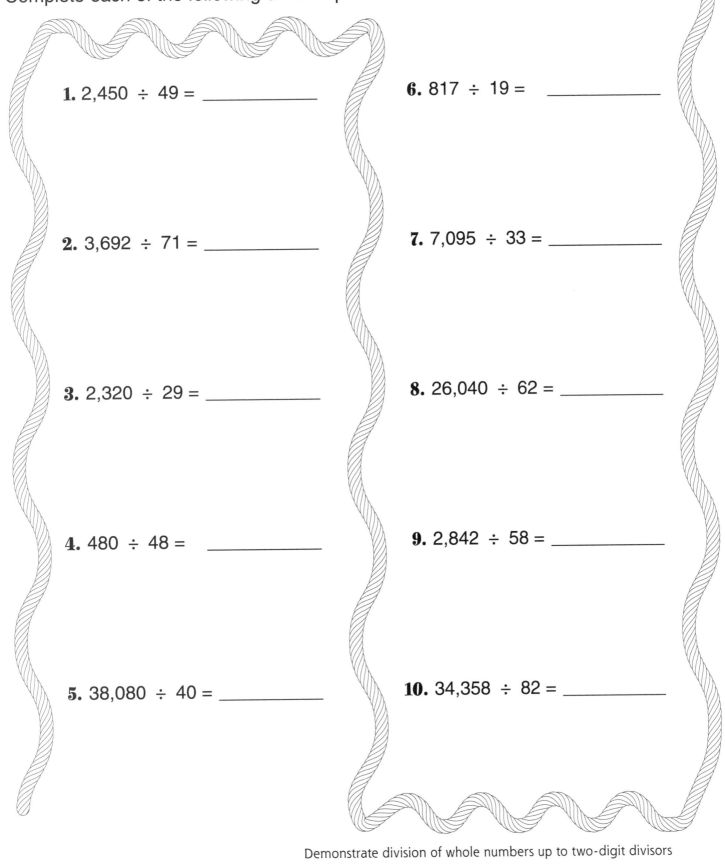

1. 2,450 ÷ 49 = _____

2. 3,692 ÷ 71 = _____

3. 2,320 ÷ 29 = _____

4. 480 ÷ 48 = _____

5. 38,080 ÷ 40 = _____

6. 817 ÷ 19 = _____

7. 7,095 ÷ 33 = _____

8. 26,040 ÷ 62 = _____

9. 2,842 ÷ 58 = _____

10. 34,358 ÷ 82 = _____

Demonstrate division of whole numbers up to two-digit divisors

Number & Operations

What's My Number (Division)?

Name_____

Use the clues to find each number.

1.
- If divided by 10, the remainder is 2.
- If divided by 4, the remainder is 0.
- It is less than 50.
- The sum of the digits is 5.

_____

2.
- If divided by 3, the remainder is 1.
- If divided by 100, the remainder is 0.
- It has three digits.
- It is less than 400.

_____

3.
- If divided by 25, the remainder is 0.
- If divided by 8, the remainder is 5.
- It is more than 500.
- It is less than 600.

_____

4.
- If divided by 3, the remainder is 0.
- If divided by 53, the remainder is 0.
- It is more than 300.
- It is less than 500.

What are TWO possible numbers so far? _____ and _____

Write a clue to narrow it down to just one of the numbers.

_____

Demonstrate division of whole numbers up to two-digit divisors

Number & Operations

EMC 3019 • Basic Math Skills, Grade 6 • ©2003 by Evan-Moor Corp.

Distribution and Displays

Name _____

Solve each problem.

1. Tim wants to put 600 marbles into bags. If he puts 30 marbles in each bag, how many bags will he need?

   _____

2. Yessenia has a collection of 327 trolls. She wants to display them on shelves in her room. She thinks that 26 trolls will fit on each shelf. How many shelves does she need to display all her trolls?

   _____

3. Kellie has a collection of 1,942 stamps. She has figured that 48 stamps will fit nicely on each side of a page. How many pages does she need to display all the stamps if she puts them on both sides of the paper?

   _____

4. Frank has been collecting baseball cards and now has 3,750. He is putting them in display sheets that allow him to put 18 in each sheet, 9 on each side of the sheet. How many display sheets does he need to put all his cards in sheets?

   _____

5. Rudy has packages of Chewies to share with his class. He has 20 packages, and each package has 45 pieces. If there are 29 people in his class and he wants to divide the chewies as evenly as possible among them, how many pieces of candy should each person get?

   _____

Demonstrate division of whole numbers up to two-digit divisors

Math Test

Fill in the circle next to the correct answer.

1. 49 ÷ 7 = _____

  Ⓐ 6   Ⓒ 8
  Ⓑ 7   Ⓓ 9

2. 56 ÷ 8 = _____

  Ⓐ 6   Ⓒ 8
  Ⓑ 7   Ⓓ 9

3. 48 ÷ 6 = _____

  Ⓐ 6   Ⓒ 8
  Ⓑ 7   Ⓓ 9

4. 45 ÷ 5 = _____

  Ⓐ 6   Ⓒ 8
  Ⓑ 7   Ⓓ 9

5. 250 ÷ 25 = _____

  Ⓐ 1   Ⓒ 100
  Ⓑ 10   Ⓓ none of the above

6. 884 ÷ 34 = _____

  Ⓐ 20   Ⓒ 26
  Ⓑ 206   Ⓓ none of the above

7. 1,188 ÷ 54 = _____

  Ⓐ 1,080   Ⓒ 22
  Ⓑ 202   Ⓓ none of the above

8. 3,087 ÷ 63 = _____

  Ⓐ 49   Ⓒ 56
  Ⓑ 252   Ⓓ none of the above

9. Luis has 2,528 baseball cards. He is putting them into a book, and each page will hold 18 cards. How many pages does he need to put all his cards into the book?

_____

_____

10. There are 476 students at Jackson School. They are all going on a field trip along with 35 additional sponsors (teachers and parents). If each bus holds 60 people, how many buses do they need for the field trip?

_____

_____

Demonstrate division of whole numbers up to two-digit divisors

EMC 3019 • Basic Math Skills, Grade 6 • ©2003 by Evan-Moor Corp.

Riddle

What do you get if you cross a tape measure with a steamroller?

To solve the riddle, complete each of the following problems. Then write the corresponding letter on the line in front of each problem. Read the letters from top to bottom and they will spell out the solution to the riddle.

_____ $2\frac{1}{4} + 3\frac{1}{2} =$ _____

_____ $2\frac{2}{3} + 1\frac{2}{3} =$ _____

___A___ $7\frac{1}{3} - 2 \quad =$ $5\frac{1}{3}$ _____

_____ $8\frac{1}{3} - 3\frac{1}{12} =$ _____

_____ $2\frac{1}{3} + 3\frac{5}{12} =$ _____

_____ $2\frac{1}{4} + 2\frac{1}{4} =$ _____

_____ $6\frac{1}{3} - 1\frac{5}{6} =$ _____

_____ $9\frac{3}{4} - 4\frac{1}{2} =$ _____

$5\frac{1}{3}$	**A**
$4\frac{1}{2}$	**E**
$5\frac{3}{4}$	**F**
$4\frac{1}{3}$	**L**
$5\frac{1}{4}$	**T**

Demonstrate addition and subtraction of fractions including mixed numbers and unlike denominators

Which Is Faster, Hot or Cold?

Name_____

To solve the riddle, complete each of the following problems. Then write the corresponding letter on the line in front of each problem. Read the letters from top to bottom starting on the left and they will spell out the solution to the riddle.

H $2\frac{1}{4} + 2\frac{1}{4} =$ _____ $4\frac{1}{2}$

_____ $2\frac{2}{3} + 2\frac{2}{3} =$ _____

_____ $3\frac{1}{2} + 2\frac{1}{3} =$ _____

_____ $1\frac{1}{2} + 2 =$ _____

_____ $5\frac{1}{3} - 1\frac{1}{3} =$ _____

_____ $7 - 3\frac{1}{4} =$ _____

_____ $4\frac{6}{7} - 1\frac{6}{7} =$ _____

_____ $3\frac{1}{3} + 2\frac{2}{3} =$ _____

_____ $3\frac{1}{4} + 2\frac{1}{4} =$ _____

_____ $5\frac{1}{3} - 1\frac{1}{3} =$ _____

_____ $7\frac{3}{4} - 1\frac{1}{4} =$ _____

_____ $8\frac{1}{2} - 3\frac{1}{6} =$ _____

_____ $8\frac{1}{3} - 2\frac{2}{6} =$ _____

_____ $5\frac{1}{3} - 1\frac{7}{12} =$ _____

_____ $5\frac{1}{3} - 2\frac{3}{9} =$ _____

_____ $8\frac{1}{3} - 3\frac{4}{9} =$ _____

_____ $5\frac{3}{4} - 2 =$ _____

_____ $2\frac{1}{3} + \frac{2}{3} =$ _____

_____ $3\frac{1}{2} + 2\frac{1}{3} =$ _____

_____ $1\frac{1}{2} + 2\frac{1}{4} =$ _____

_____ $3\frac{3}{4} + \frac{3}{4} =$ _____

_____ $1\frac{1}{2} + 1\frac{1}{2} =$ _____

_____ $6\frac{1}{3} - 2\frac{7}{12} =$ _____

_____ $3 + 2\frac{1}{3} =$ _____

_____ $2\frac{1}{4} + 2\frac{1}{2} =$ _____

_____ $1\frac{1}{2} + 2\frac{3}{8} =$ _____

3	**A**	$5\frac{1}{2}$	**S**
$3\frac{1}{2}$	**B**	$5\frac{5}{6}$	**T**
$3\frac{3}{4}$	**C**	6	**U**
$3\frac{7}{8}$	**D**	$6\frac{1}{2}$	**Y**
4	**E**		
$4\frac{1}{2}$	**H**		
$4\frac{3}{4}$	**L**		
$4\frac{8}{9}$	**N**		
$5\frac{1}{3}$	**O**		

Demonstrate addition and subtraction of fractions including mixed numbers and unlike denominators

Number & Operations

EMC 3019 • Basic Math Skills, Grade 6 • ©2003 by Evan-Moor Corp.

Sum Fractions

Name _____

Find the sum of each of the following problems.

1. $2\frac{1}{3} + 4\frac{2}{3} =$ _____

2. $5\frac{3}{8} + 2\frac{2}{8} =$ _____

3. $4\frac{3}{7} + 2\frac{5}{7} =$ _____

4. $2\frac{2}{3} + 4\frac{2}{3} =$ _____

5. $4\frac{2}{5} + 3 =$ _____

6. $\frac{1}{4} + \frac{1}{3} =$ _____

7. $\frac{3}{7} + \frac{2}{5} =$ _____

8. $\frac{2}{9} + \frac{1}{3} =$ _____

9. $1\frac{4}{5} + 2\frac{1}{3} =$ _____

10. $6\frac{4}{5} + 4\frac{2}{3} =$ _____

Demonstrate addition and subtraction of fractions including mixed numbers and unlike denominators

Fraction Difference

Find the difference of each of the following.

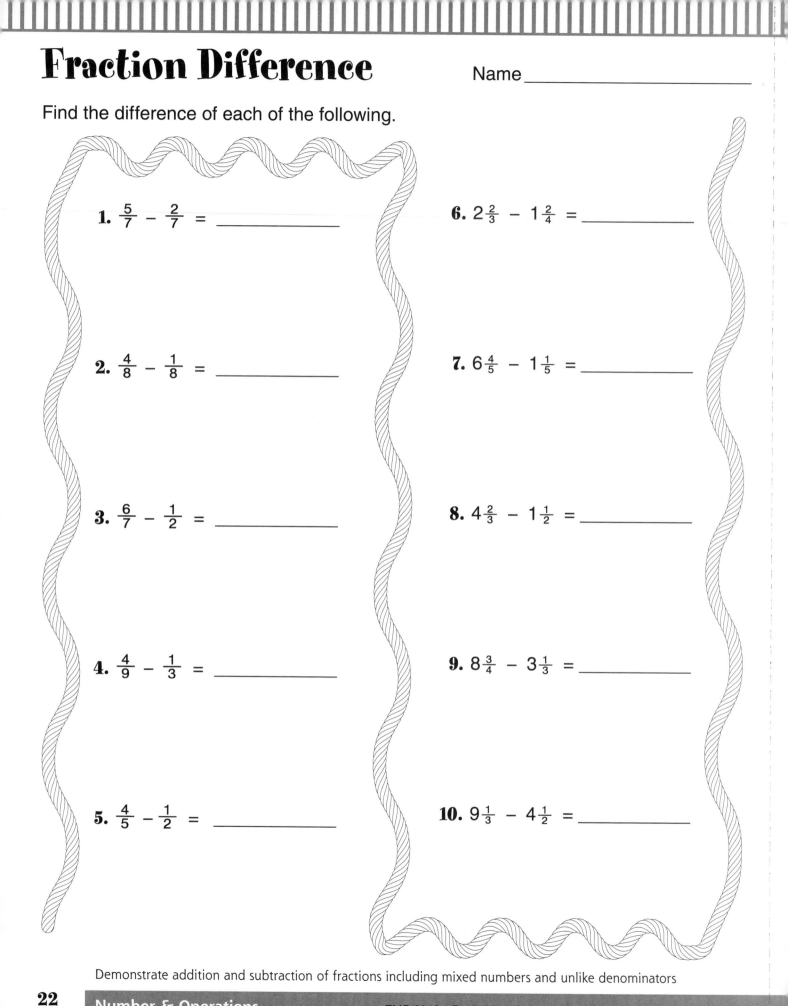

1. $\frac{5}{7} - \frac{2}{7} =$ _____

2. $\frac{4}{8} - \frac{1}{8} =$ _____

3. $\frac{6}{7} - \frac{1}{2} =$ _____

4. $\frac{4}{9} - \frac{1}{3} =$ _____

5. $\frac{4}{5} - \frac{1}{2} =$ _____

6. $2\frac{2}{3} - 1\frac{2}{4} =$ _____

7. $6\frac{4}{5} - 1\frac{1}{5} =$ _____

8. $4\frac{2}{3} - 1\frac{1}{2} =$ _____

9. $8\frac{3}{4} - 3\frac{1}{3} =$ _____

10. $9\frac{1}{3} - 4\frac{1}{2} =$ _____

Demonstrate addition and subtraction of fractions including mixed numbers and unlike denominators

EMC 3019 • Basic Math Skills, Grade 6 • ©2003 by Evan-Moor Corp.

Cooking in the Kitchen

Name_____

Solve each problem.

1. Jimmy is baking a cake. The recipe calls for a total of $1\frac{1}{2}$ cups of sugar. One of the first steps asks him to put $\frac{1}{4}$ cup of sugar into the bowl. Then later on, he is supposed to put the rest of the sugar in, but he doesn't know how much to put in. How much sugar is left to put in at the end?

   _____

2. Suzanne is making a batch of cookies. She is trying to figure out how big of a bowl she needs. She knows the recipe calls for $2\frac{1}{2}$ cups of flour, $1\frac{1}{2}$ cups of sugar, $1\frac{1}{4}$ cups of butter, $\frac{1}{2}$ cup of peanut butter, and about $\frac{2}{3}$ cup of other stuff. How many cups of ingredients does she need her bowl to hold?

   _____

3. Ian is baking cookies, and he made 18 cookies from the first $2\frac{1}{2}$ cups of the batter. If he started with 10 cups of batter, how much batter is left? How many cookies will he be able to make from the 10 cups of batter?

   _____

4. Brandon is making pancakes. He made 4 pancakes from the first $\frac{3}{4}$ cup of batter. He started with $2\frac{1}{2}$ cups of batter. How much batter does he have left?

   _____

5. Julie is making some brownies and has just a little oil left. The recipe calls for $1\frac{1}{3}$ cup of oil. She has only $\frac{3}{4}$ cup of oil. She is going to substitute applesauce for the remaining oil. How much applesauce does she need to add to her recipe?

   _____

Demonstrate addition and subtraction of fractions including mixed numbers and unlike denominators

Fabric World

Name _____

Solve each problem.

1. Ricky was buying some fabric to make his vampire costume. He found one piece of fabric that was $2\frac{3}{4}$ yards long and another one that was $1\frac{1}{3}$ yards long. He wasn't worried about the seam, but he needs 4 yards of fabric. Does he have enough with these two pieces? Why or why not?

   _____

2. Helen is making new throw pillows to put on her bed. She needs 6 yards of fabric. She found one color that had $2\frac{1}{2}$ yards, another with $1\frac{1}{3}$ yards, and a third with $1\frac{3}{4}$ yards. Does she have enough fabric? Why or why not?

   _____

3. Mary Alice has $15\frac{1}{2}$ yards of ribbon. She needs $2\frac{1}{3}$ yards for one project and $3\frac{3}{4}$ yards for another. She needs 9 yards for her last project and she's wondering if there's enough. Does she have enough left? Why or why not?

   _____

4. Brian found $\frac{1}{2}$ spool of thread in his mom's sewing box. He found another spool in a junk drawer that had $\frac{1}{3}$ of the thread used up. He found a third spool in the garage with $\frac{1}{4}$ of the spool left. Does he have more than one full spool? Why or why not?

   _____

5. Derrick is making new curtains for his bedroom. The fabric he wants for the windows is $3\frac{3}{4}$ yards long, and he wants to put up $1\frac{3}{4}$ yards of fabric on each of his 3 windows. Does he have enough? Why or why not?

   _____

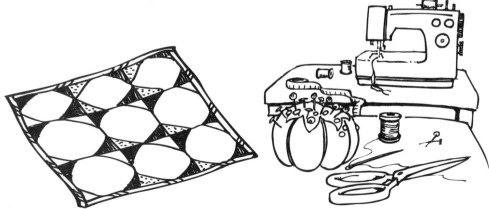

Demonstrate addition and subtraction of fractions including mixed numbers and unlike denominators

Number & Operations

EMC 3019 • Basic Math Skills, Grade 6 • ©2003 by Evan-Moor Corp.

Math Test

Name _____

Fill in the circle next to the correct answer. Simplify your answer if possible.

1. $\frac{3}{5} + \frac{1}{5} =$ _____

   Ⓐ $\frac{4}{10}$　　　　Ⓒ $\frac{4}{5}$

   Ⓑ $\frac{2}{5}$　　　　Ⓓ $\frac{3}{5}$

2. $\frac{3}{4} + \frac{5}{6} =$ _____

   Ⓐ $1\frac{7}{12}$　　　　Ⓒ $\frac{4}{3}$

   Ⓑ $\frac{8}{10}$　　　　Ⓓ $\frac{4}{5}$

3. $3\frac{1}{3} + 2\frac{3}{7} =$ _____

   Ⓐ $5\frac{4}{7}$　　　　Ⓒ $5\frac{4}{10}$

   Ⓑ $5\frac{16}{21}$　　　　Ⓓ $5\frac{2}{5}$

4. $5\frac{3}{4} + 4\frac{1}{2} =$ _____

   Ⓐ $9\frac{1}{4}$　　　　Ⓒ $9\frac{2}{3}$

   Ⓑ $9\frac{4}{6}$　　　　Ⓓ $10\frac{1}{4}$

5. $\frac{6}{7} - \frac{5}{7} =$ _____

   Ⓐ $\frac{1}{7}$　　　　Ⓒ $\frac{2}{7}$

   Ⓑ 1　　　　Ⓓ $\frac{11}{7}$

6. $5\frac{2}{3} - 2\frac{2}{9} =$ _____

   Ⓐ $3\frac{4}{6}$　　　　Ⓒ 3

   Ⓑ $3\frac{4}{9}$　　　　Ⓓ $3\frac{1}{3}$

7. $5\frac{1}{3} - 2\frac{2}{3} =$ _____

   Ⓐ $3\frac{2}{3}$　　　　Ⓒ $2\frac{1}{3}$

   Ⓑ $3\frac{1}{3}$　　　　Ⓓ $2\frac{2}{3}$

8. $4\frac{1}{3} - 2\frac{6}{7} =$ _____

   Ⓐ $2\frac{10}{21}$　　　　Ⓒ $1\frac{10}{21}$

   Ⓑ $2\frac{5}{4}$　　　　Ⓓ $2\frac{5}{21}$

9. Sally has two papers that she wants to tape end to end. She hopes that the total length is at least $24\frac{1}{2}$ inches long. One piece of paper is $12\frac{3}{4}$ inches long and the other one is $11\frac{7}{8}$ inches long. Will the papers taped together be long enough? Why or why not?

   _____

   _____

   _____

10. Jimmy started with a string that was $25\frac{1}{3}$ feet long. He cut off a piece to give to his friend that was $6\frac{3}{4}$ feet long. How much string does Jimmy have left?

    _____

    _____

    _____

Demonstrate addition and subtraction of fractions including mixed numbers and unlike denominators

What Never Gets Locked Out?

To solve this riddle, complete each of the following multiplication problems. Then write the corresponding letter on the line in front of the problem. The letters will spell out the solution to the riddle when read from **bottom to top**, starting from right.

S ___ $\frac{1}{2} \times \frac{1}{2} =$ ___ $\frac{1}{4}$ ___ $2\frac{2}{3} \times \frac{1}{3} =$ ___

___ $\frac{3}{5} \times \frac{1}{2} =$ ___   ___ $\frac{1}{5} \times 2\frac{1}{2} =$ ___

___ $\frac{2}{5} \times 2 =$ ___

___ $1\frac{1}{2} \times \frac{1}{2} =$ ___   ___ $1\frac{2}{5} \times \frac{1}{2} =$ ___

___ $3 \times \frac{1}{5} =$ ___

___ $1\frac{1}{3} \times \frac{2}{3} =$ ___   ___ $2 \times \frac{1}{3} =$ ___

___ $1\frac{2}{3} \times \frac{1}{3} =$ ___   ___ $\frac{3}{4} \times \frac{2}{3} =$ ___

___ $1\frac{3}{4} \times \frac{1}{2} =$ ___   ___ $\frac{1}{5} \times \frac{1}{2} =$ ___

___ $1 \times \frac{1}{2} =$ ___

___ $2 \times \frac{2}{5} =$ ___   ___ $\frac{2}{5} \times 1\frac{2}{3} =$ ___

___ $\frac{3}{5} \times \frac{1}{2} =$ ___

___ $2\frac{2}{3} \times \frac{1}{3} =$ ___

___ $1 \times \frac{5}{9} =$ ___

___ $1\frac{3}{4} \times \frac{1}{2} =$ ___

___ $2 \times \frac{1}{4} =$ ___

___ $\frac{1}{5} \times 4 =$ ___

___ $\frac{1}{2} \times \frac{1}{2} =$ ___

___ $\frac{1}{3} \times 2 =$ ___

___ $5 \times \frac{1}{9} =$ ___

$\frac{2}{3}$	A
$\frac{4}{5}$	E
$\frac{7}{8}$	G
$\frac{5}{9}$	H
$\frac{1}{2}$	I
$\frac{3}{4}$	K
$\frac{3}{5}$	N
$\frac{7}{10}$	O
$\frac{1}{10}$	P
$\frac{1}{4}$	S
$\frac{8}{9}$	T
$\frac{3}{10}$	Y

Demonstrate multiplication of fractions including mixed numbers

Tongue Twister #3

Name _____

Complete each of the following multiplication problems. Then write the corresponding letter on the line in front of the problem. The letters will spell out a tongue twister. How many times can you say it in 15 seconds?

_____ S $\frac{1}{4} \times 2 =$ _____ $\frac{1}{2}$

_____ $\frac{2}{7} \times 3 =$ _____

_____ $2\frac{1}{2} \times \frac{1}{4} =$ _____

_____ $\frac{1}{6} \times 2 =$ _____

_____ $\frac{2}{11} \times 5 =$ _____

_____ $\frac{2}{7} \times 2 =$ _____

_____ $1\frac{1}{4} \times \frac{1}{2} =$ _____

_____ $\frac{3}{5} \times \frac{5}{6} =$ _____

_____ $\frac{1}{3} \times \frac{1}{3} =$ _____

_____ $\frac{4}{5} \times \frac{5}{8} =$ _____

_____ $1\frac{1}{2} \times \frac{1}{2} =$ _____

_____ $\frac{3}{5} \times 1\frac{1}{2} =$ _____

_____ $\frac{1}{5} \times 1\frac{2}{3} =$ _____

_____ $\frac{1}{3} \times \frac{2}{3} =$ _____

$\frac{3}{4}$	A
$\frac{1}{3}$	C
$\frac{2}{9}$	E
$\frac{4}{7}$	F
$\frac{1}{9}$	H
$\frac{5}{8}$	I
$\frac{6}{7}$	P
$\frac{1}{2}$	S
$\frac{9}{10}$	U
$\frac{10}{11}$	Y

Demonstrate multiplication of fractions including mixed numbers

Fraction Products

Name _____

Complete each multiplication problem. Write your answer in simplest form.

1. $\frac{2}{5} \times \frac{1}{3} =$ _____

2. $\frac{1}{4} \times \frac{3}{7} =$ _____

3. $\frac{1}{2} \times \frac{3}{8} =$ _____

4. $\frac{3}{5} \times \frac{2}{7} =$ _____

5. $\frac{3}{7} \times \frac{3}{4} =$ _____

6. $\frac{5}{9} \times \frac{1}{3} =$ _____

7. $\frac{1}{2} \times \frac{3}{5} =$ _____

8. $\frac{5}{2} \times \frac{1}{9} =$ _____

9. $\frac{4}{3} \times \frac{4}{9} =$ _____

10. $\frac{5}{8} \times \frac{1}{3} =$ _____

11. $\frac{4}{5} \times \frac{3}{2} =$ _____

12. $\frac{2}{5} \times \frac{5}{9} =$ _____

13. $\frac{5}{2} \times \frac{4}{7} =$ _____

14. $\frac{3}{2} \times \frac{2}{3} =$ _____

15. $\frac{5}{7} \times \frac{3}{5} =$ _____

16. $\frac{1}{3} \times \frac{3}{4} =$ _____

17. $\frac{2}{5} \times \frac{1}{2} =$ _____

18. $\frac{4}{9} \times \frac{3}{2} =$ _____

19. $\frac{5}{8} \times \frac{4}{5} =$ _____

20. $\frac{8}{9} \times \frac{3}{4} =$ _____

Demonstrate multiplication of fractions including mixed numbers

EMC 3019 • Basic Math Skills, Grade 6 • ©2003 by Evan-Moor Corp.

Multiply My Fraction

Name _____

Complete each multiplication problem. Write your answer in simplest form.

1. $1\frac{2}{5} \times 3\frac{3}{4} =$ _____

2. $2\frac{5}{6} \times 3 =$ _____

3. $4\frac{2}{7} \times \frac{1}{2} =$ _____

4. $3\frac{3}{5} \times 2\frac{6}{7} =$ _____

5. $1\frac{2}{5} \times 2\frac{3}{4} =$ _____

6. $4\frac{1}{2} \times 3\frac{1}{2} =$ _____

7. $2\frac{1}{4} \times 4\frac{1}{3} =$ _____

8. $3\frac{3}{4} \times 2\frac{4}{5} =$ _____

9. $5\frac{1}{4} \times 3\frac{2}{3} =$ _____

10. $2\frac{1}{2} \times 2\frac{4}{5} =$ _____

Demonstrate multiplication of fractions including mixed numbers

What's My Fraction (Multiplication)?

Name _____

Use the clues to find each number.

1.
- My fraction is a mixed number.
- When my fraction is multiplied by $\frac{3}{4}$, the product is $1\frac{1}{8}$.

_____

2.
- My fraction is a mixed number.
- When my fraction is divided by $\frac{2}{5}$, the answer is $8\frac{1}{2}$.

_____

3.
- My fraction is a mixed number.
- When my fraction is multiplied by $\frac{1}{3}$, the product is $1\frac{2}{5}$.

_____

4.
- My fraction is NOT a mixed number.
- My fraction is equivalent to $\frac{1}{2}$.
- When my fraction is divided by $\frac{1}{3}$, the answer is $1\frac{1}{2}$.
- The numerator of my fraction is a 4.

_____

Demonstrate multiplication of fractions including mixed numbers

Tim's Painting

Name _____

Tim is painting several different surfaces and needs to know the area needing paint so that he can buy the correct amount of paint. For each of the following rectangles, multiply the length by the width to find the area needing paint.

1. Tim wants to paint one side of a door that is $6\frac{1}{4}$ feet tall and 3 feet wide. What is the area of the door?

    _____

2. Tim wants to paint a tabletop that is $6\frac{2}{3}$ feet by $3\frac{3}{4}$ feet. What is the area of the tabletop?

    _____

3. Tim wants to paint a sign with dimensions of 20 inches by $14\frac{1}{2}$ inches. What is the area of the sign?

    _____

4. Tim wants to paint a shelf in his bedroom. The top of the shelf measures $\frac{3}{4}$ foot by $2\frac{2}{3}$ feet. If he paints the top and the bottom of the shelf, what is the total area to be painted?

    _____

5. Tim wants to paint the ceiling in his bedroom. The room is rectangular in shape. The length of the room is $13\frac{1}{2}$ feet and the width is $10\frac{2}{3}$ feet. What is the area of the ceiling to be painted?

    _____

Demonstrate multiplication of fractions including mixed numbers

Math Test

Name_____

Fill in the circle next to the correct answer. If possible, simplify each fraction.

1. $\frac{1}{2} \times \frac{1}{3} = $ _____

   Ⓐ $\frac{1}{6}$ Ⓒ $\frac{2}{5}$

   Ⓑ $\frac{1}{2}$ Ⓓ $\frac{1}{3}$

2. $\frac{3}{5} \times \frac{2}{3} = $ _____

   Ⓐ $1\frac{1}{5}$ Ⓒ $\frac{2}{5}$

   Ⓑ $1\frac{4}{15}$ Ⓓ $2\frac{1}{2}$

3. $\frac{4}{5} \times \frac{5}{8} = $ _____

   Ⓐ $\frac{9}{40}$ Ⓒ $\frac{1}{10}$

   Ⓑ $\frac{1}{2}$ Ⓓ $\frac{1}{8}$

4. $2\frac{1}{2} \times 3 = $ _____

   Ⓐ $6\frac{1}{2}$ Ⓒ $21\frac{1}{2}$

   Ⓑ $3\frac{1}{2}$ Ⓓ $7\frac{1}{2}$

5. $4 \times 5\frac{1}{3} = $ _____

   Ⓐ $20\frac{1}{3}$ Ⓒ $5\frac{1}{3}$

   Ⓑ $21\frac{1}{3}$ Ⓓ $1\frac{1}{3}$

6. $3\frac{1}{3} \times 1\frac{1}{2} = $ _____

   Ⓐ 5 Ⓒ 4

   Ⓑ $3\frac{1}{6}$ Ⓓ $4\frac{1}{5}$

7. $7\frac{1}{3} \times 3\frac{3}{4} = $ _____

   Ⓐ $27\frac{1}{4}$ Ⓒ $27\frac{1}{2}$

   Ⓑ $21\frac{1}{4}$ Ⓓ $21\frac{4}{7}$

8. $1\frac{5}{6} \times 1\frac{1}{4} = $ _____

   Ⓐ $\frac{11}{24}$ Ⓒ $1\frac{5}{24}$

   Ⓑ $2\frac{5}{24}$ Ⓓ $2\frac{7}{24}$

9. Show all the steps when you multiply the following problem.

$$3\frac{3}{4} \times 3 = \text{_____}$$

10. Juan needs to find the area of a picture he plans to paint. The canvas is $9\frac{1}{3}$ inches across by $12\frac{1}{4}$ inches high. He knows that he has to multiply the length by the width to get the area. What is the area of the canvas?

_____

_____

Demonstrate multiplication of fractions including mixed numbers

       EMC 3019 • Basic Math Skills, Grade 6 • ©2003 by Evan-Moor Corp.

Riddle

What do you call a horse that stays up very late?

To solve the riddle, complete each division problem below. Then write the corresponding letter on the line in front of each problem. The letters will spell out the solution when read from top to bottom.

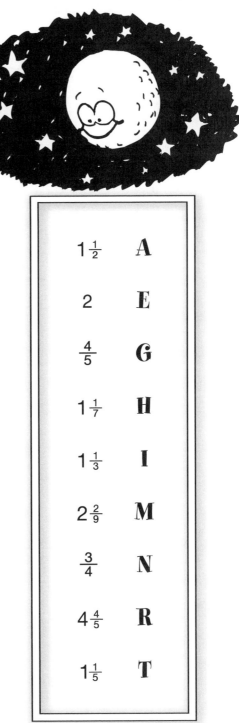

__A__ $\frac{3}{4} \div \frac{1}{2} =$ __$1\frac{1}{2}$__

_____ $\frac{1}{2} \div \frac{2}{3} =$ _____

_____ $\frac{4}{5} \div \frac{3}{5} =$ _____

_____ $\frac{2}{3} \div \frac{5}{6} =$ _____

_____ $\frac{4}{7} \div \frac{1}{2} =$ _____

_____ $\frac{4}{5} \div \frac{2}{3} =$ _____

_____ $\frac{5}{9} \div \frac{1}{4} =$ _____

_____ $\frac{1}{2} \div \frac{1}{3} =$ _____

_____ $\frac{4}{5} \div \frac{1}{6} =$ _____

_____ $\frac{4}{5} \div \frac{2}{5} =$ _____

$1\frac{1}{2}$	**A**
2	**E**
$\frac{4}{5}$	**G**
$1\frac{1}{7}$	**H**
$1\frac{1}{3}$	**I**
$2\frac{2}{9}$	**M**
$\frac{3}{4}$	**N**
$4\frac{4}{5}$	**R**
$1\frac{1}{5}$	**T**

Demonstrate division of fractions including mixed numbers

Number & Operations

What Must You Pay When You Go to School?

Name_____

Complete each division problem below and simplify the answer. Then write the corresponding letter on the line in front of the problem. The letters will spell out the solution to the riddle when read from top to bottom.

_____ $\frac{1}{3} \div 1 =$ _____

_____ $\frac{1}{4} \div \frac{1}{2} =$ _____

_____ $\frac{2}{5} \div \frac{4}{5} =$ _____

_____ $\frac{3}{4} \div 3 =$ _____

_____ $\frac{1}{3} \div \frac{5}{6} =$ _____

_____ $\frac{1}{2} \div 1 =$ _____

_____ $\frac{2}{5} \div \frac{3}{5} =$ _____

_____ $\frac{1}{2} \div \frac{2}{3} =$ _____

_____ $\frac{1}{4} \div \frac{5}{8} =$ _____

$\frac{1}{3}$	**A**	$\frac{2}{5}$	**N**
$\frac{1}{4}$	**E**	$\frac{3}{4}$	**O**
$\frac{2}{3}$	**I**	$\frac{1}{2}$	**T**

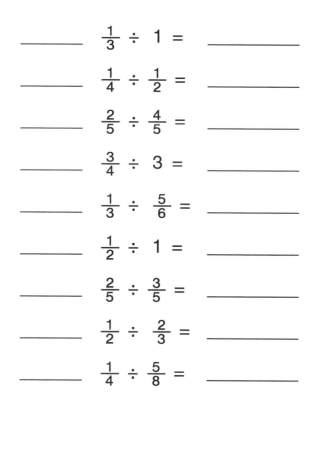

Demonstrate division of fractions including mixed numbers

Number & Operations

EMC 3019 • Basic Math Skills, Grade 6 • ©2003 by Evan-Moor Corp.

Fraction Division

Name _____

Complete each of the following division problems. Write your answer in simplest form.

1. $\frac{1}{2} \div \frac{1}{3} =$ _____

2. $\frac{2}{3} \div \frac{3}{4} =$ _____

3. $\frac{2}{5} \div \frac{1}{2} =$ _____

4. $\frac{4}{5} \div \frac{2}{3} =$ _____

5. $\frac{3}{5} \div \frac{1}{5} =$ _____

6. $\frac{4}{7} \div \frac{3}{7} =$ _____

7. $\frac{2}{5} \div \frac{2}{3} =$ _____

8. $\frac{4}{3} \div \frac{1}{3} =$ _____

9. $\frac{5}{2} \div \frac{3}{4} =$ _____

10. $\frac{2}{3} \div \frac{3}{2} =$ _____

11. $\frac{6}{7} \div \frac{5}{2} =$ _____

12. $\frac{4}{9} \div \frac{2}{3} =$ _____

13. $\frac{4}{7} \div \frac{2}{5} =$ _____

14. $\frac{3}{8} \div \frac{4}{3} =$ _____

15. $\frac{1}{5} \div \frac{8}{3} =$ _____

Demonstrate division of fractions including mixed numbers

Fraction Division II
(with Mixed Numbers)

Name_____

Complete each of the following division problems. Write your answer in simplest form.

1. $2\frac{1}{5} \div 1\frac{1}{2} =$ _____

2. $3\frac{3}{4} \div 1\frac{1}{3} =$ _____

3. $2\frac{1}{2} \div 1\frac{1}{4} =$ _____

4. $3\frac{3}{5} \div 1\frac{1}{5} =$ _____

5. $2\frac{2}{7} \div 3\frac{5}{7} =$ _____

6. $4\frac{1}{3} \div 6\frac{2}{3} =$ _____

7. $3\frac{1}{2} \div 4\frac{1}{2} =$ _____

8. $7\frac{1}{2} \div 8 =$ _____

9. $5 \div 2\frac{1}{2} =$ _____

10. $1\frac{1}{9} \div 6 =$ _____

11. $7 \div 2\frac{1}{3} =$ _____

12. $8\frac{1}{2} \div 4\frac{1}{5} =$ _____

13. $9\frac{4}{5} \div 6\frac{2}{5} =$ _____

14. $7\frac{1}{3} \div 6\frac{1}{3} =$ _____

15. $4\frac{1}{5} \div 2\frac{1}{10} =$ _____

Demonstrate division of fractions including mixed numbers

EMC 3019 • Basic Math Skills, Grade 6 • ©2003 by Evan-Moor Corp.

Pizza Parlor

Name _____

Solve each problem.

1. Tim has one-half of a pizza that he wants to divide equally between two people. Draw a picture of this problem and tell how much pizza each will get. Write the math sentence that goes with the problem.

_____

2. George has three-fourths of a pizza. He is going to divide it into six equal pieces. Draw a picture of this problem and tell how much of the whole pizza each slice will be. Write the math sentence that goes with the problem.

_____

3. Kelley has two whole pizzas. She is going to divide all of the pizzas into pieces that are one-third of a whole pizza. Draw a picture of this problem and tell how many pieces she can make. Write the math sentence that goes with the problem.

_____

4. Linda has five and one-third pizzas. She is going to divide them between some people who each request one and one-third pizzas. Draw a picture of this problem and tell how many one and one-third pizzas she can make. Write the math sentence that goes with the problem.

_____

Demonstrate division of fractions including mixed numbers

What's My Fraction (Division)?

Use the clues to find each number.

1. • My fraction is NOT a mixed number.

   • When my fraction is divided by $\frac{2}{4}$, the answer is $\frac{4}{5}$.

   _____

2. • My fraction is NOT a mixed number.

   • When my fraction is divided by $1\frac{1}{4}$, the answer is $\frac{8}{45}$.

   _____

3. • My fraction is a mixed number.

   • When my fraction is divided by $1\frac{1}{2}$, the answer is $1\frac{1}{15}$.

   _____

4. • My fraction is a mixed number.

   • When my fraction is divided by $1\frac{2}{5}$, the answer is $1\frac{27}{28}$.

   _____

Demonstrate division of fractions including mixed numbers

Number & Operations EMC 3019 • Basic Math Skills, Grade 6 • ©2003 by Evan-Moor Corp.

Math Test

Name _____

Fill in the circle next to the correct answer. If possible, simplify the fraction.

1. $\frac{1}{2} \div \frac{1}{2} =$ _____

   Ⓐ $\frac{1}{4}$ Ⓒ 1

   Ⓑ 2   Ⓓ $\frac{2}{5}$

2. $\frac{2}{3} \div \frac{2}{5} =$ _____

   Ⓐ $\frac{4}{15}$ Ⓒ $1\frac{5}{6}$

   Ⓑ $1\frac{2}{3}$ Ⓓ $\frac{3}{5}$

3. $\frac{3}{4} \div \frac{7}{8} =$ _____

   Ⓐ $\frac{6}{7}$ Ⓒ $\frac{3}{7}$

   Ⓑ $\frac{1}{2}$ Ⓓ $\frac{7}{6}$

4. $\frac{4}{5} \div \frac{2}{3} =$ _____

   Ⓐ $\frac{8}{15}$ Ⓒ $1\frac{1}{5}$

   Ⓑ $\frac{1}{2}$ Ⓓ $\frac{3}{5}$

5. $1\frac{1}{5} \div \frac{3}{5} =$ _____

   Ⓐ $1\frac{1}{5}$ Ⓒ $\frac{3}{5}$

   Ⓑ $\frac{1}{2}$ Ⓓ 2

6. $4\frac{2}{7} \div 2\frac{6}{7} =$ _____

   Ⓐ $1\frac{1}{2}$ Ⓒ $1\frac{1}{3}$

   Ⓑ $8\frac{12}{49}$ Ⓓ $\frac{2}{3}$

7. $4 \div 2\frac{1}{5} =$ _____

   Ⓐ $2\frac{1}{5}$ Ⓒ 2

   Ⓑ $1\frac{9}{11}$ Ⓓ $\frac{11}{20}$

8. $1\frac{5}{8} \div \frac{7}{8} =$ _____

   Ⓐ $1\frac{6}{7}$ Ⓒ $\frac{7}{13}$

   Ⓑ $1\frac{27}{64}$ Ⓓ $1\frac{5}{7}$

9. Show all the steps to complete the following problem.

$$3\frac{3}{5} \div 2\frac{1}{2} = \text{_____}$$

10. Jimmy has three and one-half pizzas. He wants to divide them into pieces that are each one-fourth of a pizza. How many slices will he get? Draw a picture of this situation and write the math sentence being shown.

_____

_____

Demonstrate division of fractions including mixed numbers

Tongue Twister #4

Name_____

Complete each addition problem below. Write the corresponding letter on the line above the correct answer. The letters will spell out a tongue twister. Try to say it fast three times. Good Luck!

A $3.5 + 2.6 =$ ___6.1___   **M** $6.39 + 0.2 =$ _____

B $2.1 + 4.26 =$ _____   **N** $5.5 + 0.04 =$ _____

I $5.2 + 0.42 =$ _____   **P** $4.9 + 0.24 =$ _____

L $4.20 + 1.31 =$ _____   **U** $4.2 + 1.02 =$ _____

___	___	_A_	___	___		___	___	___
5.14	5.51	6.1	5.62	5.54		6.36	5.22	5.54

___	___	___	___		___	___	___
5.14	5.51	5.22	6.59		6.36	5.22	5.54

Demonstrate addition and subtraction of decimals to the thousandths

Riddle

What do you get if you cross a cat and a lemon?

Complete each problem below. Write the letter that corresponds to the answer on the line in front of the problem. The letters will spell out the solution to the riddle if read from **bottom to top**.

___S___ 2.5 + 2.802 = __5.302__

_____ 5.11 + 0.192 = _____

_____ 5.2 + 0.05 = _____

_____ 3.426 + 2.1 = _____

_____ 8.6 − 3.09 = _____

_____ 8.45 − 3.2 = _____

_____ 9.421 − 4.06 = _____

_____ 3.4 + 1.902 = _____

_____ 5.12 + 0.165 = _____

5.285	A
5.361	O
5.526	P
5.51	R
5.302	S
5.25	U

Demonstrate addition and subtraction of decimals to the thousandths

Sum Decimals

Name _____

Complete each of the following addition problems.

1. $2.0 + 3.5 =$ _____

2. $5.0 + 6.4 =$ _____

3. $2.3 + 4.0 =$ _____

4. $1.9 + 2.0 =$ _____

5. $3.4 + 9.0 =$ _____

6. $1.2 + 5.6 =$ _____

7. $5.4 + 9.4 =$ _____

8. $6.7 + 2.9 =$ _____

9. $9.5 + 4.6 =$ _____

10. $1.2 + 5.16 =$ _____

11. $4.2 + 8.49 =$ _____

12. $4.52 + 6.62 =$ _____

13. $5.42 + 9.5 =$ _____

14. $5.106 + 4.51 =$ _____

15. $5.0 + 6.125 =$ _____

16. $5.424 + 9.81 =$ _____

17. $12.4 + 5.216 =$ _____

18. $5.42 + 95.41 =$ _____

19. $5.0 + 5.106 =$ _____

20. $6.0 + 0.009 =$ _____

Demonstrate addition and subtraction of decimals to the thousandths

EMC 3019 • Basic Math Skills, Grade 6 • ©2003 by Evan-Moor Corp.

Decimal Difference

Name_____

Complete each of the following subtraction problems.

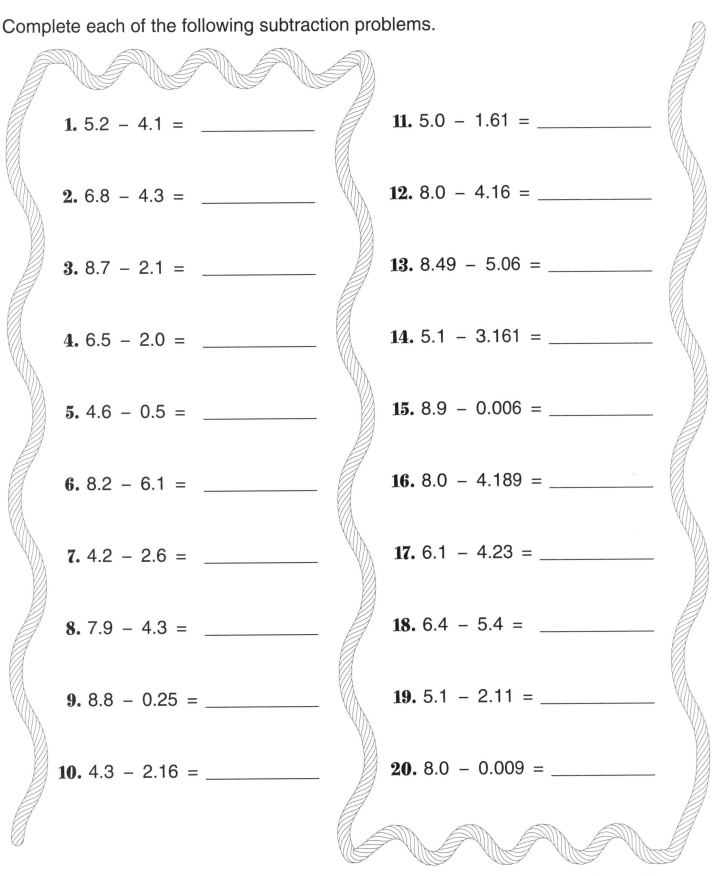

1. 5.2 − 4.1 = _____

2. 6.8 − 4.3 = _____

3. 8.7 − 2.1 = _____

4. 6.5 − 2.0 = _____

5. 4.6 − 0.5 = _____

6. 8.2 − 6.1 = _____

7. 4.2 − 2.6 = _____

8. 7.9 − 4.3 = _____

9. 8.8 − 0.25 = _____

10. 4.3 − 2.16 = _____

11. 5.0 − 1.61 = _____

12. 8.0 − 4.16 = _____

13. 8.49 − 5.06 = _____

14. 5.1 − 3.161 = _____

15. 8.9 − 0.006 = _____

16. 8.0 − 4.189 = _____

17. 6.1 − 4.23 = _____

18. 6.4 − 5.4 = _____

19. 5.1 − 2.11 = _____

20. 8.0 − 0.009 = _____

Demonstrate addition and subtraction of decimals to the thousandths

Number & Operations

Book Costs

Solve each problem.

Name_____

1. Georgia is buying three books. They cost $14.00, $15.95 and $17.50. What is the total cost of the three books?

    _____

2. Sally bought three books at the store yesterday, one for herself and two for her mother. The total bill came to $45.90 prior to tax. The book that Sally bought for herself cost $17.95. What was the total for the two books she bought for her mother?

    _____

3. Walker Book Store can purchase a book for $12.93 and then sell the same book for $14.50. How much profit do they make from the sale of this book?

    _____

4. Timothy bought four books and one journal. The books cost $4.95, $5.75, $10.25, and $14.99. The total of the five items was $44.39. How much was the journal?

    _____

5. Patricia bought a book at the store for a certain amount. She got $2.00 from her mom to buy the book, $3.25 from her dad, and $4.00 from her older sister. Patricia had to kick in the last $2.49. How much did the book cost?

    _____

Demonstrate addition and subtraction of decimals to the thousandths

EMC 3019 • Basic Math Skills, Grade 6 • ©2003 by Evan-Moor Corp.

Stormy Decimals

Name _____

Solve each problem.

1. The first day of the snowstorm, there were 9.2 centimeters of snow. During the second day of the storm, another 18.2 centimeters fell. If the total snowfall for the three-day snowstorm was 39.1 centimeters, how much snow fell on the third day?

   _____

2. The tornado that came through Lucerne caused 1.32 million dollars worth of damage. The same tornado went on to Smithville and caused another 3.221 million dollars worth of damage. What was the total damage caused by this tornado?

   _____

3. The total rainfall for two days was 11.9 inches. The first day's total was 5.4 inches less than the second day's. How much rain fell on each day?

   _____

4. Greeley experienced an unusual amount of hail during last week's storm. There were 6.1 inches of hail, and with that came an additional 1.2 inches of rain. The next day, there was 4.2 inches of hail and only 0.9 inch of rain. The third day didn't have any hail, but had 2.8 inches of rain. What was the total amount of rain for the three days?

   _____

5. South Fork had an ice storm come through that left 0.35 inch of ice on every car windshield. The sun came out for a little while and melted 0.2 inch of ice away, but then another ice storm came through and left an additional 0.39 inch of ice on the windshield. What was the total amount of ice on the windshield at the end of this ice storm?

   _____

Demonstrate addition and subtraction of decimals to the thousandths

Math Test

Fill in the circle next to the correct answer.

1. 4.5 + 0.7 = _____
   - Ⓐ 5.2
   - Ⓑ 4.2
   - Ⓒ 4.12
   - Ⓓ 4.7

2. 2.3 + 0.42 = _____
   - Ⓐ 6.5
   - Ⓑ 0.65
   - Ⓒ 2.72
   - Ⓓ 2.45

3. 9.45 + 0.095 = _____
   - Ⓐ 9.14
   - Ⓑ 10.4
   - Ⓒ 9.54
   - Ⓓ 9.545

4. 16.2 + 1.62 = _____
   - Ⓐ 17.64
   - Ⓑ 32.4
   - Ⓒ 17.82
   - Ⓓ 3.24

5. 3.5 − 1.3 = _____
   - Ⓐ 2.2
   - Ⓑ 2.3
   - Ⓒ 2.5
   - Ⓓ 25.0

6. 4.2 − 1.9 = _____
   - Ⓐ 3.7
   - Ⓑ 2.3
   - Ⓒ 3.3
   - Ⓓ 2.7

7. 6.3 − 4.09 = _____
   - Ⓐ 2.39
   - Ⓑ 2.21
   - Ⓒ 2.29
   - Ⓓ 2.31

8. 5.1 − 0.008 = _____
   - Ⓐ 5.102
   - Ⓑ 5.002
   - Ⓒ 5.092
   - Ⓓ 5.992

9. Shelley's roof has three layers of shingles on it. The bottom layer is 0.24 inch thick. The second and third layers are each 0.21 inch thick. What is the total thickness of the three layers of shingles?

   _____

   _____

10. When Tina woke up this morning, there was 25.4 centimeters of snow on the ground. By noon, there was only 8.3 centimeters of snow left on the ground. How much had melted between the time Tina woke up and noon?

    _____

Demonstrate addition and subtraction of decimals to the thousandths

Number & Operations

EMC 3019 • Basic Math Skills, Grade 6 • ©2003 by Evan-Moor Corp.

Trivia #1

Name _____

What is the world's largest animal? To figure out what kind of animal this is, solve each of the multiplication problems below. Write the letter that corresponds to the answer on the line in front of each problem. The letters will spell out the answer to the trivia question.

__A__ 0.7 × 0.4 = __0.28__

_____ 0.2 × 0.3 = _____

_____ 0.9 × 0.4 = _____

_____ 1.2 × 0.6 = _____

_____ 4.3 × 0.09 = _____

_____ 1.2 × 1.3 = _____

_____ 5.1 × 2.6 = _____

_____ 1.4 × 0.2 = _____

_____ 0.6 × 0.6 = _____

_____ 1.29 × 0.3 = _____

0.28	**A**	13.26	**H**
0.06	**B**	0.36	**L**
0.387	**E**	0.72	**U**
		1.56	**W**

Demonstrate multiplication of decimals to the thousandths

Number & Operations

What Year Do Frogs Like Best?

Name_____

Complete each of the multiplication problems below. On the line above the product, write the letter that corresponds to the problem. The letters will spell out the solution to the riddle.

A 2.3 × 5.2 = _11.96_

A 4.0 × 1.2 = _____

E 5.2 × 0.8 = _____

E 1.07 × 5.2 = _____

L 3.08 × 4.02 = _____

P 2.94 × 9.2 = _____

R 2.001 × 5.0 = _____

Y 9.0 × 0.004 = _____

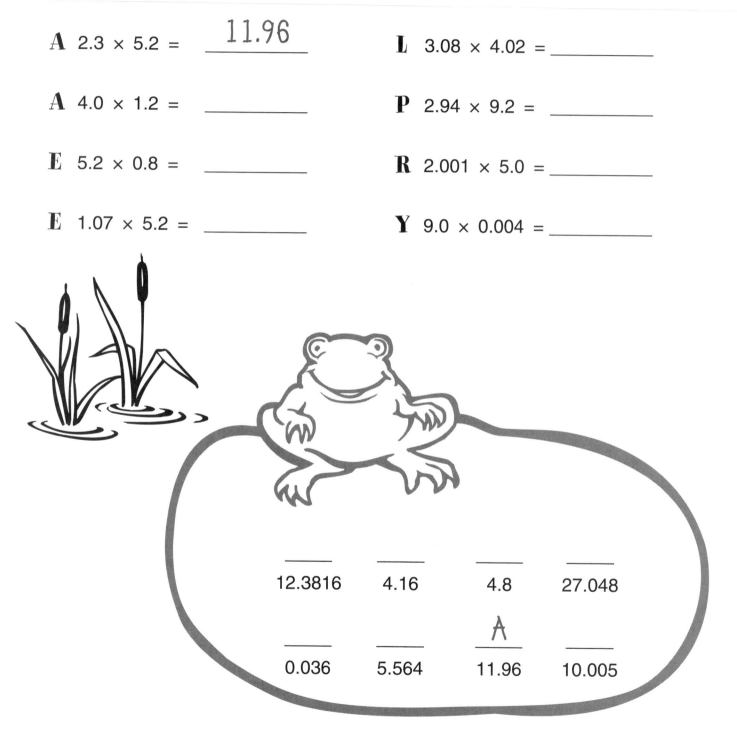

___   ___   ___   ___
12.3816   4.16   4.8   27.048

             A

___   ___   ___   ___
0.036   5.564   11.96   10.005

Demonstrate multiplication of decimals to the thousandths

EMC 3019 • Basic Math Skills, Grade 6 • ©2003 by Evan-Moor Corp.

Decimal Multiplication

Name _____

Complete each of the following multiplication problems.

1. $4.5 \times 2.1 =$ _____

2. $1.2 \times 6.3 =$ _____

3. $5.0 \times 2.6 =$ _____

4. $8.0 \times 1.9 =$ _____

5. $1.3 \times 9.0 =$ _____

6. $1.6 \times 9.4 =$ _____

7. $6.2 \times 6.1 =$ _____

8. $9.0 \times 1.26 =$ _____

9. $2.0 \times 4.42 =$ _____

10. $1.2 \times 6.25 =$ _____

11. $12.3 \times 0.061 =$ _____

12. $1.2 \times 1.003 =$ _____

13. $4.9 \times 1.106 =$ _____

14. $6.05 \times 5.2 =$ _____

15. $1.23 \times 0.006 =$ _____

16. $6.0 \times 9.126 =$ _____

17. $5.0 \times 6.421 =$ _____

18. $5.263 \times 5.26 =$ _____

19. $9.321 \times 1.23 =$ _____

20. $0.233 \times 4.562 =$ _____

Demonstrate multiplication of decimals to the thousandths

Decimal Multiplication II

Name_____

Complete each of the following multiplication problems.

1. $2.2 \times 3.0 =$ _____

2. $8.6 \times 4.0 =$ _____

3. $1.0 \times 5.3 =$ _____

4. $5.0 \times 2.3 =$ _____

5. $6.9 \times 6.5 =$ _____

6. $1.2 \times 6.4 =$ _____

7. $8.2 \times 6.5 =$ _____

8. $11.0 \times 5.2 =$ _____

9. $2.6 \times 6.2 =$ _____

10. $37.2 \times 1.1 =$ _____

11. $9.9 \times 5.42 =$ _____

12. $4.16 \times 6.23 =$ _____

13. $1.2 \times 6.23 =$ _____

14. $31.2 \times 0.006 =$ _____

15. $0.006 \times 0.003 =$ _____

16. $8.2 \times 5.016 =$ _____

17. $1.3 \times 6.0 =$ _____

18. $2.294 \times 3.0 =$ _____

19. $6.2 \times 5.12 =$ _____

20. $3.29 \times 1.009 =$ _____

Demonstrate multiplication of decimals to the thousandths

Number & Operations

EMC 3019 • Basic Math Skills, Grade 6 • ©2003 by Evan-Moor Corp.

What's My Decimal (Multiplication)?

Use the clues to find each decimal number.

---

1. • My number has three digits.

   • When it is divided by 0.3, the answer is 19.1.

   • There are digits in the ones place, the tenths place, and the hundredths place.   _____

---

2. • My number has three digits.

   • When it is divided by 0.03, the answer is 87.

   • There are digits in the ones place, tenths place, and the hundredths place.   _____

---

3. • My number has four digits.

   • When it is divided by 0.6, the answer is 7.29.

   • There are digits in the ones place, tenths place, hundredths place, and thousandths place.   _____

---

4. • My number has five digits, two to the left of the decimal and three to the right.

   • When it is divided by 0.5, the answer is 152.49.   _____

Demonstrate multiplication of decimals to the thousandths

Multiplication with Money

Name _____

Solve each problem.

1. Chuck's class is going on a field trip this next Thursday. There are 95 students going on the field trip, and each one is paying their teacher $3.75. How much money will be collected?   _____

2. Rodney and his class are collecting money for a local charity. They figure if each of the 28 students in their class brings in $3.58, then they will reach their goal. What do you think the class's goal is? Why?

_____

3. The school store is selling 280 pencils for $0.15 each and 250 erasers for $0.10 each. If they sell all of these items, can they pay a bill they have for $75.00? Why or why not?

_____

4. Frank is teaching a lesson about money to 12 first-grade students. Each student has a bowl with the following coins in it: 6 quarters, 15 dimes, 20 nickels, and 15 pennies. What is the total value of the money for all 12 students?

_____

5. Raquel is buying 23 new CDs. The average price of the CDs is $14.95. What is the total value of the 23 CDs?   _____

Demonstrate multiplication of decimals to the thousandths

Math Test

Name _____

Fill in the circle next to the correct answer.

1. $0.2 \times 3.0 =$ _____
   - Ⓐ 6.0
   - Ⓑ 0.6
   - Ⓒ 0.06
   - Ⓓ 0.23

2. $5.0 \times 0.4 =$ _____
   - Ⓐ 0.2
   - Ⓑ 2.0
   - Ⓒ 0.05
   - Ⓓ 0.02

3. $0.2 \times 0.4 =$ _____
   - Ⓐ 0.08
   - Ⓑ 8.0
   - Ⓒ 0.8
   - Ⓓ 0.24

4. $0.6 \times 0.8 =$ _____
   - Ⓐ 4.8
   - Ⓑ 0.048
   - Ⓒ 0.48
   - Ⓓ 48.0

5. $1.2 \times 5.2 =$ _____
   - Ⓐ 60.0
   - Ⓑ 6.0
   - Ⓒ 224.0
   - Ⓓ 6.24

6. $6.42 \times 0.25 =$ _____
   - Ⓐ 16.05
   - Ⓑ 1.65
   - Ⓒ 16.5
   - Ⓓ 1.605

7. $1.052 \times 0.1 =$ _____
   - Ⓐ 1.052
   - Ⓑ 10.52
   - Ⓒ 0.1052
   - Ⓓ 0.01052

8. $1.2 \times 2.311 =$ _____
   - Ⓐ 2.7732
   - Ⓑ 0.27732
   - Ⓒ 277.32
   - Ⓓ 27.732

9. Deirdre is buying 5 CDs for $14.95 each. How much will the 5 CDs total?

   _____

   _____

10. What is my number? When it is divided by 2.45 the answer is 3.21.

   _____

   _____

Demonstrate multiplication of decimals to the thousandths

Where Do Cows Go on Vacation?

Name_____

To answer the riddle, complete each division problem on the left side of the paper. Draw a straight line between each problem and its answer on the right. Each line you draw will go through a number. Match the corresponding letter in front of each problem with the numbered lines at the bottom of the page. The letters will spell out the solution to the riddle.

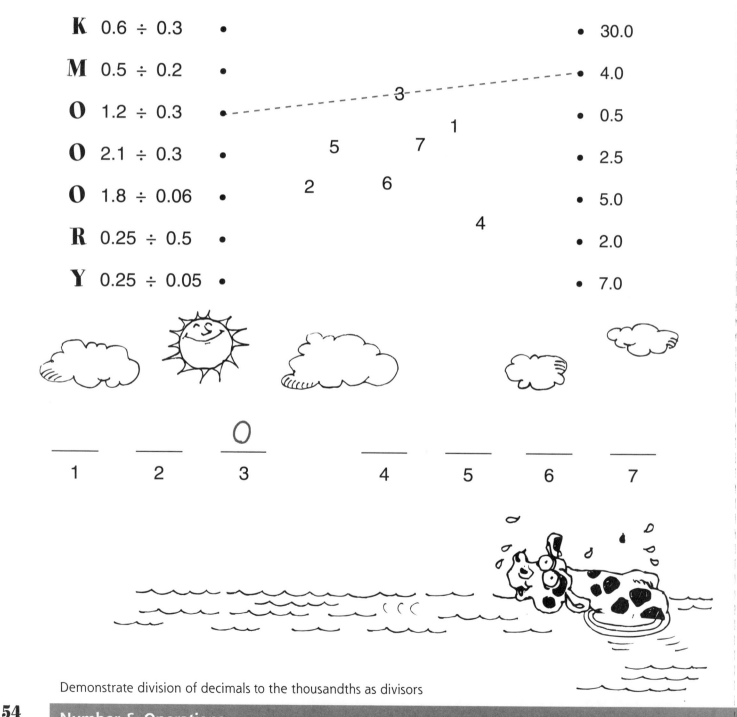

K 0.6 ÷ 0.3   •

M 0.5 ÷ 0.2   •

O 1.2 ÷ 0.3   •

O 2.1 ÷ 0.3   •

O 1.8 ÷ 0.06   •

R 0.25 ÷ 0.5   •

Y 0.25 ÷ 0.05 •

• 30.0

• 4.0

• 0.5

• 2.5

• 5.0

• 2.0

• 7.0

3   1   5   7   2   6   4

___   ___   _O_   ___   ___   ___   ___
 1   2   3   4   5   6   7

Demonstrate division of decimals to the thousandths as divisors

Tongue Twister #5

Name _____

Complete each division problem below. Write the corresponding letter on the line above the correct answer. The letters will spell out a tongue twister. Once you have the tongue twister completed, try to say it fast three times. Good luck!

A 2.4 ÷ 2.0 = _____1.2_____

D 2.0 ÷ 5.0 = _____

E 2.4 ÷ 4.0 = _____

H 28.8 ÷ 6.0 = _____

L 1.2 ÷ 0.4 = _____

O 0.5 ÷ 0.2 = _____

R 0.1 ÷ 0.5 = _____

T 1.26 ÷ 0.6 = _____

W 0.96 ÷ 0.3 = _____

Y 0.18 ÷ 0.2 = _____

		A				
	0.2	0.6	0.4			
3.0	0.6	1.2	2.1	4.8	0.6	0.2

0.9	0.6	3.0	3.0	2.5	3.2

3.0	0.6	1.2	2.1	4.8	0.6	0.2

Demonstrate division of decimals to the thousandths as divisors

Number & Operations

Decimal Division

Name _____

Complete each of the following division problems. Do not give a remainder!
Continue dividing until you get a decimal answer.

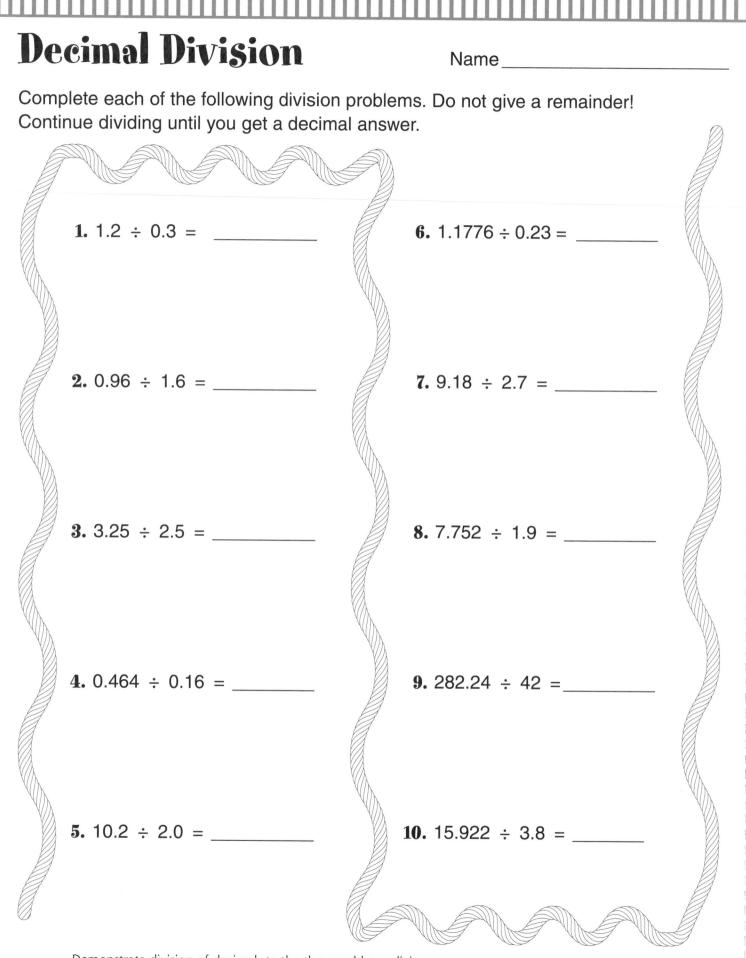

1. 1.2 ÷ 0.3 = _____

2. 0.96 ÷ 1.6 = _____

3. 3.25 ÷ 2.5 = _____

4. 0.464 ÷ 0.16 = _____

5. 10.2 ÷ 2.0 = _____

6. 1.1776 ÷ 0.23 = _____

7. 9.18 ÷ 2.7 = _____

8. 7.752 ÷ 1.9 = _____

9. 282.24 ÷ 42 = _____

10. 15.922 ÷ 3.8 = _____

Demonstrate division of decimals to the thousandths as divisors

Number & Operations

EMC 3019 • Basic Math Skills, Grade 6 • ©2003 by Evan-Moor Corp.

Decimal Division II

Name _____

Complete each of the following division problems. Do not give a remainder!
Continue dividing until you get a decimal answer.

1. $6.72 \div 2.1 =$ _____

2. $23.0 \div 5.0 =$ _____

3. $17.836 \div 3.43 =$ _____

4. $1.5696 \div 0.24 =$ _____

5. $13.552 \div 6.16 =$ _____

6. $1.1477 \div 4.99 =$ _____

7. $10.78 \div 98.0 =$ _____

8. $192.0 \div 0.96 =$ _____

9. $15.897 \div 4.542 =$ _____

10. $6.3388 \div 1.219 =$ _____

Demonstrate division of decimals to the thousandths as divisors

Store Sales

Solve each problem.

1. One case of chips comes with 48 little bags inside. The case costs
   the store $16.80. How much did each bag cost?

   _____

   If the store sells a case of chips for $24.00, how much profit will
   the store make on each bag?

   _____

2. One box of peanuts comes with 24 bags inside. The box costs
   $8.16. How much did each bag cost?

   _____

   If the store sells a box of peanuts for $12.00, how much profit will
   the store make on each bag?

   _____

3. A case of soda has 24 cans or 4 six-packs. One case of orange
   soda costs $7.44. A six-pack of orange soda costs $1.92.
   Which is the better price per soda?

   _____

   How much could be saved by buying 24 cans of the better-priced
   soda?

   _____

Demonstrate division of decimals to the thousandths as divisors

Number & Operations

EMC 3019 • Basic Math Skills, Grade 6 • ©2003 by Evan-Moor Corp.

What's My Number (Division with Decimals)?

Name _____

Use the clues to find each decimal number.

1. • My number has three digits.
    • The digits add up to 9.
    • When multiplied by 0.3, the answer is 3.78.   _____

2. • My number has three digits.
    • The sum of the digits is 15.
    • The digits are all different odd numbers.
    • If divided by 0.25, the answer is a whole number.
    • The number is greater than 3 and less than 4.   _____

3. • My number is more than 10 and less than 20.
    • It has 3 digits.
    • The sum of the digits is 11.
    • If multiplied by 0.7, the answer is 10.22.   _____

4. • My number has four digits.
    • All the digits are odd numbers.
    • It is less than 20, but more than 10.
    • The ones digit and the tenths digit are the same.
    • The sum of the digits is 12.
    • The hundredths digit is four more than the digit in the tens place.
    • If multiplied by 0.2, the answer is 2.67.   _____

Demonstrate division of decimals to the thousandths as divisors

Math Test

Fill in the circle next to the correct answer.

1. $0.8 \div 2.0 =$ _____
   - Ⓐ 4.0
   - Ⓒ 40.0
   - Ⓑ 0.04
   - Ⓓ 0.4

2. $9.0 \div 0.3 =$ _____
   - Ⓐ 3.0
   - Ⓒ 30.0
   - Ⓑ 300.0
   - Ⓓ 0.3

3. $0.6 \div 0.2 =$ _____
   - Ⓐ 3.0
   - Ⓒ 30.0
   - Ⓑ 300.0
   - Ⓓ 0.3

4. $3.0 \div 1.2 =$ _____
   - Ⓐ 2.5
   - Ⓒ 0.4
   - Ⓑ 25.0
   - Ⓓ 0.25

5. $13.02 \div 3.1 =$ _____
   - Ⓐ 0.042
   - Ⓒ 4.2
   - Ⓑ 0.42
   - Ⓓ 42.0

6. $4.68 \div 5.2 =$ _____
   - Ⓐ 9.0
   - Ⓒ 0.09
   - Ⓑ 0.9
   - Ⓓ 0.009

7. $0.096 \div 1.2 =$ _____
   - Ⓐ 80.0
   - Ⓒ 0.8
   - Ⓑ 8.0
   - Ⓓ 0.08

8. $2.63 \div 5.26 =$ _____
   - Ⓐ 2.0
   - Ⓒ 0.02
   - Ⓑ 5.0
   - Ⓓ 0.5

9. Shelley has 16.5 ounces of frosting that she wants to divide into 4 equal servings to frost four different cupcakes. How many ounces of frosting should she put on each cupcake? (Give the answer in decimal form, with no remainders.)

   _____

   _____

10. A case of candy bars contains 24 bars. If the case costs $8.88, what is the cost per candy bar?

    _____

    _____

Demonstrate division of decimals to the thousandths as divisors

Riddle

What's the time when the clock strikes thirteen?

To solve the riddle, solve each problem below. Write the letter that corresponds to the answer in front of the problem. When completed, read the solution from top to bottom, starting on the left.

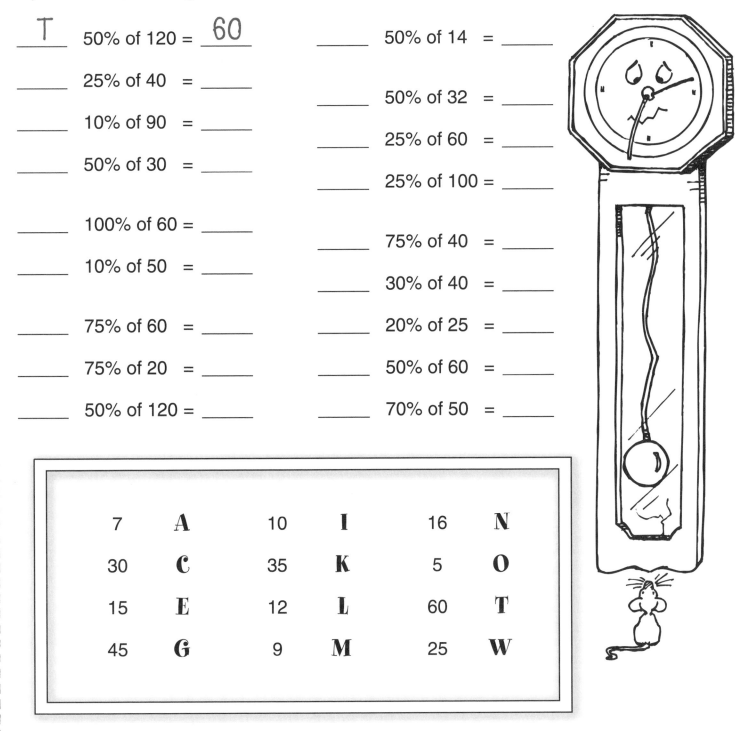

__T__ 50% of 120 = _60_

_____ 25% of 40 = _____

_____ 10% of 90 = _____

_____ 50% of 30 = _____

_____ 100% of 60 = _____

_____ 10% of 50 = _____

_____ 75% of 60 = _____

_____ 75% of 20 = _____

_____ 50% of 120 = _____

_____ 50% of 14 = _____

_____ 50% of 32 = _____

_____ 25% of 60 = _____

_____ 25% of 100 = _____

_____ 75% of 40 = _____

_____ 30% of 40 = _____

_____ 20% of 25 = _____

_____ 50% of 60 = _____

_____ 70% of 50 = _____

7	A	10	I	16	N
30	C	35	K	5	O
15	E	12	L	60	T
45	G	9	M	25	W

Utilize percents

Why Is Tennis a Waiter's Favorite Sport?

Name_____

To solve the riddle, solve each problem below. Write the corresponding letter in front of the problem. When completed, read the solution from **bottom to top**, starting from the right.

__E__ 20% of 50 = _10_   ____ 50% of 24 = ____

____ 10% of 50 = ____   ____ 10% of 100 = ____

____ 75% of 12 = ____   ____ 25% of 28 = ____

____ 50% of 14 = ____   ____ 50% of 26 = ____

____ 40% of 50 = ____   ____ 50% of 40 = ____

____ 25% of 40 = ____   ____ 10% of 60 = ____

____ 20% of 60 = ____   ____ 25% of 56 = ____

                              ____ 20% of 45 = ____

____ 75% of 16 = ____

____ 25% of 36 = ____   ____ 100% of 60 = ____

____ 100% of 32 = ____   ____ 50% of 18 = ____

5	C
10	E
32	H
9	I
14	M
15	N
13	O
6	P
20	R
12	S
60	T
7	V

Utilize percents

Percents 1

Name _____

Answer the following questions about percent.

1. What is 100% of 25? _____

2. What is 10% of 60? _____

3. What is 25% of 48? _____

4. What is 70% of 50? _____

5. What is 75% of 32? _____

6. What is 90% of 40? _____

7. What is 20% of 35? _____

8. What is 50% of 32? _____

9. What is 40% of 55? _____

10. What is 25% of 64? _____

11. What is 100% of 42? _____

12. What is 25% of 20? _____

13. What is 70% of 90? _____

14. What is 75% of 36? _____

15. What is 10% of 50? _____

16. What is 10% of 70? _____

17. What is 40% of 60? _____

18. What is 90% of 70? _____

19. What is 50% of 24? _____

20. What is 50% of 82? _____

Utilize percents

Percents II

What is 50% of each number?

1. 6 _____   **3.** 28 _____

2. 50 _____   **4.** 300 _____

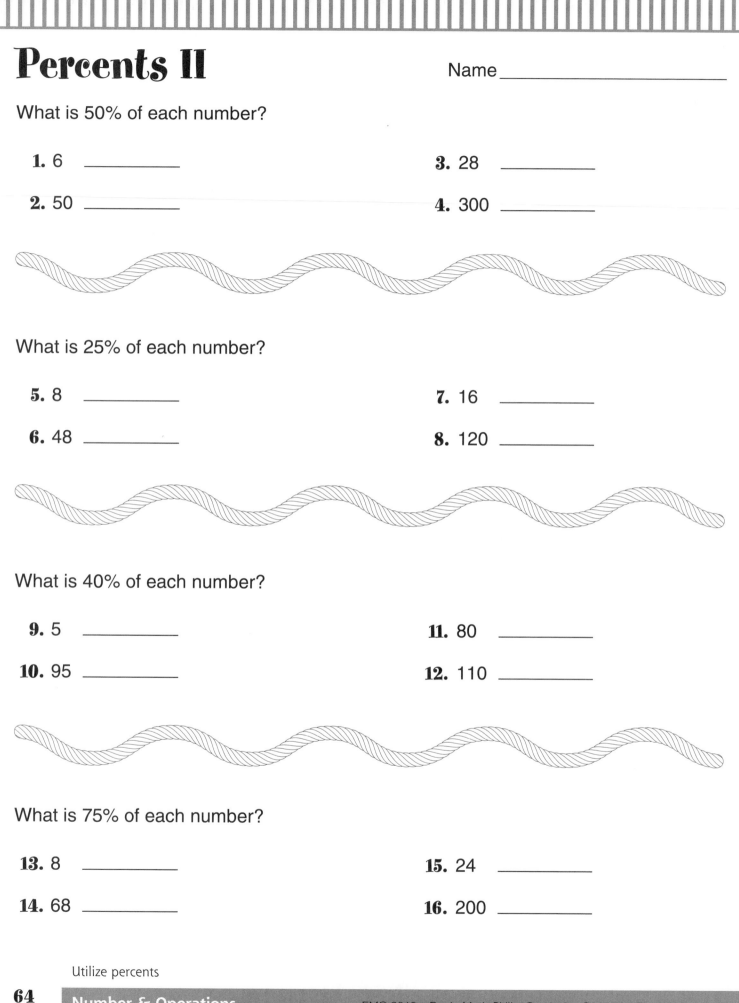

What is 25% of each number?

5. 8 _____   **7.** 16 _____

6. 48 _____   **8.** 120 _____

What is 40% of each number?

9. 5 _____   **11.** 80 _____

10. 95 _____   **12.** 110 _____

What is 75% of each number?

13. 8 _____   **15.** 24 _____

14. 68 _____   **16.** 200 _____

Utilize percents

On Sale!

Name _____

Solve each problem. Be sure to show your work on each problem.

1. Tim found a new jacket on sale. The original price was $96.
   The tag said that it was 25% off. What was the sale price?

   _____

2. Julia was shopping at a store that advertised 50% off everything.
   She found a new CD player originally priced at $76. What was
   the sale price?

   _____

3. Roberto bought a new shirt that was 25% off. The original price
   was $60. How much did he save?

   _____

4. Amy Beth found a new pair of shoes that were 30% off the original
   price. The original price was $60. How much did she save?

   _____

5. Andy and his brother found a new video game advertised at
   25% off. They split the cost of the new game between the two of
   them. The original price was $60. How much did each of them
   pay with the discount?

   _____

Utilize percents

Car Sales

Solve each problem.

1. Tim is planning to buy a used car for $5,000. The tax on the new car is 6%. How much will he pay for the car including tax?

   _____

2. Dorothy and her twin sister will split the cost of a car when they are 16. Their parents have agreed to pay 10% of the cost of the car. If they buy a car for $7,500, how much will each sister pay?

   _____

3. Jack's parents and grandparents have each offered to pay a portion of his new car that costs $9,000. His grandparents will pay 10%, and his parents will pay 20%. How much will Jack have to pay?

   _____

4. Juanita's older sister Ramona is buying a car that she will share with her mom. They have figured that Ramona will use the car about 20% of the time, so she will pay 20% of the cost of the car. Her mom will pay the remaining amount. The car costs $12,000. How much of the car's cost will each of them pay?

   _____

5. Tim is thinking about getting a new car, and he wants to know what his insurance costs will be. He will have to pay 13% of the cost of the car annually as his insurance costs. He is considering two different cars: one that costs $15,000 and one that costs $8,000. What would his monthly insurance costs be for each vehicle?

   _____

Utilize percents

Math Test

Fill in the circle next to the correct answer.

1. What is 100% of 25?

Ⓐ 25   Ⓒ 20

Ⓑ 5   Ⓓ 50

2. What is 25% of 24?

Ⓐ 25   Ⓒ 6

Ⓑ 12   Ⓓ 4

3. What is 50% of 16?

Ⓐ 50   Ⓒ 8

Ⓑ 16   Ⓓ 4

4. What is 50% of 64?

Ⓐ 8   Ⓒ 64

Ⓑ 16   Ⓓ 32

5. What is 75% of 32?

Ⓐ 75   Ⓒ 25

Ⓑ 24   Ⓓ 16

6. What is 10% of 90?

Ⓐ 10   Ⓒ 8

Ⓑ 9   Ⓓ 7

7. What is 80% of 40?

Ⓐ 32   Ⓒ 30

Ⓑ 40   Ⓓ 20

8. What is 90% of 200?

Ⓐ 90   Ⓒ 18

Ⓑ 9   Ⓓ 180

9. Tim found a jacket that was 25% off. The original price was $45.00. What was the sale price?

_____

_____

10. Jennifer saw a new CD player that was 10% off. The original price was $72.00. How much will she save?

_____

_____

Utilize percents

Tongue Twister #6

Name_____

Answer each question below. Then write the corresponding letter above each answer. The letters will spell out a tongue twister. Try to say it fast three times.

B What is the fraction form of 0.5? _____   **M** What is the percent form of 0.48? _____

C What is the decimal form of 30%? _____   **N** What is the fraction form of 30%? _____

D What is the percent form of 0.8? _____   **R** What is the decimal form of 70%? _____

E What is the fraction form of 0.4? _____   **S** What is the percent form of 0.08? _____

G What is the decimal form of 14%? _____   **T** What is the fraction form of 0.9? _____

H What is the percent form of $\frac{1}{2}$? _____   **U** What is the decimal form of 29%? _____

I What is the fraction form of 0.75? _____   **W** What is the percent form of $\frac{1}{4}$? _____

L What is the decimal form of $\frac{1}{8}$? _____

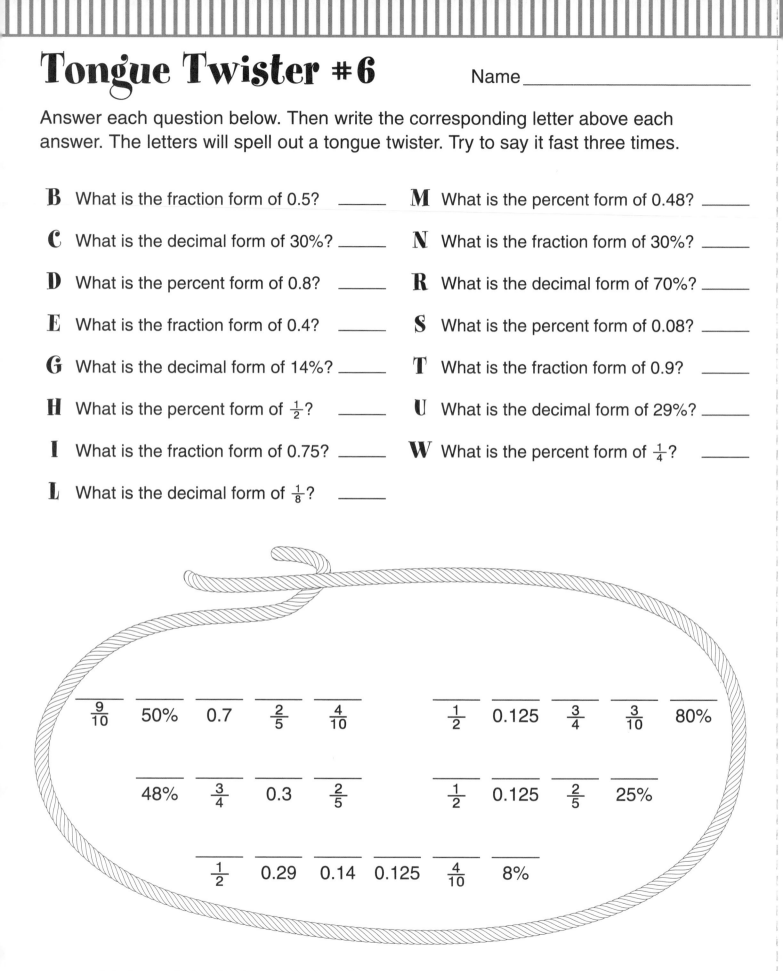

$\frac{9}{10}$ 50%   0.7 $\frac{2}{5}$ $\frac{4}{10}$ $\frac{1}{2}$ 0.125 $\frac{3}{4}$ $\frac{3}{10}$ 80%

48% $\frac{3}{4}$ 0.3 $\frac{2}{5}$ $\frac{1}{2}$ 0.125 $\frac{2}{5}$ 25%

$\frac{1}{2}$ 0.29   0.14   0.125 $\frac{4}{10}$ 8%

Calculate equivalent fractions, decimals, and percents

EMC 3019 • Basic Math Skills, Grade 6 • ©2003 by Evan-Moor Corp.

What Has Fifty Heads and No Tails?

Name _____

Answer each question below. Then write the corresponding letter above each answer. The letters will spell out the answer to the riddle.

A   What is the decimal form of $\frac{1}{2}$?   _____

B   What is the fraction form of 0.25?   _____

C   What is the percent form of $\frac{1}{2}$?   _____

E   What is the decimal form of 40%?   _____

F   What is the fraction form of 75%?   _____

H   What is the percent form of 0.9?   _____

M   What is the decimal form of 43%?   _____

O   What is the fraction form of 80%?   _____

S   What is the percent form of 0.09?   _____

T   What is the decimal form of 80%?   _____

X   What is the fraction form of 30%?   _____

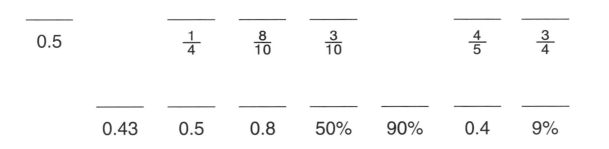

| ____ | | ____ | ____ | ____ | | ____ | ____ |
| 0.5 | | $\frac{1}{4}$ | $\frac{8}{10}$ | $\frac{3}{10}$ | | $\frac{4}{5}$ | $\frac{3}{4}$ |

| | ____ | ____ | ____ | ____ | ____ | ____ | ____ |
| | 0.43 | 0.5 | 0.8 | 50% | 90% | 0.4 | 9% |

Calculate equivalent fractions, decimals, and percents

Number & Operations

That's Equivalent

Name _____

Complete the table below so that each row shows three representations of the same value.

	Fraction	Decimal	Percent
1.	$\frac{1}{4}$	0.25	25%
2.		0.5	50%
3.	$\frac{7}{10}$		
4.			75%
5.		0.8	
6.	$\frac{2}{5}$		
7.	$\frac{1}{8}$		
8.			37.5%
9.		0.9	
10.		0.625	

Calculate equivalent fractions, decimals, and percents

Number & Operations

EMC 3019 • Basic Math Skills, Grade 6 • ©2003 by Evan-Moor Corp.

That's Equivalent, Too

Name_____

Complete the table below so that each row shows three representations of the same value.

	Fraction	Decimal	Percent
1.			50%
2.	$\frac{1}{8}$		
3.		0.875	
4.	$\frac{1}{4}$		
5.			62.5%
6.	$\frac{7}{10}$		
7.		0.3	
8.		0.75	
9.			90%
10.		0.375	

Calculate equivalent fractions, decimals, and percents

Number & Operations

Sales

Solve each problem.

1. Helena was shopping and found a suit that she really liked.
   The sale at the store was 40% off. In order to figure out how much
   the discount was, she needed to convert the percent into
   a decimal. What is 40% as a decimal?

   _____

2. Fred found a jersey that he really liked that was $\frac{1}{5}$ off. At another
   store, he found the same jersey listed at the same original price,
   but it was discounted 15% off. Which was the better buy
   (cheaper for Fred)?

   _____

3. Tax for Northglenn City is calculated at 6.5%. Shawn is working
   at a convenience store with his mom and needs to convert the
   percent into a decimal to input it on his calculator. What decimal
   number should he use?

   _____

4. Jasmine used her calculator to find the percent of discount
   that she got when she bought a sweater. The calculator read
   0.4117647. What percent discount was the sweater?
   (Round the value to the nearest percent.)

   _____

5. Steven saw a sweatshirt at one store for $\frac{1}{4}$ off. He saw the
   same sweatshirt at another store discounted by 25%, and he is
   wondering which one is cheaper. What additional information do
   you need to answer this question? If you had this information,
   how would these discounts compare?

   _____

Calculate equivalent fractions, decimals, and percents

Number & Operations

EMC 3019 • Basic Math Skills, Grade 6 • ©2003 by Evan-Moor Corp.

Spelling Tests

Name_____

1. Julia got 19 out of the 20 spelling words on her test.
   What percent did she get correct?   _____

2. Hector got 12 out of the 20 spelling words on his test.
   What percent did he get wrong?   _____

3. Rebecca got 17 out of the 20 spelling words on her test.
   What percent did she get correct?   _____

4. Edward got 19 out of the 25 spelling words on his test.
   What percent did he get correct?   _____

5. Regina got 24 out of the 25 spelling words on her test.
   What percent did she get wrong?   _____

6. Wesley got 40% of the words on his spelling test correct.
   What fraction of the words did he get correct?   _____

7. Waldo got 50% of the words on his spelling test correct.
   What fraction of the words did he get correct?   _____

8. Aaron got 25% of the words on his spelling test correct.
   What fraction of the words did he get correct?   _____

Calculate equivalent fractions, decimals, and percents

Math Test

Name _____

Fill in the circle next to the correct answer.

1. What is the decimal form of $\frac{1}{2}$?

   Ⓐ 0.25   Ⓒ 0.12

   Ⓑ 0.5   Ⓓ 0.1

2. What is the decimal form of 25%?

   Ⓐ 2.5   Ⓒ 0.25

   Ⓑ 0.025   Ⓓ 25.0

3. What is the decimal form of $\frac{2}{5}$?

   Ⓐ 0.25   Ⓒ 0.4

   Ⓑ 0.2   Ⓓ 0.5

4. What is the fraction form of 75%?

   Ⓐ $\frac{1}{2}$ Ⓒ $\frac{5}{7}$

   Ⓑ $\frac{2}{3}$ Ⓓ $\frac{3}{4}$

5. What is the fraction form of 0.8?

   Ⓐ $\frac{4}{5}$ Ⓒ $\frac{1}{2}$

   Ⓑ $\frac{8}{15}$ Ⓓ $\frac{3}{4}$

6. What is the fraction form of 20%?

   Ⓐ $\frac{2}{5}$ Ⓒ $\frac{1}{5}$

   Ⓑ $\frac{4}{9}$ Ⓓ $\frac{2}{9}$

7. What is the percent form of 0.15?

   Ⓐ 15%   Ⓒ 1.5%

   Ⓑ 0.15%   Ⓓ 150%

8. What is the percent form of $\frac{9}{10}$?

   Ⓐ 9%   Ⓒ 10%

   Ⓑ 90%   Ⓓ 91%

9. Give two other values that are equivalent to 25%.

_____

_____

10. Explain how to change a decimal into a percent.

_____

_____

_____

Calculate equivalent fractions, decimals, and percents

Number & Operations   EMC 3019 • Basic Math Skills, Grade 6 • ©2003 by Evan-Moor Corp.

What Did Noah Use to See in the Dark?

Name _____

To solve the riddle, complete each of the following math sentences with either the <, =, or > symbol. Then draw a straight line from the problem to the correct symbol. Each line will pass through at least one number. Write the letter that corresponds to each number on the line(s) at the bottom of the page. The letters will spell out the solution to the riddle.

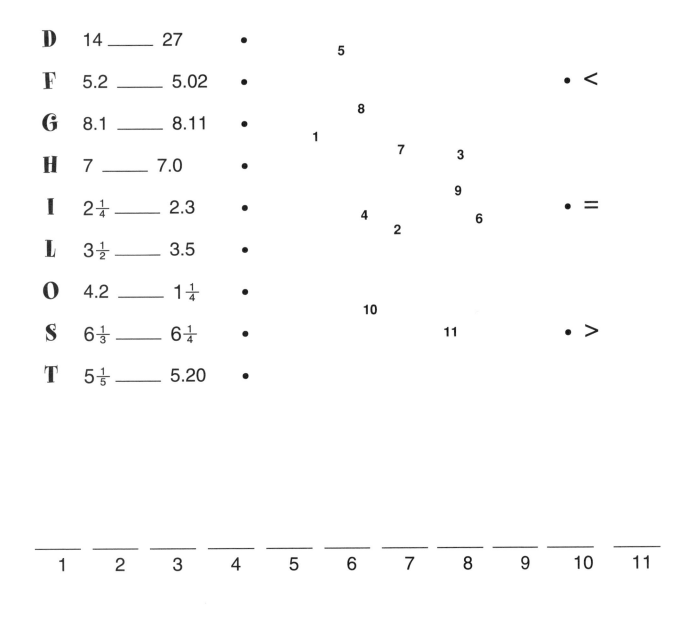

D 14 _____ 27

F 5.2 _____ 5.02

G 8.1 _____ 8.11

H 7 _____ 7.0

I $2\frac{1}{4}$ _____ 2.3

L $3\frac{1}{2}$ _____ 3.5

O 4.2 _____ $1\frac{1}{4}$

S $6\frac{1}{3}$ _____ $6\frac{1}{4}$

T $5\frac{1}{5}$ _____ 5.20

5

<

8
1
7   3
9
4   6   =
2

10
11   >

___ ___ ___ ___ ___ ___ ___ ___ ___ ___ ___
1   2   3   4   5   6   7   8   9   10   11

Compare values using <, >, ≤, ≥, and =

What Relation Is a Doorstep to a Doormat?

Name _____

To solve the riddle, complete each of the following math sentences with either the <, =, or > symbol. Then draw a straight line from the problem to the correct symbol. Each line will pass through at least one number. Write the letter that corresponds to each number on the line(s) at the bottom of the page. The letters will spell out the solution to the riddle.

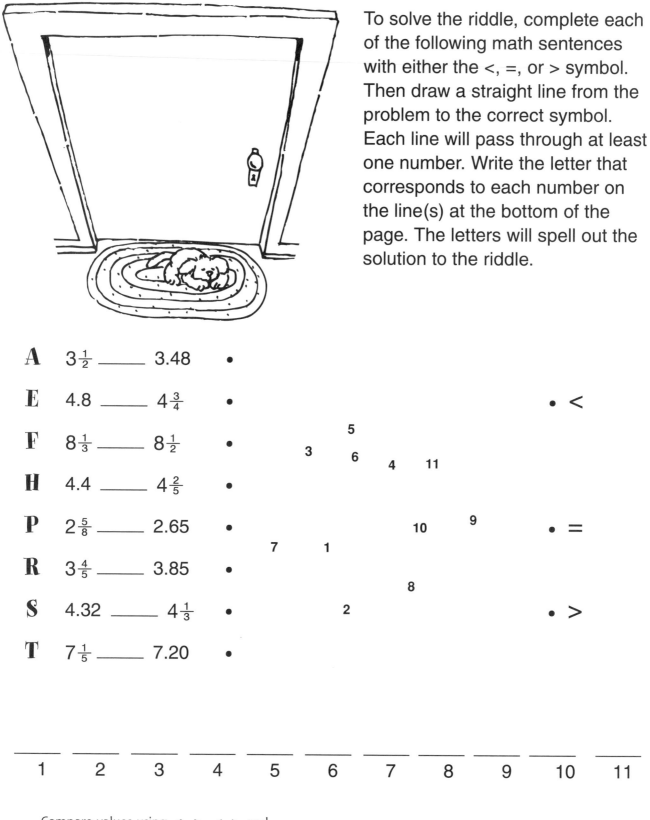

A $3\frac{1}{2}$ ____ 3.48   •

E   4.8 ____ $4\frac{3}{4}$ •

F $8\frac{1}{3}$ ____ $8\frac{1}{2}$ •

H   4.4 ____ $4\frac{2}{5}$ •

P $2\frac{5}{8}$ ____ 2.65   •

R $3\frac{4}{5}$ ____ 3.85   •

S   4.32 ____ $4\frac{1}{3}$ •

T $7\frac{1}{5}$ ____ 7.20   •

• <

5

3

6

4   11

10   9

• =

7   1

8

2

• >

___ ___ ___ ___ ___ ___ ___ ___ ___ ___ ___
 1   2   3   4   5   6   7   8   9   10 11

Compare values using <, >, ≤, ≥, and =

Number & Operations

EMC 3019 • Basic Math Skills, Grade 6 • ©2003 by Evan-Moor Corp.

Inequalities: True or False?

Name_____

Next to each math sentence, write *True* if the sentence is correct, and *False* if the sentence is NOT correct.

1. $5 < 8$ _____

2. $4 = 4.0$ _____

3. $3.3 > 3.4$ _____

4. $2.15 > 2.3$ _____

5. $5.16 < 6.2$ _____

6. $6.4 \geq 9.2$ _____

7. $6.5 \leq 6.50$ _____

8. $4.2 < 4.21$ _____

9. $9.05 = 9.5$ _____

10. $4.2 \leq 4.21$ _____

11. $4.32 < 4.23$ _____

12. $8.51 \geq 8.5$ _____

13. $9.2 > 9.29$ _____

14. $4.9 < 6.5$ _____

15. $4.5 \leq 4.15$ _____

16. $6.5 > 6.95$ _____

17. $4.2 \geq 3.99$ _____

18. $88.2 < 8.92$ _____

19. $4.169 \leq 41.6$ _____

20. $15.42 = 15.402$ _____

Compare values using $<$, $>$, $\leq$, $\geq$, and $=$

Inequalities

Complete each problem with one of the following symbols: <, =, or >

1. 2.63 _____ 2.603

2. 5.2 _____ 5.3

3. 4.9 _____ 4.19

4. 3.2 _____ 3.20

5. 4.5 _____ 4.05

6. 6.2 _____ 6.9

7. 4.15 _____ 4.5

8. 9.8 _____ 10.2

9. 6.3 _____ 6.93

10. 4.1 _____ 4.10

11. 63.25 _____ 63.25

12. 10.8 _____ 8.912

13. 5.2 _____ 14.9

14. 264.2 _____ 264.9

15. 429.5 _____ 430.9

16. 516.3 _____ 516.8

17. 520 _____ 520.0

18. 640.5 _____ 645.5

19. 420.9 _____ 420.89

20. 1,509.266 _____ 1,510.12

Compare values using <, >, ≤, ≥, and =

EMC 3019 • Basic Math Skills, Grade 6 • ©2003 by Evan-Moor Corp.

Sign Me Up

1. Normando can't remember the difference between the following two symbols: < and ≤. Write a note to Normando explaining the difference between them.

   _____

2. Mary has the problem 6.14 ___ 6.2. She is supposed to write a symbol on the line that makes a true math sentence. She reasons that 614 is much larger than 62, so it must be a > symbol. Write a note to Mary telling her if you agree with her or not and why.

   _____

3. Lucy was confused about the following math sentence: 4.8 ___ 4.80. She was asked to list more than one symbol that could be used to complete the math sentence correctly. List all the symbols she could use.

   _____

4. Luke has the problem 7.50 ___ $7\frac{1}{2}$. He is supposed to write a symbol on the line that makes a true math sentence. He reasons that in terms of money, 50 cents is the same as a half-dollar, so it must be an = symbol. Write a note to Luke telling him if he is correct or not and why.

   _____

Compare values using <, >, ≤, ≥, and =

Number & Operations   79

Better Buy

Name _____

In each of the following situations, determine which one is the better buy or the cheaper purchase. Write the values from the problem in a math sentence using the < or > symbols.

1. Rachel saw two different CD players. One was originally priced at $75 and was $\frac{1}{4}$ off. The other one was originally priced at $90 and was 30% off. Find the final price of each CD player, and then list them in order from the cheapest to most expensive using the correct inequality symbol.

    _____

2. Charity saw two different videos. One was originally priced at $30 and was $\frac{1}{5}$ off. The other was originally priced at $20 and was $\frac{1}{10}$ off. Find the final price of each video, and then list them in order from the cheapest to most expensive using the correct inequality symbol.

    _____

3. Ben was shopping for a new video game and saw two different sales. One had an original price of $45 and was $\frac{1}{10}$ off. The other was originally priced at $70 and was $\frac{1}{4}$ off. Find the final price of each jacket, and then list them in order from the cheapest to most expensive using the correct inequality symbol.

    _____

4. Ed and Cindy wanted to buy their father a new sweater for Father's Day. They found two different sales and didn't know which was better. One had an original price of $49 and was 20% off. The other store had one originally priced at $62 and was $\frac{1}{3}$ off. Find the final price of each sweater, and then list them in order from the cheapest to most expensive using the correct inequality symbol.

    _____

5. Jennifer, Kellie, and George each bought a new jacket. Jennifer's was originally priced at $80 and was 15% off. Kellie's was originally priced at $75 and was $\frac{1}{10}$ off. George's was originally priced at $90 and was $\frac{1}{5}$ off. Find the final price of each jacket, and then list them in order from the cheapest to most expensive using the correct inequality symbol.

    _____

Compare values using <, >, ≤, ≥, and =

EMC 3019 • Basic Math Skills, Grade 6 • ©2003 by Evan-Moor Corp.

Math Test

Name _____

Fill in the circle next to the correct answer.

1. Which math sentence is true?

- Ⓐ 5.30 = 5.3
- Ⓑ 6.2 = 6.201
- Ⓒ 5.03 = 5.3
- Ⓓ 15.2 = 1.52

2. Which math sentence is true?

- Ⓐ 5.4 > 5.51
- Ⓑ 2.49 > 2.5
- Ⓒ 3.52 > 3.49
- Ⓓ 6.12 > 6.23

3. Which math sentence is true?

- Ⓐ 5.16 < 5.151
- Ⓑ 5.49 < 5.481
- Ⓒ 13.0 < 12.99
- Ⓓ 2.19 < 2.2

4. Which symbol could complete the following?

$$4.7 \underline{} 4.24$$

- Ⓐ ≤
- Ⓑ =
- Ⓒ ≥
- Ⓓ any of the above

5. Which symbol could complete the following?

$$2.6 \underline{} 2.600$$

- Ⓐ ≤
- Ⓑ =
- Ⓒ ≥
- Ⓓ any of the above

6. Which symbol could complete the following?

$$4.116 \underline{} 4.12$$

- Ⓐ ≤
- Ⓑ =
- Ⓒ ≥
- Ⓓ any of the above

7. Which of the following is NOT true?

- Ⓐ 8.5 > 8.49
- Ⓑ 9.3 < 9.29
- Ⓒ 4.19 ≥ 4.155
- Ⓓ 19.25 ≤ 19.250

8. Which of the following is NOT true?

- Ⓐ 41.285 ≤ 41.285
- Ⓑ 15.261 < 15.262
- Ⓒ 51.254 ≥ 51.26
- Ⓓ 4.162 > 4.1

9. Use the numbers 3.5 and 3.51 and the > symbol to write a true math sentence.

_____

10. Use the numbers 15.82 and 15.8201 and the < symbol to write a true math sentence.

_____

Compare values using <, >, ≤, ≥, and =

©2003 by Evan-Moor Corp. • Basic Math Skills, Grade 6 • EMC 3019

Number & Operations   **81**

Riddle

What happened when the frog parked its car in a "No Parking" zone?

Find the prime factorization for each number below. Then write the corresponding letter on the line in front of the number. The letters will spell out the solution when read from **bottom to top**, starting on the right.

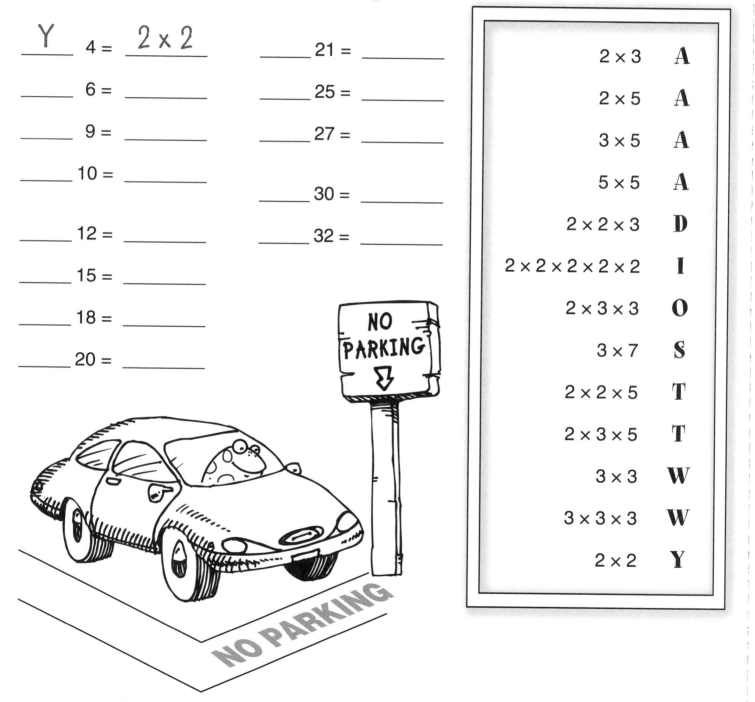

_Y_ 4 = _2 × 2_

_____ 6 = _____

_____ 9 = _____

_____ 10 = _____

_____ 12 = _____

_____ 15 = _____

_____ 18 = _____

_____ 20 = _____

_____ 21 = _____

_____ 25 = _____

_____ 27 = _____

_____ 30 = _____

_____ 32 = _____

2 × 3	**A**
2 × 5	**A**
3 × 5	**A**
5 × 5	**A**
2 × 2 × 3	**D**
2 × 2 × 2 × 2 × 2	**I**
2 × 3 × 3	**O**
3 × 7	**S**
2 × 2 × 5	**T**
2 × 3 × 5	**T**
3 × 3	**W**
3 × 3 × 3	**W**
2 × 2	**Y**

NO PARKING

NO PARKING

Calculate prime factorization for numbers less than 250

82

What Has Six Legs, but Can't Walk?

Name_____

Find the prime factorization for each number below. Then write the corresponding letter on the line in front of the number. The letters will spell out the solution when read from **bottom to top**.

___S___ 25 = ___5 x 5___

_____ 27 = _____

_____ 28 = _____

_____ 12 = _____

_____ 16 = _____

_____ 30 = _____

_____ 42 = _____

_____ 25 = _____

_____ 48 = _____

_____ 72 = _____

_____ 12 = _____

_____ 16 = _____

_____ 64 = _____

_____ 64 = _____

_____ 48 = _____

_____ 90 = _____

_____ 27 = _____

2 × 2 × 3	**A**
2 × 2 × 2 × 2 × 2 × 2	**E**
2 × 3 × 5	**F**
2 × 3 × 3 × 5	**H**
2 × 2 × 2 × 3 × 3	**I**
2 × 2 × 7	**N**
2 × 3 × 7	**O**
2 × 2 × 2 × 2	**P**
2 × 2 × 2 × 2 × 3	**R**
5 × 5	**S**
3 × 3 × 3	**T**

Calculate prime factorization for numbers less than 250

Number & Operations

83

Prime Factorization I

Name_____

Find the prime factorization for each of the following numbers.

1. 25 = _____

2. 32 = _____

3. 64 = _____

4. 50 = _____

5. 48 = _____

6. 49 = _____

7. 24 = _____

8. 16 = _____

9. 72 = _____

10. 68 = _____

11. 30 = _____

12. 8 = _____

13. 12 = _____

14. 76 = _____

15. 80 = _____

16. 9 = _____

17. 10 = _____

18. 36 = _____

19. 27 = _____

20. 81 = _____

Calculate prime factorization for numbers less than 250

Prime Factorization II

Name_____

Find the prime factorization for each of the following numbers.

1. 200 = _____

2. 198 = _____

3. 105 = _____

4. 180 = _____

5. 168 = _____

6. 102 = _____

7. 160 = _____

8. 184 = _____

9. 108 = _____

10. 132 = _____

11. 204 = _____

12. 120 = _____

13. 210 = _____

14. 175 = _____

15. 144 = _____

16. 147 = _____

17. 225 = _____

18. 121 = _____

19. 156 = _____

20. 215 = _____

Calculate prime factorization for numbers less than 250

Factor Trees

Factor trees can be used to find the prime factorization of any number. The following is an example of a factor tree used to find the prime factorization of the number 18.

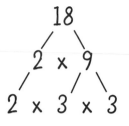

Draw a factor tree to find the prime factorization of each of the following numbers.

1. 15	**2.** 14	**3.** 25
4. 24	**5.** 45	**6.** 80
7. 32	**8.** 40	**9.** 16

Calculate prime factorization for numbers less than 250

EMC 3019 • Basic Math Skills, Grade 6 • ©2003 by Evan-Moor Corp.

Dividing by Primes

You can find the prime factorization of a number by dividing by prime numbers as shown below.

$$
\begin{array}{r|l}
2 & 12 \\
\hline
2 & 6 \\
\hline
& 3
\end{array}
$$

The prime factorization of 12 is 2 × 2 × 3.

Divide by prime numbers to find the prime factorization of each number.

1. 18	**2.** 20	**3.** 24
4. 15	**5.** 30	**6.** 22
7. 27	**8.** 60	**9.** 48

Calculate prime factorization for numbers less than 250

Math Test

Fill in the circle next to the correct answer.

For Numbers 1 through 8, find the prime factorization of the given number.

1. 24

   Ⓐ $2 \times 2 \times 2 \times 3$
   Ⓑ $2 \times 2 \times 3 \times 3$
   Ⓒ $2 \times 2 \times 3 \times 5$
   Ⓓ $2 \times 3 \times 3 \times 5$

2. 60

   Ⓐ $2 \times 2 \times 2 \times 3$
   Ⓑ $2 \times 2 \times 3 \times 3$
   Ⓒ $2 \times 2 \times 3 \times 5$
   Ⓓ $2 \times 3 \times 3 \times 5$

3. 36

   Ⓐ $2 \times 2 \times 3$
   Ⓑ $2 \times 2 \times 3 \times 3$
   Ⓒ $2 \times 2 \times 2 \times 3$
   Ⓓ $2 \times 3 \times 3$

4. 45

   Ⓐ $3 \times 5 \times 5$
   Ⓑ $2 \times 3 \times 5$
   Ⓒ 3×5
   Ⓓ $3 \times 3 \times 5$

5. 30

   Ⓐ $2 \times 2 \times 3$
   Ⓑ $2 \times 3 \times 5$
   Ⓒ $2 \times 2 \times 3 \times 5$
   Ⓓ $2 \times 3 \times 3 \times 5$

6. 42

   Ⓐ 3×7
   Ⓑ $2 \times 3 \times 3 \times 7$
   Ⓒ $2 \times 3 \times 7$
   Ⓓ $2 \times 2 \times 3 \times 7$

7. 21

   Ⓐ 3×7
   Ⓑ $2 \times 3 \times 3$
   Ⓒ $2 \times 3 \times 5$
   Ⓓ 2×7

8. 54

   Ⓐ $2 \times 3 \times 3 \times 3$
   Ⓑ $2 \times 2 \times 3$
   Ⓒ $2 \times 3 \times 3 \times 5$
   Ⓓ $2 \times 2 \times 3 \times 3$

---

9. Draw a factor tree to find the prime factorization of 20.

10. Divide by primes to find the prime factorization of 30.

Calculate prime factorization for numbers less than 250

Tongue Twister #7

Name _____

Find the Greatest Common Factor (GCF) for each pair of numbers. Then write the corresponding letter above each answer. The letters will spell out a tongue twister. Try to say it fast three times.

A GCF of 25 and 30 = _____   M GCF of 16 and 26 = _____

E GCF of 35 and 42 = _____   O GCF of 12 and 15 = _____

F GCF of 30 and 50 = _____   R GCF of 64 and 16 = _____

I GCF of 24 and 56 = _____   S GCF of 12 and 28 = _____

L GCF of 7 and 15   = _____   Y GCF of 18 and 54 = _____

___ ___ ___ ___ ___
10   1   7   5   4

___ ___ ___
10   1   18

___ ___ ___ ___
10   16   3   2

___ ___ ___ ___ ___
10   1   8   7   4

Calculate Greatest Common Factor (GCF) for up to three numbers less than 150

What Is Served but Never Eaten?

Name_____

To solve the riddle, find the GCF (Greatest Common Factor) for each of the following sets of numbers. Then write the corresponding letter in front of the set of numbers. The letters will spell out the solution when read from **bottom to top**.

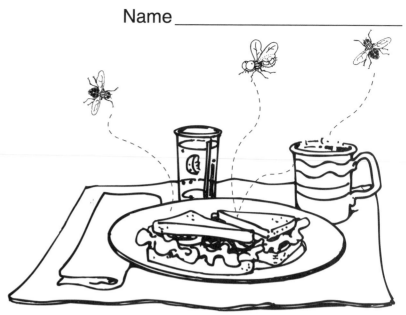

_____ What is the GCF of 10 and 15? _____

_____ What is the GCF of 5 and 20? _____

_____ What is the GCF of 7 and 9? _____

_____ What is the GCF of 4 and 14? _____

_____ What is the GCF of 16 and 24? _____

_____ What is the GCF of 12 and 20? _____

_____ What is the GCF of 14 and 21? _____

_____ What is the GCF of 28 and 7? _____

_____ What is the GCF of 12 and 15? _____

_____ What is the GCF of 18 and 45? _____

_____ What is the GCF of 11 and 21? _____

1	A
2	B
3	E
4	I
5	L
6	M
7	N
8	S
9	T

Calculate Greatest Common Factor (GCF) for up to three numbers less than 150

EMC 3019 • Basic Math Skills, Grade 6 • ©2003 by Evan-Moor Corp.

What's Your GCF?

Name _____

Find the Greatest Common Factor (GCF) for each of the following sets of numbers.

1. 2, 4 = _____

2. 3, 9 = _____

3. 5, 15 = _____

4. 4, 12 = _____

5. 6, 8 = _____

6. 4, 6 = _____

7. 3, 5 = _____

8. 2, 10 = _____

9. 4, 11 = _____

10. 5, 7 = _____

11. 6, 15 = _____

12. 10, 15 = _____

13. 20, 24 = _____

14. 32, 60 = _____

15. 100, 120 = _____

16. 90, 140 = _____

17. 100, 125 = _____

18. 99, 144 = _____

19. 18, 102 = _____

20. 22, 97 = _____

Calculate Greatest Common Factor (GCF) for up to three numbers less than 150

What's Your GCF II?

Name _____

Find the Greatest Common Factor (GCF) for each of the following sets of numbers.

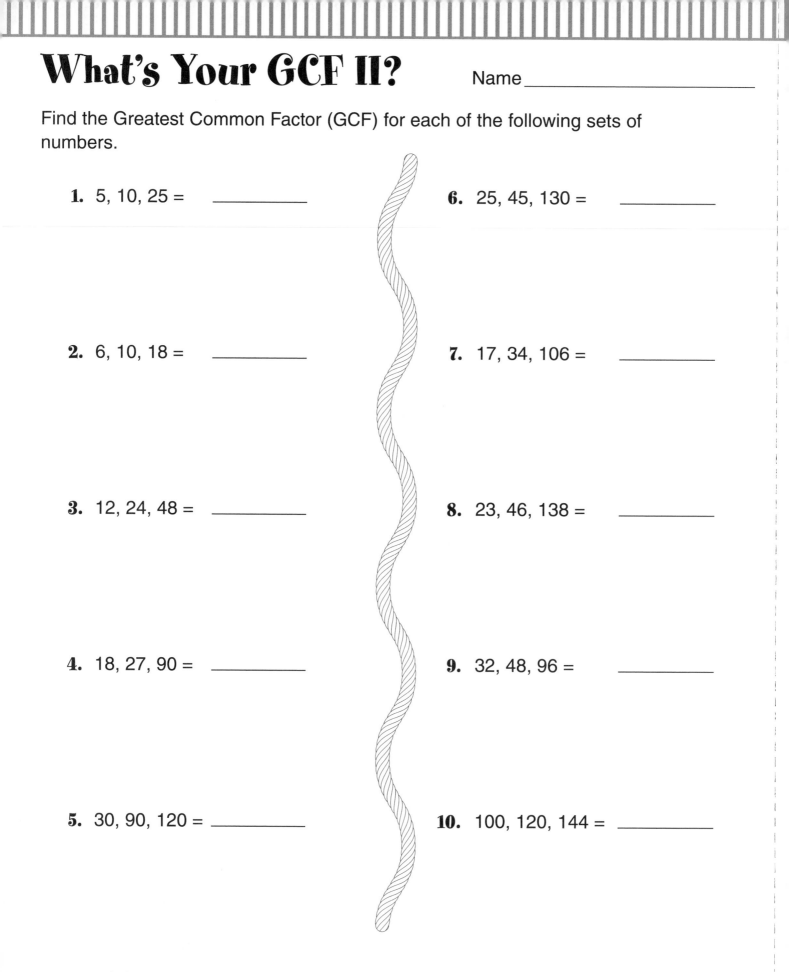

1. 5, 10, 25 = _____

2. 6, 10, 18 = _____

3. 12, 24, 48 = _____

4. 18, 27, 90 = _____

5. 30, 90, 120 = _____

6. 25, 45, 130 = _____

7. 17, 34, 106 = _____

8. 23, 46, 138 = _____

9. 32, 48, 96 = _____

10. 100, 120, 144 = _____

Calculate Greatest Common Factor (GCF) for up to three numbers less than 150

Number & Operations   EMC 3019 • Basic Math Skills, Grade 6 • ©2003 by Evan-Moor Corp.

Brendan's Test

Name _____

Brendan took a test on Greatest Common Factors. His work is below, and you need to be the teacher and check his paper. If he got it correct, write a *C* next to the problem. If he got it wrong, make a check mark and write the correct answer next to the check mark.

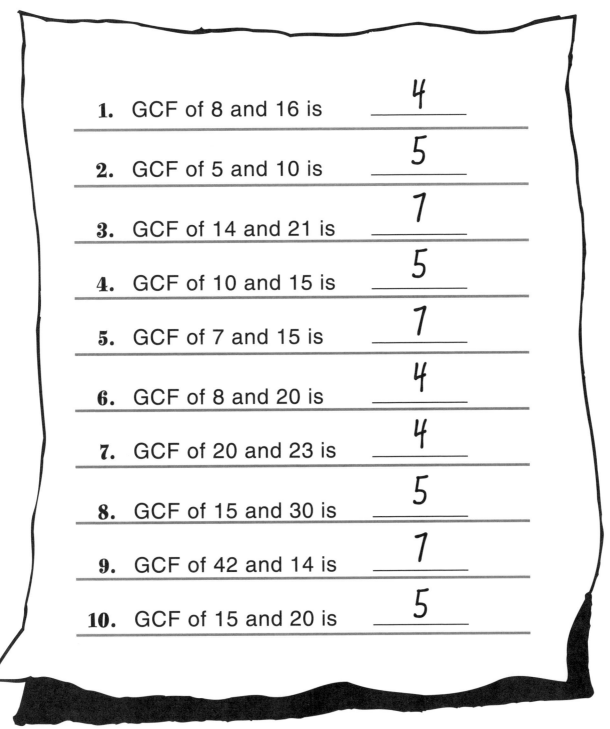

1. GCF of 8 and 16 is ____4____

2. GCF of 5 and 10 is ____5____

3. GCF of 14 and 21 is ____7____

4. GCF of 10 and 15 is ____5____

5. GCF of 7 and 15 is ____7____

6. GCF of 8 and 20 is ____4____

7. GCF of 20 and 23 is ____4____

8. GCF of 15 and 30 is ____5____

9. GCF of 42 and 14 is ____7____

10. GCF of 15 and 20 is ____5____

Calculate Greatest Common Factor (GCF) for up to three numbers less than 150

Reducing Fractions

One way to reduce fractions to their lowest terms is to find the GCF of the numerator and the denominator. Then divide both by the GCF and you have reduced the fraction into lowest terms.

GCF of 4 and 20 is 4. Divide both the numerator and denominator by 4.

$$\frac{4}{20} = \frac{4 \div 4}{20 \div 4} = \frac{1}{5}$$

Find the GCF of each numerator and denominator and reduce the fraction.

1. $\frac{3}{9}$ = _____

2. $\frac{4}{12}$ = _____

3. $\frac{5}{10}$ = _____

4. $\frac{15}{20}$ = _____

5. $\frac{4}{7}$ = _____

6. $\frac{2}{6}$ = _____

7. $\frac{12}{15}$ = _____

8. $\frac{20}{24}$ = _____

9. $\frac{15}{45}$ = _____

10. $\frac{36}{42}$ = _____

Calculate Greatest Common Factor (GCF) for up to three numbers less than 150

EMC 3019 • Basic Math Skills, Grade 6 • ©2003 by Evan-Moor Corp.

Math Test

Name _____

Fill in the circle next to the correct answer.

1. What does GCF stand for?

  Ⓐ Greatest Continuous Figure

  Ⓑ Geometric Circular Figure

  Ⓒ General Combination Factor

  Ⓓ Greatest Common Factor

2. What is the GCF of 3 and 6?

  Ⓐ 1

  Ⓑ 3

  Ⓒ 18

  Ⓓ 6

3. What is the GCF of 8 and 12?

  Ⓐ 8

  Ⓑ 2

  Ⓒ 4

  Ⓓ 24

4. What is the GCF of 15 and 32?

  Ⓐ 1

  Ⓑ 2

  Ⓒ 3

  Ⓓ 5

5. What is the GCF of 9 and 27?

  Ⓐ 1

  Ⓑ 3

  Ⓒ 27

  Ⓓ 9

6. What is the GCF of 16, 8, and 12?

  Ⓐ 4

  Ⓑ 2

  Ⓒ 8

  Ⓓ 48

7. What is the GCF of 15, 40, and 30?

  Ⓐ 10

  Ⓑ 3

  Ⓒ 5

  Ⓓ 120

8. What is the GCF of 3, 4, and 12?

  Ⓐ 3

  Ⓑ 1

  Ⓒ 2

  Ⓓ 12

9. What are all the common factors of 24 and 32?

_____

_____

10. What is the GCF of 24 and 32? Why?

_____

_____

_____

Calculate Greatest Common Factor (GCF) for up to three numbers less than 150

Trivia #2

How many teeth can a shark grow in its lifetime?

To find the answer, determine the Least Common Multiple (LCM) for each set of numbers below. Then write the corresponding letter on the line above the LCM. The letters will spell out the answer.

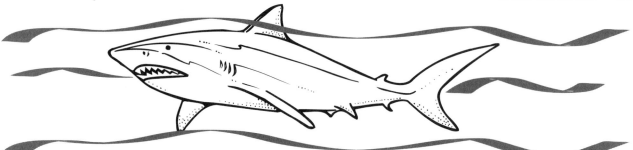

A What is the LCM of 1 and 5? _____

D What is the LCM of 2 and 3? _____

E What is the LCM of 3 and 9? _____

F What is the LCM of 1 and 11? _____

H What is the LCM of 16 and 2? _____

N What is the LCM of 17 and 1? _____

O What is the LCM of 13 and 1? _____

R What is the LCM of 18 and 3? _____

S What is the LCM of 14 and 2? _____

T What is the LCM of 3 and 5? _____

U What is the LCM of 1 and 7? _____

W What is the LCM of 2 and 5? _____

Y What is the LCM of 8 and 2? _____

___ ___ ___ ___ ___ ___
15   10   9   17   15   8

___ ___ ___ ___
11   13   7   18

___ ___ ___ ___ ___ ___ ___ ___
15   16   13   7   14   5   17   6

Calculate Least Common Multiple (LCM) for up to three numbers less than 25

EMC 3019 • Basic Math Skills, Grade 6 • ©2003 by Evan-Moor Corp.

What's Best for a Sick Bird?

Name _____

To solve the riddle, find the Least Common Multiple (LCM) for each set of numbers. Then write the corresponding letter on the line above the LCM. The letters will spell out the solution to the riddle.

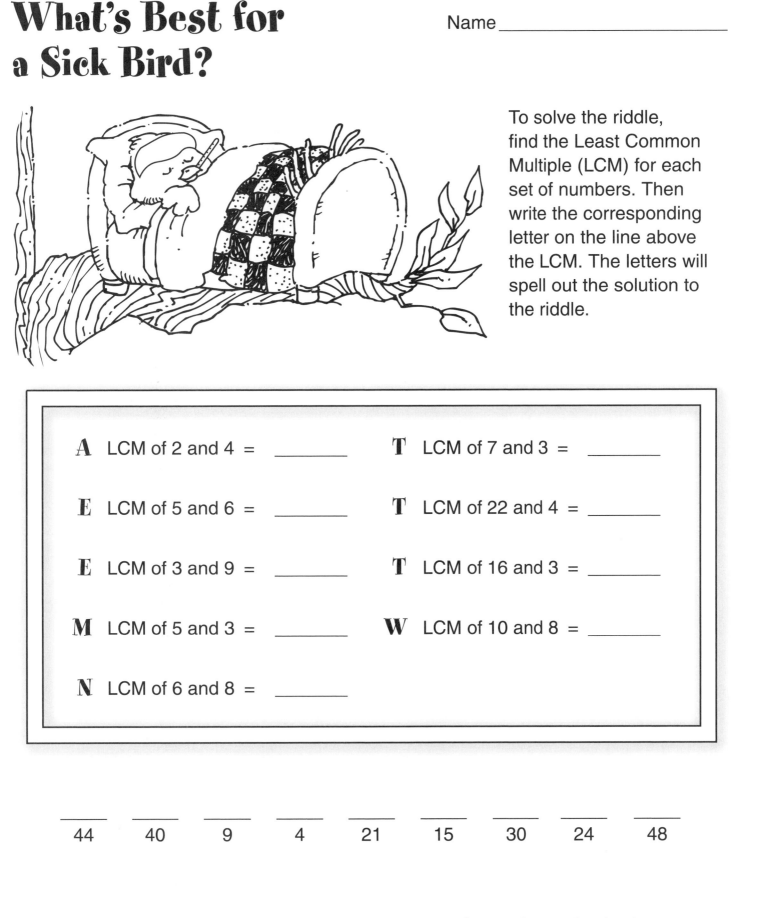

A LCM of 2 and 4 = _____

E LCM of 5 and 6 = _____

E LCM of 3 and 9 = _____

M LCM of 5 and 3 = _____

N LCM of 6 and 8 = _____

T LCM of 7 and 3 = _____

T LCM of 22 and 4 = _____

T LCM of 16 and 3 = _____

W LCM of 10 and 8 = _____

___ ___ ___ ___ ___ ___ ___ ___ ___
44   40   9   4   21   15   30   24   48

Calculate Least Common Multiple (LCM) for up to three numbers less than 25

LCM 1

Find the Least Common Multiple (LCM) for each set of numbers below.

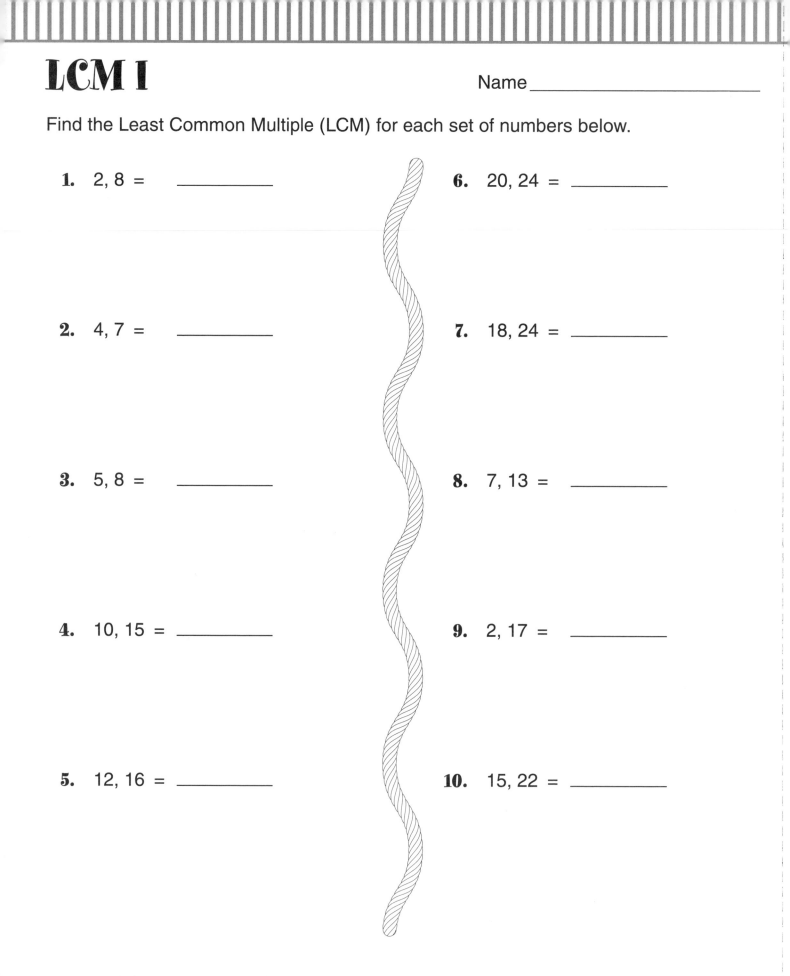

1. 2, 8 = _____

2. 4, 7 = _____

3. 5, 8 = _____

4. 10, 15 = _____

5. 12, 16 = _____

6. 20, 24 = _____

7. 18, 24 = _____

8. 7, 13 = _____

9. 2, 17 = _____

10. 15, 22 = _____

Calculate Least Common Multiple (LCM) for up to three numbers less than 25

LCM II

Name_____

Find the Least Common Multiple (LCM) for each set of numbers below.

1. 2, 4, 6 = _____

2. 3, 6, 9 = _____

3. 2, 4, 7 = _____

4. 1, 6, 9 = _____

5. 3, 5, 10 = _____

6. 4, 9, 24 = _____

7. 2, 15, 20 = _____

8. 4, 12, 15 = _____

9. 6, 8, 10 = _____

10. 3, 5, 11 = _____

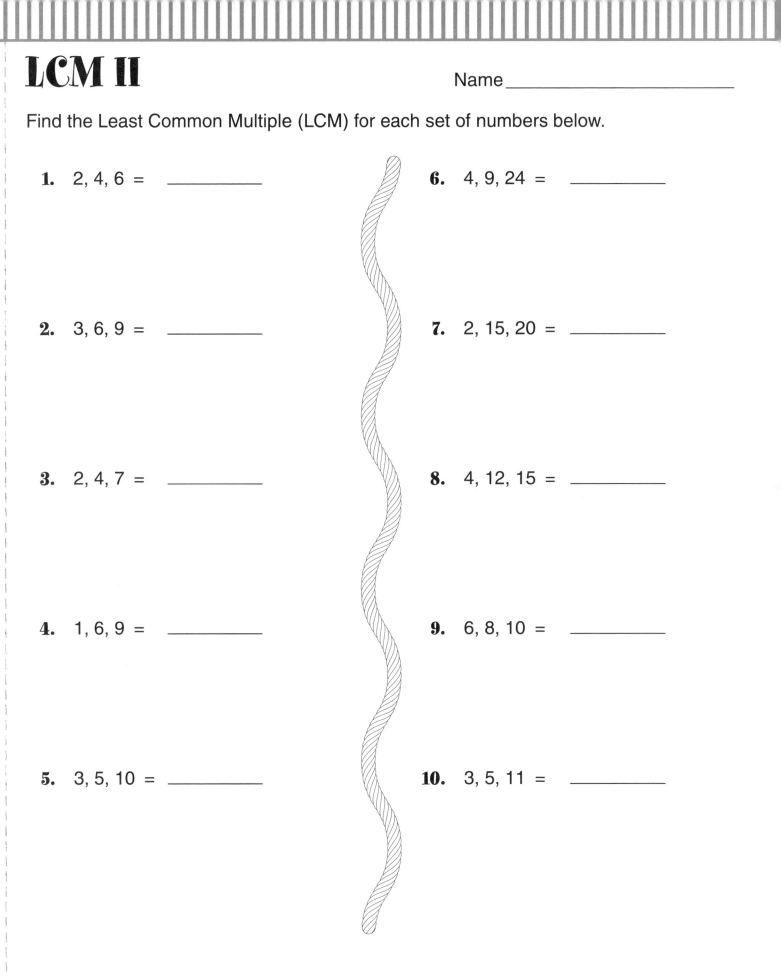

Calculate Least Common Multiple (LCM) for up to three numbers less than 25

Number & Operations

LCD

Tim's teacher mentioned that he would need to use the concept of Least Common Multiples (LCM) when adding and subtracting fractions with unlike denominators. She said that he would need to look at the denominators of all the fractions and find the Least Common Denominator (LCD) for the fractions that are being added or subtracted. Look at each set of fractions below and find the LCD (the LCM of the denominators).

1. $\dfrac{1}{5}$, $\dfrac{2}{3}$ _____

2. $\dfrac{4}{5}$, $\dfrac{2}{7}$ _____

3. $\dfrac{5}{6}$, $\dfrac{1}{3}$ _____

4. $\dfrac{3}{4}$, $\dfrac{9}{10}$ _____

5. $\dfrac{3}{5}$, $\dfrac{5}{9}$ _____

6. $\dfrac{13}{15}$, $\dfrac{1}{20}$ _____

7. $\dfrac{19}{20}$, $\dfrac{1}{24}$ _____

8. $\dfrac{4}{9}$, $\dfrac{3}{5}$ _____

9. $\dfrac{7}{9}$, $\dfrac{5}{11}$ _____

10. $\dfrac{5}{18}$, $\dfrac{3}{16}$ _____

Calculate Least Common Multiple (LCM) for up to three numbers less than 25

Venn Diagrams for LCM

Name _____

The Venn diagram shows the first 6 multiples of 2 and 4. The center section shows the common multiples. The Least Common Multiple (LCM) of 2 and 4 is 4.

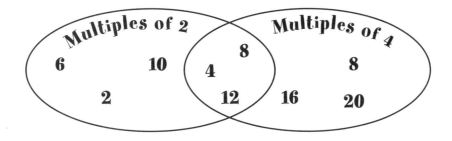

Write the first 5 multiples of each number in the Venn diagram. Write the common multiples in the center section. Circle the LCM.

1. 2, 3

2. 3, 5

3. 2, 5

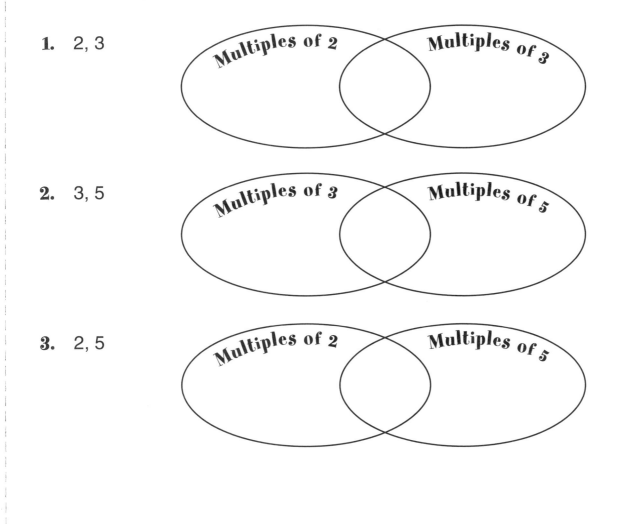

Calculate Least Common Multiple (LCM) for up to three numbers less than 25

Math Test

Fill in the circle next to the correct answer.

1. What does LCM stand for?

  Ⓐ Lowest Computed Multiple
  Ⓑ Least Computed Measurement
  Ⓒ Least Common Multiple
  Ⓓ Longitudinal Cartesian Measurement

2. What is the LCM of 3 and 4?

  Ⓐ 12
  Ⓑ 3
  Ⓒ 4
  Ⓓ 1

3. What is the LCM of 2 and 10?

  Ⓐ 2
  Ⓑ 10
  Ⓒ 5
  Ⓓ 20

4. What is the LCM of 9 and 12?

  Ⓐ 72
  Ⓑ 3
  Ⓒ 1
  Ⓓ 36

5. What is the LCM of 24 and 36?

  Ⓐ 72
  Ⓑ 12
  Ⓒ 24
  Ⓓ 36

6. What is the LCM of 2, 3, and 5?

  Ⓐ 2
  Ⓑ 30
  Ⓒ 1
  Ⓓ 60

7. What is the LCM of 4, 6, and 9?

  Ⓐ 36
  Ⓑ 216
  Ⓒ 1
  Ⓓ 12

8. What is the LCM of 12, 15, and 16?

  Ⓐ 180
  Ⓑ 2,880
  Ⓒ 1
  Ⓓ 240

9. What are the first seven multiples of 4 and the first seven multiples of 7?

_____

_____

_____

10. What is the LCM of 4 and 7?

_____

_____

_____

Calculate equivalent fractions, decimals, and percents

Algebra

Function Tables

Number Lines and the Coordinate System

Equations

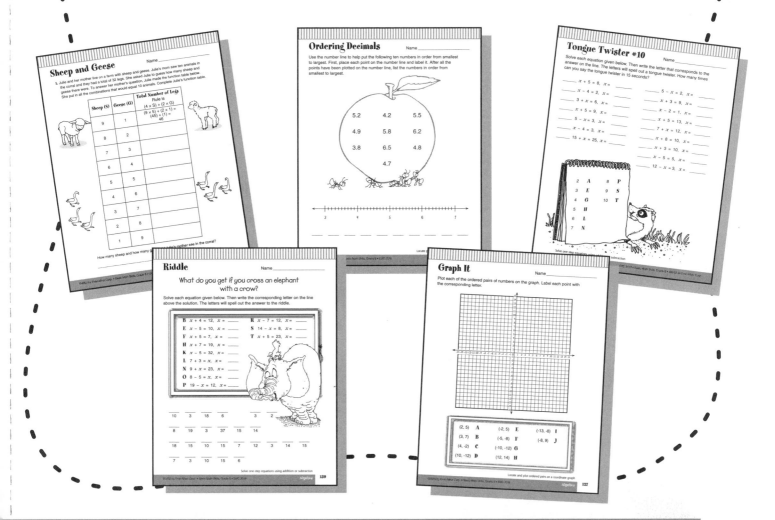

What Runs Around the Garden Without Moving?

Name_____

Complete each function table using the given rule. On the line above the output value, write the corresponding letter from the chart. The letters will spell out the answer to the riddle.

Rule is ×3 +2	
Input	**Output**
2	8
4	
9	
12	

A
C
E

Rule is ×2 −3	
Input	**Output**
2	1
4	
9	
11	

E
F
N

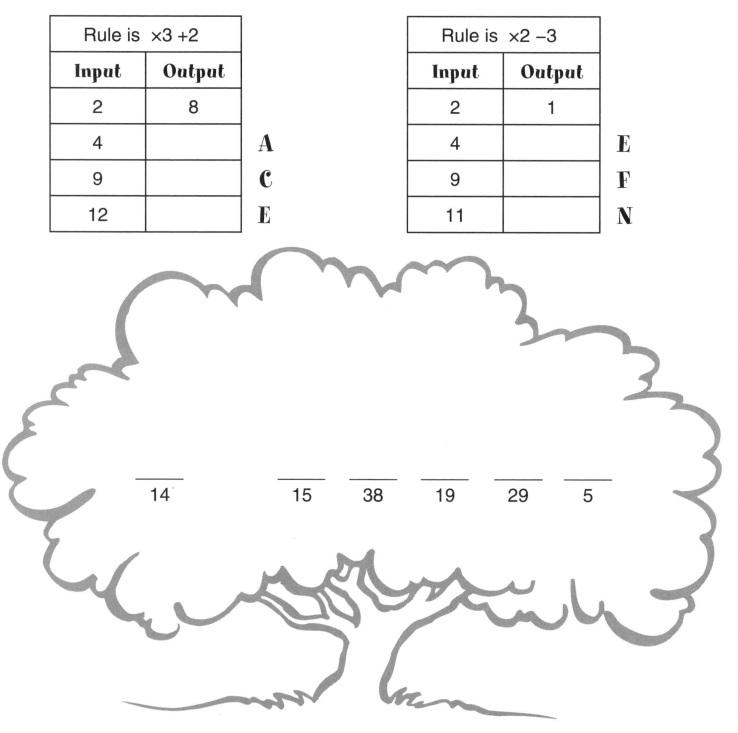

___   ___ ___ ___ ___ ___
14   15   38   19   29   5

Complete a function table with up to two operations

Algebra

EMC 3019 • Basic Math Skills, Grade 6 • ©2003 by Evan-Moor Corp.

Tongue Twister #8

Name _____

Complete each function table using the given rule. On the line above the output value, write the corresponding letter from the chart. The letters will spell out a tongue twister. How many times can you say it in 20 seconds?

Rule is ×2 −1	
Input	**Output**
4	7
9	
10	
14	

A
A
C

Rule is ÷2 +1	
Input	**Output**
4	3
10	
12	
16	

C
E
L

Rule is ×3 +2	
Input	**Output**
2	8
4	
6	
9	
10	

L
M
N
S

___ ___ ___ ___ ___
6   14   7   19   29

___ ___ ___ ___ ___
27   9   17   20   32

Complete a function table with up to two operations

Algebra

Function Tables 1

Complete each of the following function tables using the given rule.

1.

Rule = +27	
Input	**Output**
1	
11	
16	
23	

2.

Rule = −15	
Input	**Output**
25	
19	
15	
13	

3.

Rule = +4 −3	
Input	**Output**
4	
15	
23	
34	

4.

Rule = ×2 +3	
Input	**Output**
2	
4	
9	
15	

5.

Rule = ÷2 +1	
Input	**Output**
4	
16	
	13
38	

6.

Rule = ×3 −5	
Input	**Output**
19	
	40
8	
1	

7.

Rule = ×3 −12	
Input	**Output**
12	
8	
	3
3	

8.

Rule = ÷3 −2	
Input	**Output**
12	
15	
	5
39	

9.

Rule = ×5 +1	
Input	**Output**
	16
	21
	41
	51

Complete a function table with up to two operations

EMC 3019 • Basic Math Skills, Grade 6 • ©2003 by Evan-Moor Corp.

Function Tables II
(with positive rational numbers)

Name _____

Complete each of the following function tables using the given rule.

1.

Rule = +2.45	
Input	**Output**
3	
2.1	
4.16	
	5.2

2.

Rule = −3.25	
Input	**Output**
5	
6.19	
7.4	
	3.5

3.

Rule = +1 −3	
Input	**Output**
5	
13	
19	
	20

4.

Rule = ×2 +1$\frac{1}{2}$	
Input	**Output**
5	
1$\frac{1}{2}$	
3$\frac{1}{4}$	
	1$\frac{1}{2}$

5.

Rule = ÷2 +1	
Input	**Output**
8	
12	
15	
	15.5

6.

Rule = ×3.2 +4.9	
Input	**Output**
1.2	
0.8	
2	
	10.02

7.

Rule = ÷2 +6.41	
Input	**Output**
4	
5	
8	
	11.91

8.

Rule = ×$\frac{1}{3}$ +$\frac{1}{4}$	
Input	**Output**
3	
6	
9	
	4$\frac{1}{4}$

9.

Rule = ×$\frac{1}{2}$ +$\frac{1}{2}$	
Input	**Output**
8	
9	
13	
	8$\frac{1}{2}$

Complete a function table with up to two operations

Algebra

Pathways

Name_____

Helen's family is planning to put a paving stone path through their garden. They want the path to look like this:

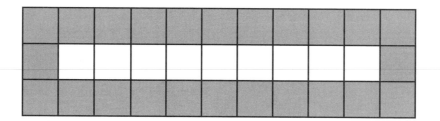

They aren't sure how long the path will be, so they created a function table to determine the number of gray and white stones that would be needed for different lengths of the path. There are two outputs in the table, one for the number of gray stones and the other for the number of white stones. Helen wrote the rules for each output column in the table. Help Helen by completing the table for her. The first row has been completed for you.

Total Length of Path Input	Number of Gray Stones Rule = input ×2 +2	Number of White Stones Rule = input −2
11 stones	24	9
15 stones		
20 stones		
45 stones		
100 stones		
240 stones		
	64	
	122	
		60
		150

Complete a function table with up to two operations

Algebra   EMC 3019 • Basic Math Skills, Grade 6 • ©2003 by Evan-Moor Corp.

Sheep and Geese

Name_____

Julie and her mother live on a farm with sheep and geese. Julie's mom saw 10 animals in the corral, and they had a total of 32 legs. She asked Julie to guess how many sheep and geese there were. To answer her mother's question, Julie made the function table below. She put in all the combinations that would equal 10 animals. Complete Julie's function table.

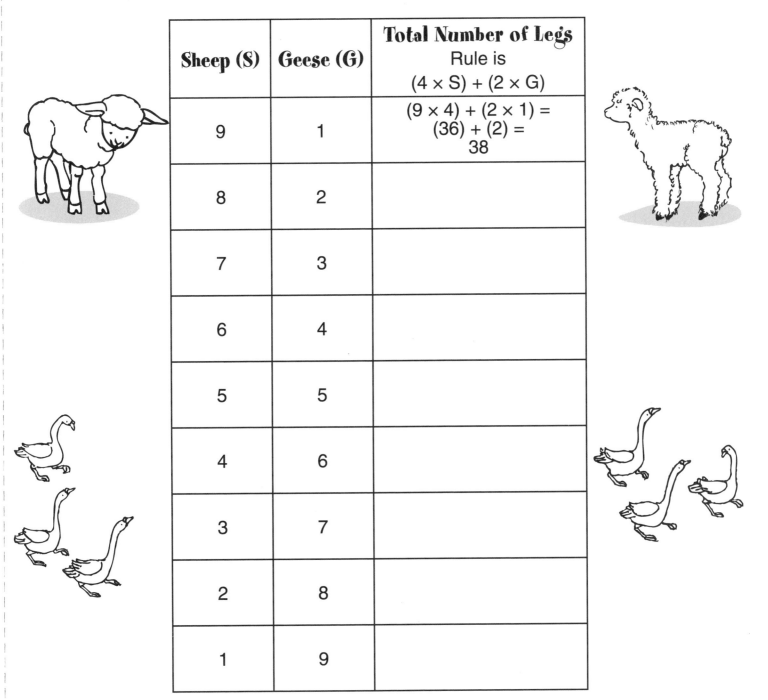

Sheep (S)	Geese (G)	Total Number of Legs Rule is (4 × S) + (2 × G)
9	1	(9 × 4) + (2 × 1) = (36) + (2) = 38
8	2	
7	3	
6	4	
5	5	
4	6	
3	7	
2	8	
1	9	

How many sheep and how many geese did Julie's mother see in the corral?

_____

Complete a function table with up to two operations

Math Test

Fill in the circle next to the correct answer.

Use this function table for Numbers 1 through 4.

Rule = ÷2 +4		
	Input	Output
	2	5
1.	4	
2.	7	
3.		16
4.		22.5

Use this function table for Numbers 5 through 8.

Rule = ×3 −5		
	Input	Output
5.	6	
6.	1	
7.		10
8.		70

1. What is the output if the input is 4?

Ⓐ 2   Ⓒ 8

Ⓑ 6   Ⓓ 10

2. What is the output if the input is 7?

Ⓐ 6   Ⓒ 6.5

Ⓑ 7   Ⓓ 7.5

3. What is the input if the output is 16?

Ⓐ 24   Ⓒ 16

Ⓑ 20   Ⓓ 12

4. What is the input if the output is 22.5?

Ⓐ 26.5   Ⓒ 36

Ⓑ 37   Ⓓ 18.5

5. What is the output if the input is 6?

Ⓐ 18   Ⓒ 13

Ⓑ 23   Ⓓ 4

6. What is the output if the input is 1?

Ⓐ 3   Ⓒ 8

Ⓑ 2   Ⓓ −2

7. What is the input if the output is 10?

Ⓐ 5   Ⓒ 15

Ⓑ 10   Ⓓ 20

8. What is the input if the output is 70?

Ⓐ 70   Ⓒ 75

Ⓑ 25   Ⓓ 50

9. Draw a function table with three inputs and three outputs using the rule ×6 −4.

10. Draw a function table with three inputs and three outputs using the rule ÷2 +1.

Complete a function table with up to two operations

Algebra

EMC 3019 • Basic Math Skills, Grade 6 • ©2003 by Evan-Moor Corp.

What Color Is a Shout?

Name_____

Write the rule used to complete each function table. Remember that the rule must be true for all inputs and outputs in the given table. Then write the corresponding letter from the function table on the line above the rule. The letters will spell out the solution to the riddle.

E Rule =

Input	Output
1	5
2	10
3	15
4	20

H Rule =

Input	Output
1	0
2	0
3	0
4	0

L Rule =

Input	Output
1	0
2	1
3	2
4	3

L Rule =

Input	Output
1	−1
2	0
3	1
4	2

O Rule =

Input	Output
1	4
2	5
3	6
4	7

Y Rule =

Input	Output
1	3
2	4
3	5
4	6

____ ____ ____ ____   ____ ____
+2   ×5   −2   −1   +3   ×0

Write rules for a function table in the form of an expression

What Is the Best Day to Cook Bacon and Eggs?

Name_____

Write the rule used to complete each function table. Remember that the rule must be true for all inputs and outputs in the given table. Then write the corresponding letter from the function table on the line above the rule. The letters will spell out the solution to the riddle.

A Rule = _____

Input	Output
3	6
4	7
6	9
8	11

D Rule = _____

Input	Output
2	0
6	0
10	0
12	0

F Rule = _____

Input	Output
4	2
5	3
9	7
10	8

R Rule = _____

Input	Output
3	7
5	9
7	11
8	12

Y Rule = _____

Input	Output
1	2
7	14
10	20
12	24

Y Rule = _____

Input	Output
6	2
9	3
21	7
30	10

_____ _____ _____   _____ _____ _____
 −2   +4   ×2   ×0   +3   ÷3

Write rules for a function table in the form of an expression

EMC 3019 • Basic Math Skills, Grade 6 • ©2003 by Evan-Moor Corp.

What's My Rule?

Name _____

Look at each function table and determine the rule for each. The rule must work for each input value.

1.

Rule =	
Input	**Output**
1	2
2	3
3	4
4	5

2.

Rule =	
Input	**Output**
1	−3
2	−2
3	−1
4	0

3.

Rule =	
Input	**Output**
1	3
2	5
3	7
4	9

4.

Rule =	
Input	**Output**
1	−1
2	2
3	5
4	8

5.

Rule =	
Input	**Output**
2	6
6	14
7	16
10	22

6.

Rule =	
Input	**Output**
3	2
6	3
9	4
12	5

7.

Rule =	
Input	**Output**
8	3
10	4
15	6.5
19	8.5

8.

Rule =	
Input	**Output**
16	49
19	58
22	67
25	76

9.

Rule =	
Input	**Output**
1	0
2	2
5	8
7	12

Write rules for a function table in the form of an expression

Algebra

What's My Rule II?

Name _____

Look at each function table and determine the rule for each. The rule must work for each input value.

1.

Rule =	
Input	Output
1	6
2	7
3	8
4	9

2.

Rule =	
Input	Output
1	−7
2	−6
3	−5
4	−4

3.

Rule =	
Input	Output
1	4
2	7
3	10
4	13

4.

Rule =	
Input	Output
1	3
2	8
3	13
4	18

5.

Rule =	
Input	Output
2	2
4	3
5	3.5
9	5.5

6.

Rule =	
Input	Output
3	−1
9	1
12	2
18	4

7.

Rule =	
Input	Output
2	2
4	4
6	6
9	9

8.

Rule =	
Input	Output
3	0
5	0
6	0
11	0

9.

Rule =	
Input	Output
9	99
10	110
11	121
12	132

Write rules for a function table in the form of an expression

EMC 3019 • Basic Math Skills, Grade 6 • ©2003 by Evan-Moor Corp.

Guess the Rule

Name _____

1. Leslie is making a function machine. She says that the output is
   24 when the input is 6. What are two different rules that could be used for
   her function machine?

   _____

2. Robert is making a function machine. He says that the output is
   15 when the input is 18. What are two different rules that could be
   used for his function machine?

   _____

3. Juanita is making a function machine. She says that the output is
   20 when the input is 12. What are two different rules that she could
   be thinking of?

   _____

4. Juan is thinking of a function machine. He says that the output is
   2 when the input is 8. What are two different rules that could be used
   for his function machine?

   _____

5. Akiko is making a function machine. She says that the output is
   8 when the input is 20. What are two different rules that could be
   used for her function machine?

   _____

Write rules for a function table in the form of an expression

Pathways and Rules

Name _____

George and his family are laying a path through their garden using colored paving stones. They would like the pathway to be three stones wide and for the stones to alternate gray and white. Here is an example of what they are planning.

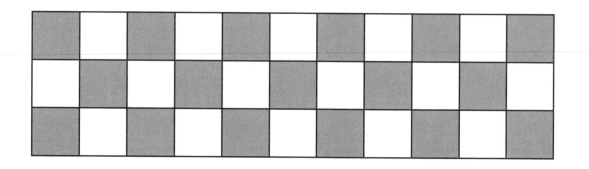

They created a function table with the length of the path as input. There are two outputs, one for the number of gray stones and one for the number of white stones. George has figured out the first few examples. He also noticed that there are 2 rules for each outcome: one rule if the input number is even, and another rule if the input number is odd. Find the rule for each output column when the input is an odd number. Then find the output for a path that is 100 stones long.

Total Length of the Path	Number of Gray Stones	Number of White Stones
Input	If the input is even, the rule is: ×3 ÷2 If the input is odd, the rule is: _____	If the input is even, the rule is: ×3 ÷2 If the input is odd, the rule is: _____
5 stones	8	7
8 stones	12	12
11 stones	17	16
100 stones		

Write rules for a function table in the form of an expression

Algebra

EMC 3019 • Basic Math Skills, Grade 6 • ©2003 by Evan-Moor Corp.

Math Test

Fill in the circle next to the correct answer.

For Numbers 1 through 4, use the function table below. The input stays the same, but the output is different for each column.

	1	2	3	4
Input	Output	Output	Output	Output
3	7	1	1	7
6	10	4	2	13
12	16	10	4	25
15	19	13	5	31

1. What is the rule for the output in column #1?

  Ⓐ ×2 +1   Ⓒ +4

  Ⓑ ×2 −2   Ⓓ −4

2. What is the rule for the output in column #2?

  Ⓐ −3   Ⓒ −1

  Ⓑ −2   Ⓓ +0

3. What is the rule for the output in column #3?

  Ⓐ ÷3   Ⓒ − 4

  Ⓑ − 2   Ⓓ ÷2 +1

4. What is the rule for the output in column #4?

  Ⓐ + 4   Ⓒ + 7

  Ⓑ × 2 +1   Ⓓ × 3 −2

For Numbers 5 through 8, use the function table below. The input stays the same, but the output is different for each column.

	5	6	7	8
Input	Output	Output	Output	Output
10	5	4	20	5
20	10	6	40	15
30	15	8	60	25
50	25	12	100	45

5. What is the rule for the output in column #5?

  Ⓐ +5   Ⓒ +10

  Ⓑ ÷2   Ⓓ ×3

6. What is the rule for the output in column #6?

  Ⓐ ÷5 +2   Ⓒ − 14

  Ⓑ − 6   Ⓓ ÷ 2 −1

7. What is the rule for the output in column #7?

  Ⓐ ×2   Ⓒ ×3 −10

  Ⓑ +10   Ⓓ +20

8. What is the rule for the output in column #8?

  Ⓐ ÷2   Ⓒ ÷10 +4

  Ⓑ ÷2 +5   Ⓓ −5

9. Julia is making a function machine. She says that the output is 5 if the input is 2. What are two rules that could be used for her function machine?

10. Tabitha is making a different function machine. She says that the output is 7 if the input is 10. What are two rules that could be used for her function machine?

Write rules for a function table in the form of an expression

©2003 by Evan-Moor Corp. • Basic Math Skills, Grade 6 • EMC 3019

Algebra   **117**

Tongue Twister #9

Name_____

Look at each value given below. Locate the value on the number line and write the corresponding letter above the number line. The letters will spell out a tongue twister when read from left to right. How many times can you say it in 15 seconds?

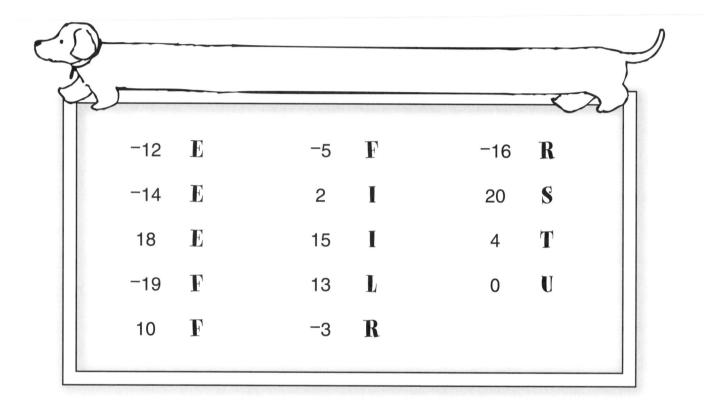

−12	**E**	−5	**F**	−16	**R**
−14	**E**	2	**I**	20	**S**
18	**E**	15	**I**	4	**T**
−19	**F**	13	**L**	0	**U**
10	**F**	−3	**R**		

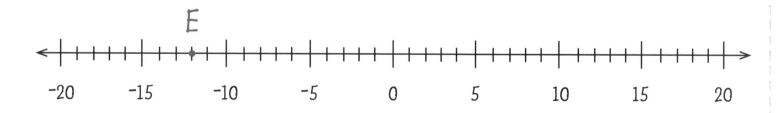

E

-20   -15   -10   -5   0   5   10   15   20

Locate points on a number line

Algebra

EMC 3019 • Basic Math Skills, Grade 6 • ©2003 by Evan-Moor Corp.

What's White on the Outside and Acts Badly?

Name_____

Look at each value given below. Locate the value on the number line and write the corresponding letter above the number line. The letters will spell out the solution to the riddle.

$8\frac{2}{3}$	**A**	$10\frac{1}{4}$	**D**	$5\frac{1}{2}$	**M**
2	**A**	$4\frac{1}{3}$	**H**	$9\frac{4}{5}$	**N**
$4\frac{3}{4}$	**A**	$13\frac{1}{2}$	**H**	8	**S**
$12\frac{7}{8}$	**C**	12	**I**	$10\frac{2}{3}$	**W**

A

0 1 2 3 4 5 6 7 8 9 10 11 12 13 14 15 16

Locate points on a number line

Algebra

Where's the Point with Integers?

Name_____

Plot each of the following points on the number line. Be sure to label each point with the corresponding letter.

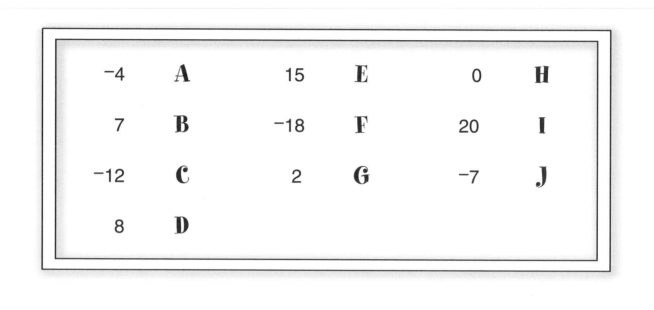

−4	**A**	15	**E**	0	**H**
7	**B**	−18	**F**	20	**I**
−12	**C**	2	**G**	−7	**J**
8	**D**				

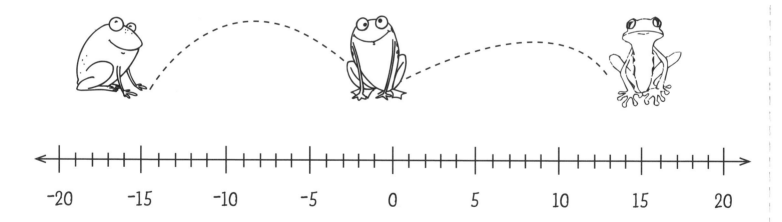

Locate points on a number line

EMC 3019 • Basic Math Skills, Grade 6 • ©2003 by Evan-Moor Corp.

Where's the Point with Fractions and Decimals?

Name_____

Plot each of the following points on the number line. Be sure to label each point with the corresponding letter.

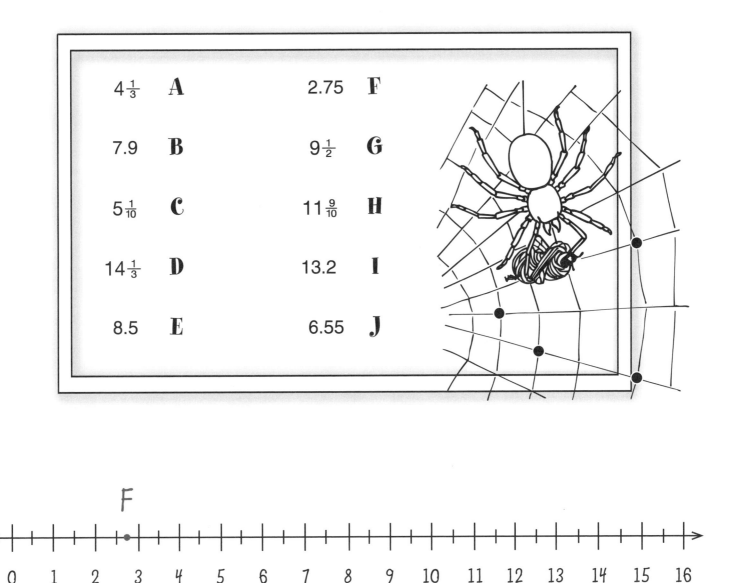

$4\frac{1}{3}$ **A**

7.9   **B**

$5\frac{1}{10}$ **C**

$14\frac{1}{3}$ **D**

8.5   **E**

2.75   **F**

$9\frac{1}{2}$ **G**

$11\frac{9}{10}$ **H**

13.2   **I**

6.55   **J**

Locate points on a number line

Ordering Fractions

Name _____

Use the number line to help order the following ten numbers from smallest to largest. First, place each point on the number line and label it. After all the points have been plotted on the number line, list the numbers in order from smallest to largest.

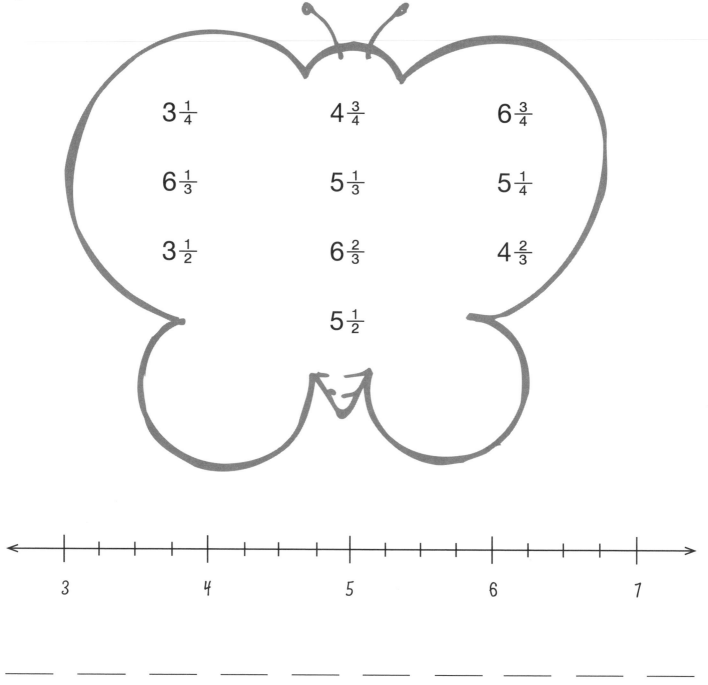

$3\frac{1}{4}$ $4\frac{3}{4}$ $6\frac{3}{4}$

$6\frac{1}{3}$ $5\frac{1}{3}$ $5\frac{1}{4}$

$3\frac{1}{2}$ $6\frac{2}{3}$ $4\frac{2}{3}$

$5\frac{1}{2}$

3   4   5   6   7

___ ___ ___ ___ ___ ___ ___ ___ ___ ___

Locate points on a number line

EMC 3019 • Basic Math Skills, Grade 6 • ©2003 by Evan-Moor Corp.

Ordering Decimals

Name _____

Use the number line to help order the following ten numbers from smallest to largest. First, place each point on the number line and label it. After all the points have been plotted on the number line, list the numbers in order from smallest to largest.

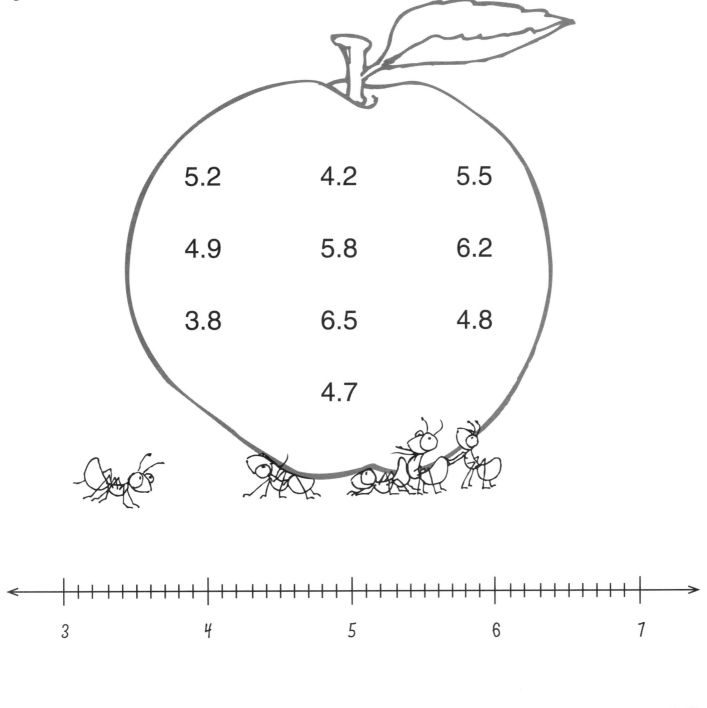

5.2	4.2	5.5
4.9	5.8	6.2
3.8	6.5	4.8
	4.7	

_____ _____ _____ _____ _____ _____ _____ _____ _____ _____

Locate points on a number line

Math Test

Name_____

Fill in the circle next to the correct answer.

Use this number line for Numbers 1 through 4.

A .... B CD

0 .... 5 10

Use this number line for Numbers 5 through 8.

A ... B ... C ... D

-4 .... 0 4

1. Which point is located at $6\frac{3}{4}$?

  Ⓐ point A   Ⓒ point C

  Ⓑ point B   Ⓓ point D

2. Which point is located at $1\frac{1}{3}$?

  Ⓐ point A   Ⓒ point C

  Ⓑ point B   Ⓓ point D

3. Which point is located at $7\frac{3}{4}$?

  Ⓐ point A   Ⓒ point C

  Ⓑ point B   Ⓓ point D

4. Which point is located at $7\frac{1}{2}$?

  Ⓐ point A   Ⓒ point C

  Ⓑ point B   Ⓓ point D

5. Which point is located at –1?

  Ⓐ point A   Ⓒ point C

  Ⓑ point B   Ⓓ point D

6. Which point is located at 3?

  Ⓐ point A   Ⓒ point C

  Ⓑ point B   Ⓓ point D

7. Which point is located at 1?

  Ⓐ point A   Ⓒ point C

  Ⓑ point B   Ⓓ point D

8. Which point is located at ⁻3?

  Ⓐ point A   Ⓒ point C

  Ⓑ point B   Ⓓ point D

9. Draw a number line and number it from 0 to 5. Write an X on the value of 2.2 and a Y on the value of 3.9.

10. Draw another number line and number it from ⁻3 to +3, with 0 right in the middle. Write an S on the value of ⁻1 and a W on the value of 2.

Locate points on a number line

Algebra   EMC 3019 • Basic Math Skills, Grade 6 • ©2003 by Evan-Moor Corp.

Favorite Pet

Name _____

Plot the ordered pairs of numbers in the order in which they are listed and connect them with straight lines. Start each new set of points with a new line.

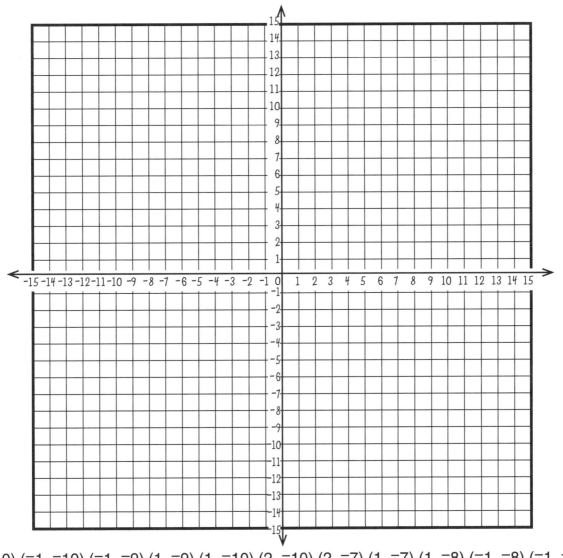

▶ (‾2, ‾10) (‾1, ‾10) (‾1, ‾9) (1, ‾9) (1, ‾10) (2, ‾10) (2, ‾7) (1, ‾7) (1, ‾8) (‾1, ‾8) (‾1, ‾7) (‾2, ‾7) (‾2, ‾10) line ends

▶ (7, ‾11) (7, ‾7) (6, ‾2) (5, 0) (4, ‾2) (3, ‾4) (1, ‾6) (‾1, ‾6) (‾3, ‾4) (‾4, ‾2) (‾5, 0) (‾6, ‾2) (‾7, ‾7) (‾7, ‾11) line ends

▶ (‾1, ‾4) (1, ‾4) (1, ‾2) (‾1, ‾2) (‾1, ‾4) line ends

▶ (2, 2) (2, 3) (4, 3) (4, 2) (2, 2) line ends

▶ (‾2, 2) (‾2, 3) (‾4, 3) (‾4, 2) (‾2, 2) line ends

▶ (5, 0) (6, 6) (7, 2) (8, 1) (9, 1) (10, 2) (10, 7) (9, 9) (7, 10) (3, 11) (‾3, 11) (‾7, 10) (‾9, 9) (‾10, 7) (‾10, 2) (‾9, 1) (‾8, 1) (‾7, 2) (‾6, 6) (‾5, 0) line ends

Locate and plot ordered pairs on a coordinate graph

Transport

Name_____

Plot the ordered pairs of numbers in the order in which they are listed and connect them with straight lines. Start each new set of points with a new line.

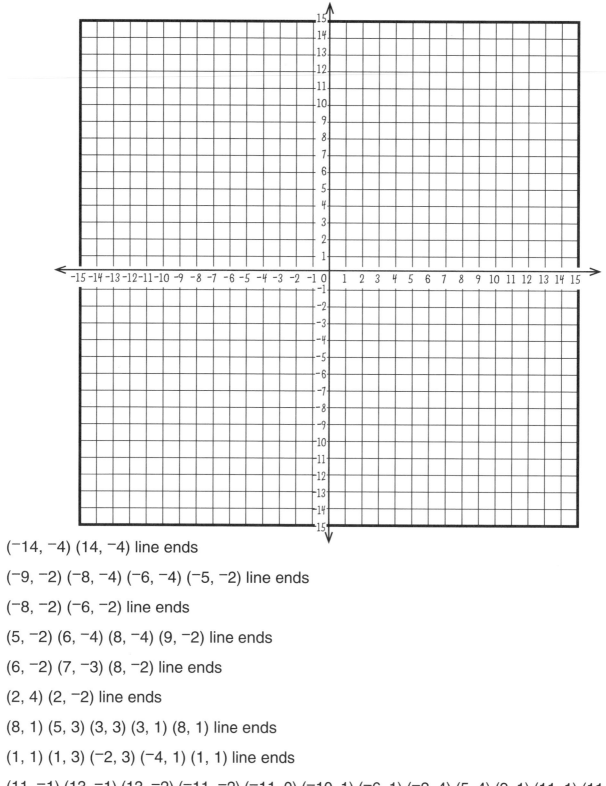

▶ (−14, −4) (14, −4) line ends

▶ (−9, −2) (−8, −4) (−6, −4) (−5, −2) line ends

▶ (−8, −2) (−6, −2) line ends

▶ (5, −2) (6, −4) (8, −4) (9, −2) line ends

▶ (6, −2) (7, −3) (8, −2) line ends

▶ (2, 4) (2, −2) line ends

▶ (8, 1) (5, 3) (3, 3) (3, 1) (8, 1) line ends

▶ (1, 1) (1, 3) (−2, 3) (−4, 1) (1, 1) line ends

▶ (11, −1) (13, −1) (13, −2) (−11, −2) (−11, 0) (−10, 1) (−6, 1) (−2, 4) (5, 4) (9, 1) (11, 1) (11, −2) line ends

Locate and plot ordered pairs on a coordinate graph

Algebra

EMC 3019 • Basic Math Skills, Grade 6 • ©2003 by Evan-Moor Corp.

Graph It

Plot each of the ordered pairs of numbers on the graph. Label each point with the corresponding letter.

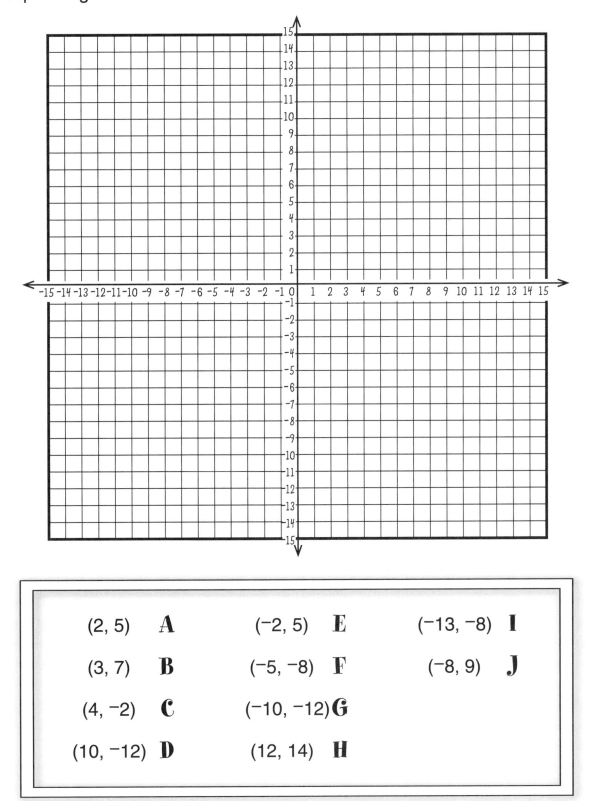

(2, 5)	**A**	(−2, 5)	**E**	(−13, −8)	**I**
(3, 7)	**B**	(−5, −8)	**F**	(−8, 9)	**J**
(4, −2)	**C**	(−10, −12)	**G**		
(10, −12)	**D**	(12, 14)	**H**		

Locate and plot ordered pairs on a coordinate graph

Algebra

Graph It, Too

Name_____

Plot each of the ordered pairs of numbers on the graph. Label each point with the corresponding letter.

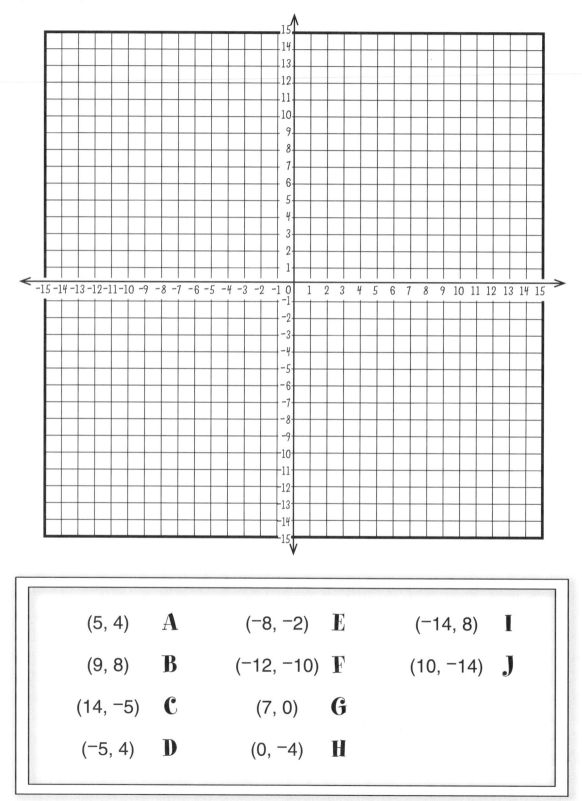

(5, 4)	**A**	(−8, −2)	**E**	(−14, 8)	**I**
(9, 8)	**B**	(−12, −10)	**F**	(10, −14)	**J**
(14, −5)	**C**	(7, 0)	**G**		
(−5, 4)	**D**	(0, −4)	**H**		

Locate and plot ordered pairs on a coordinate graph

Algebra

EMC 3019 • Basic Math Skills, Grade 6 • ©2003 by Evan-Moor Corp.

New Deli

Name_____

Pictured here is a map of New Deli. Use the map to answer the questions below.

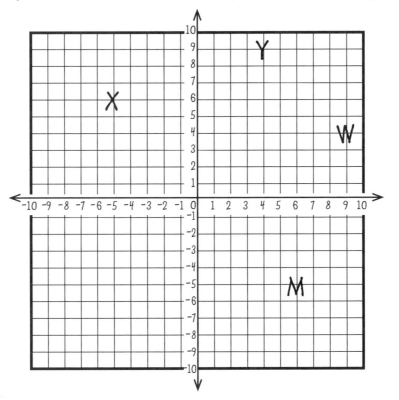

1. If the X is the town's grocery store, what is the ordered pair for that location?

    _____

2. The City Bank is located at (9, 4) and the Town Food Court is located at (4, 9). Which letter is represented for each business?

    _____

3. The M is the New Deli School. What is the ordered pair for that location?

    _____

4. Patrick lives at the intersection of (⁻2, ⁻4) and Whitney lives at the intersection of (6, ⁻8). Plot each of their homes on the map and label Patrick's house *P* and Whitney's house *W*.

5. How many blocks is it for Patrick to walk to Whitney's house without cutting diagonally through a block?

    _____

Locate and plot ordered pairs on a coordinate graph

©2003 by Evan-Moor Corp. • Basic Math Skills, Grade 6 • EMC 3019

Algebra **129**

North Bend

Name_____

Pictured here is a map of North Bend. Use the map to answer the questions below.

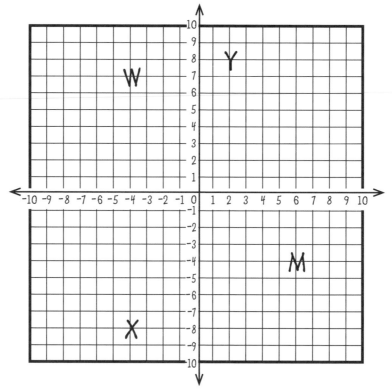

1. If the X is the town's elementary school, what is the ordered pair for that location?

_____

2. The City Market is located at (2, 8) and the Town Bank is located at (⁻4, 7). Which letter is represented for each business?

_____

3. The North Bend Middle School is located at (⁻3, 8). Plot that on the map and label it *N*.

4. Beth lives at the intersection of (⁻9, 4) and Shirley lives at the intersection of (4, ⁻5). Plot each of their homes on the map, label Beth's house *B* and Shirley's house *S*.

5. How many blocks is it for Beth to walk to Shirley's house without cutting diagonally through a block?

_____

6. Make up three other businesses that might be in the town of North Bend. Plot each one on an intersection on the map. Give the ordered pair for each business's location.

_____

_____

_____

Locate and plot ordered pairs on a coordinate graph

Algebra   EMC 3019 • Basic Math Skills, Grade 6 • ©2003 by Evan-Moor Corp.

Math Test

Name _____

Fill in the circle next to the correct answer.

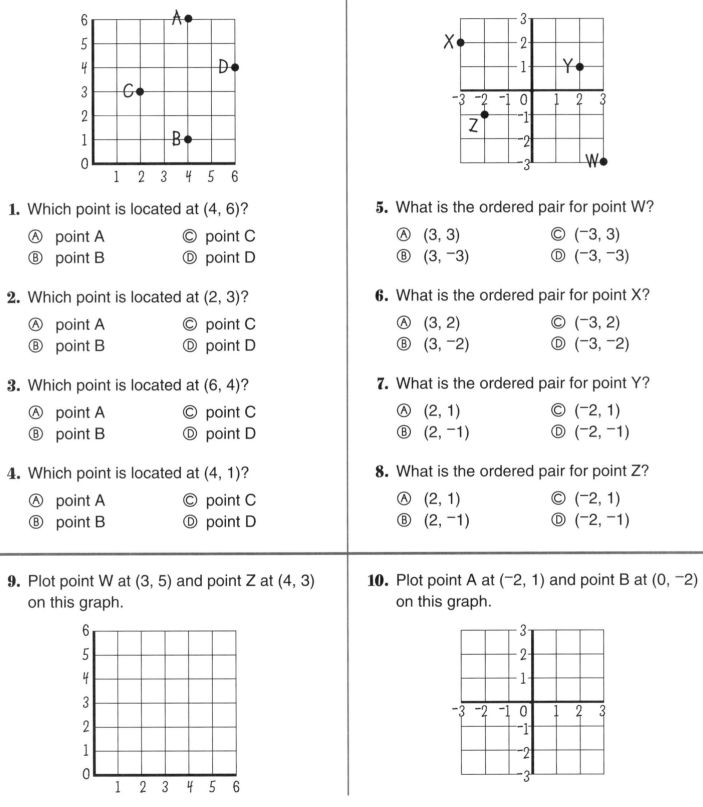

For Numbers 1 through 4, use this graph.

1. Which point is located at (4, 6)?

    Ⓐ point A   © point C

    Ⓑ point B   Ⓓ point D

2. Which point is located at (2, 3)?

    Ⓐ point A   © point C

    Ⓑ point B   Ⓓ point D

3. Which point is located at (6, 4)?

    Ⓐ point A   © point C

    Ⓑ point B   Ⓓ point D

4. Which point is located at (4, 1)?

    Ⓐ point A   © point C

    Ⓑ point B   Ⓓ point D

For Numbers 5 through 8, use this graph.

5. What is the ordered pair for point W?

    Ⓐ (3, 3)   © (⁻3, 3)

    Ⓑ (3, ⁻3)   Ⓓ (⁻3, ⁻3)

6. What is the ordered pair for point X?

    Ⓐ (3, 2)   © (⁻3, 2)

    Ⓑ (3, ⁻2)   Ⓓ (⁻3, ⁻2)

7. What is the ordered pair for point Y?

    Ⓐ (2, 1)   © (⁻2, 1)

    Ⓑ (2, ⁻1)   Ⓓ (⁻2, ⁻1)

8. What is the ordered pair for point Z?

    Ⓐ (2, 1)   © (⁻2, 1)

    Ⓑ (2, ⁻1)   Ⓓ (⁻2, ⁻1)

9. Plot point W at (3, 5) and point Z at (4, 3) on this graph.

10. Plot point A at (⁻2, 1) and point B at (0, ⁻2) on this graph.

Locate and plot ordered pairs on a coordinate graph

Riddle

What do you get if you cross a daffodil with a calculator?

Simplify each of the following math expressions using the order of operations. Then write the corresponding letter on the line in front of the expression. The letters will spell out the solution to the riddle when read from **bottom to top**, starting on the right.

Order of Operations

1. Do whatever is inside the parentheses first.
2. Next, do multiplication and division from left to right.
3. The last step is to do addition and subtraction from left to right.

_____ $7 + 4 \times 2 =$ _____

_____ $4 \div 2 \times 7 =$ _____

_____ $23 - 3 \times 2 =$ _____

_____ $5 + 6 \times 2 =$ _____

_____ $9 + 2 \times 5 =$ _____

_____ $26 - 6 \div 3 =$ _____

_____ $5 \times 2 + 9 =$ _____

_____ $8 \times 4 - 5 =$ _____

_____ $12 \div 3 + 1 =$ _____

_____ $15 \times (3 - 3) =$ _____

_____ $16 - 4 \div 4 =$ _____

_____ $14 + 2 \times 3 =$ _____

_____ $19 - (10 - 5) =$ _____

_____ $18 \times 6 \div 2 =$ _____

_____ $25 - 15 \div 5 =$ _____

_____ $26 - (9 - 2) =$ _____

_____ $6 \times (3 + 1) =$ _____

_____ $20 + 10 \div 5 =$ _____

_____ $14 + 1 \times 3 =$ _____

_____ $15 + 4 \times 2 =$ _____

_____ $50 - 4 \times 5 =$ _____

_____ $30 - 9 \div 3 =$ _____

27	A	23	L	14	T
24	E	17	O	5	U
30	F	0	Q	22	W
20	H	19	R		
54	I	15	S		

What Is a Sleeping Prehistoric Monster Called?

Name_____

Simplify each of the following math expressions using the order of operations. Then write the corresponding letter on the line in front of the expression. The letters will spell out the solution to the riddle when read from **bottom to top**.

Order of Operations

1. Do whatever is inside the parentheses first.
2. Next, do multiplication and division from left to right.
3. The last step is to do addition and subtraction from left to right.

_____ $9 + 4 \times 2 - 3 =$ _____

_____ $15 - 9 \div 3 + 4 =$ _____

_____ $4 \times 2 + 5 \times 3 =$ _____

_____ $7 \times 2 - 9 \div 3 =$ _____

_____ $4 + 6 \times 3 \div 2 =$ _____

_____ $3 \times 5 + 16 \div 2 =$ _____

_____ $5 + (5 - 3) \times 3 =$ _____

_____ $2 + 5 \times 4 + 4 =$ _____

_____ $9 \times 9 \div 3 + 6 =$ _____

_____ $38 - (5 \times 4 - 3) =$_____

21	**A**
33	**D**
14	**E**
26	**I**
11	**N**
23	**O**
16	**R**
13	**S**
10	**U**

Order of operations

by Evan-Moor Corp. • Basic Math Skills, Grade 6 • EMC 3019

Algebra 133

Follow Your Orders

Name_____

Simplify each of the following math expressions using the order of operations.

Order of Operations

1. Do whatever is inside the parentheses first.
2. Next, do multiplication and division from left to right.
3. The last step is to do addition and subtraction from left to right.

---

1. $9 + 5 - 3 =$ _____

2. $5 \times 8 - 4 =$ _____

3. $8 - 3 \times 2 =$ _____

4. $5 \times 9 + 4 =$ _____

5. $5 + 9 \times 4 =$ _____

6. $6 \div 3 + 4 =$ _____

7. $5 + 4 \times 3 =$ _____

8. $6 + 4 \times 3 =$ _____

9. $15 \div 3 - 2 =$ _____

10. $5 + 5 - 3 =$ _____

11. $18 \div 6 + 5 =$ _____

12. $6 + 3 \times 2 =$ _____

13. $4 \times 5 + 5 =$ _____

14. $18 - 5 \div 5 =$ _____

15. $20 + 4 \div 2 =$ _____

16. $4 \times 3 + 6 =$ _____

17. $15 - 4 \times 3 =$ _____

18. $5 \times 2 \div 5 =$ _____

19. $18 + 2 \times 3 =$ _____

20. $6 \times 3 - 4 =$ _____

Order of operations

EMC 3019 • Basic Math Skills, Grade 6 • ©2003 by Evan-Moor Corp.

Follow Your Orders Again

Name _____

Simplify each of the following math expressions using the order of operations.

Order of Operations

1. Do whatever is inside the parentheses first.
2. Next, do multiplication and division from left to right.
3. The last step is to do addition and subtraction from left to right.

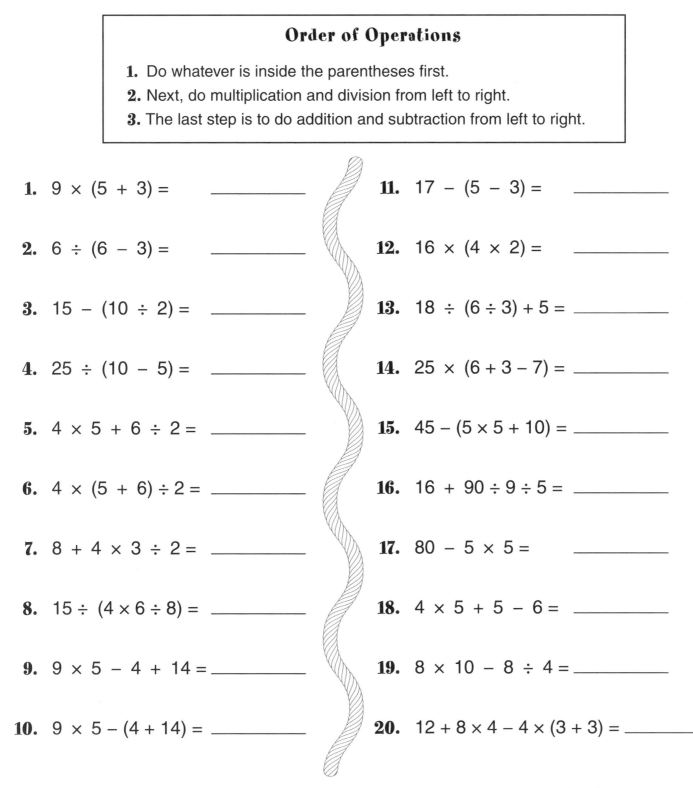

1. $9 \times (5 + 3) =$ _____

2. $6 \div (6 - 3) =$ _____

3. $15 - (10 \div 2) =$ _____

4. $25 \div (10 - 5) =$ _____

5. $4 \times 5 + 6 \div 2 =$ _____

6. $4 \times (5 + 6) \div 2 =$ _____

7. $8 + 4 \times 3 \div 2 =$ _____

8. $15 \div (4 \times 6 \div 8) =$ _____

9. $9 \times 5 - 4 + 14 =$ _____

10. $9 \times 5 - (4 + 14) =$ _____

11. $17 - (5 - 3) =$ _____

12. $16 \times (4 \times 2) =$ _____

13. $18 \div (6 \div 3) + 5 =$ _____

14. $25 \times (6 + 3 - 7) =$ _____

15. $45 - (5 \times 5 + 10) =$ _____

16. $16 + 90 \div 9 \div 5 =$ _____

17. $80 - 5 \times 5 =$ _____

18. $4 \times 5 + 5 - 6 =$ _____

19. $8 \times 10 - 8 \div 4 =$ _____

20. $12 + 8 \times 4 - 4 \times (3 + 3) =$ _____

Order of operations

Confusion with Order of Operations

Name_____

1. Timothy solved two problems and says that they have the same answer.

   a) $5 \times 4 - 3 + 2 =$

   $20 - 5 = 15$

   b) $5 \times 4 - (3 + 2) =$

   $20 - 5 = 15$

   Do you agree with Timothy? Write him a note stating if you agree or not and why. Include in your note the correct answer for each problem.

   _____

2. Francine saw the following problem and was confused about the parentheses.

   $7 + (5 \times 3) - 8$

   She understood the order of operations, but was asked the question, "Are the parentheses necessary in this problem? If the parentheses were gone, wouldn't you solve the problem the same way?" Please write a note to Francine stating if you agree or not with her thinking and why. Include in your note the correct answer for the problem.

   _____

3. Drew saw the following problem and was confused about where to start.

   $90 - (5 + 4 \times 3) + 30$

   He knew that he should start inside the parentheses, but didn't know what he should do first, $5 + 4$ or 4×3. Write a note to Drew stating the steps he should follow to solve the problem. Include in your note the correct solution and answer for the problem.

   _____

Order of operations

EMC 3019 • Basic Math Skills, Grade 6 • ©2003 by Evan-Moor Corp.

Order of Operations with Formulas

Name _____

Julie's older sister is working a geometry homework problem. She is finding the area of a trapezoid.

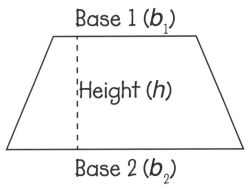

Base 1 (b_1)

Height (h)

Base 2 (b_2)

Her sister explains that the formula for finding the area of the trapezoid is

$$A = \tfrac{1}{2} \times (b_1 + b_2) \times h$$

This formula means that you first add the lengths of the two bases (since they are in parentheses) and then multiply that sum by $\tfrac{1}{2}$. Then you multiply the result by the height. This gives you the area of the trapezoid.

Use this formula and follow the order of operations to complete the table below for the area of three different trapezoids.

	Base 1	Base 2	Height	Area
Trapezoid 1	4 inches	6 inches	3 inches	
Trapezoid 2	5 inches	8 inches	4 inches	
Trapezoid 3	10 inches	15 inches	6 inches	

Order of operations

Algebra

Math Test

Simplify each of the following expressions. Fill in the circle next to the correct answer.

1. $28 \div 4 + 3 =$ _____

- Ⓐ 4
- Ⓑ 7
- Ⓒ 10
- Ⓓ 11

2. $6 - 3 \times 2 =$ _____

- Ⓐ 6
- Ⓑ 0
- Ⓒ 1
- Ⓓ 5

3. $5 \times 3 + 6 =$ _____

- Ⓐ 15
- Ⓑ 45
- Ⓒ 20
- Ⓓ 21

4. $3 + 5 \times 2 =$ _____

- Ⓐ 13
- Ⓑ 16
- Ⓒ 10
- Ⓓ 8

5. $7 \times (5 + 2) =$ _____

- Ⓐ 7
- Ⓑ 37
- Ⓒ 49
- Ⓓ 56

6. $12 \div (4 - 2) =$ _____

- Ⓐ 6
- Ⓑ 2
- Ⓒ 1
- Ⓓ 0

7. $12 \div 3 + 4 \times 3 =$ _____

- Ⓐ 4
- Ⓑ 16
- Ⓒ 12
- Ⓓ 13

8. $12 - (4 \times 2 + 2) + 3 \times 5 =$ _____

- Ⓐ 17
- Ⓑ 16
- Ⓒ 15
- Ⓓ 14

9. Write an expression with at least three numbers and any operations you choose that has an answer of 5.

_____

_____

10. Write an expression that when simplified equals 10. The expression may have any numbers in it, but it must have at least one multiplication sign, one addition sign, and one subtraction sign.

_____

_____

Order of operations

Riddle

Name _____

What do you get if you cross an elephant with a crow?

Solve each equation given below. Then write the corresponding letter on the line above the solution. The letters will spell out the answer to the riddle.

B $x + 4 = 12$, $x =$ _____

E $x - 5 = 10$, $x =$ _____

F $x + 5 = 7$, $x =$ _____

H $x + 7 = 19$, $x =$ _____

K $x - 5 = 32$, $x =$ _____

L $7 + 3 = x$, $x =$ _____

N $9 + x = 23$, $x =$ _____

O $8 - 5 = x$, $x =$ _____

P $19 - x = 12$, $x =$ _____

R $x - 7 = 12$, $x =$ _____

S $14 - x = 8$, $x =$ _____

T $x + 5 = 23$, $x =$ _____

___ ___ ___ ___   ___ ___
10   3   18   6   3   2

___ ___ ___ ___ ___ ___
8   19   3   37   15   14

___ ___ ___ ___ ___ ___ ___ ___ ___
18   15   10   15   7   12   3   14   15

___ ___ ___ ___ ___
7   3   10   15   6

Solve one-step equations using addition or subtraction

Tongue Twister #10

Name _____

Solve each equation given below. Then write the letter that corresponds to the answer on the line. The letters will spell out a tongue twister when read from left to right. How many times can you say it in 15 seconds?

_____ $x + 5 = 8$, $x =$ _____   _____ $5 - x = 2$, $x =$ _____

_____ $x - 4 = 2$, $x =$ _____   _____ $x + 3 = 9$, $x =$ _____

_____ $3 + x = 6$, $x =$ _____   _____ $x - 2 = 1$, $x =$ _____

_____ $x + 5 = 9$, $x =$ _____   _____ $x + 5 = 13$, $x =$ _____

_____ $5 - x = 3$, $x =$ _____   _____ $7 + x = 12$, $x =$ _____

_____ $x - 4 = 3$, $x =$ _____   _____ $x + 8 = 10$, $x =$ _____

_____ $15 + x = 25$, $x =$ _____   _____ $x + 3 = 10$, $x =$ _____

_____ $x - 5 = 5$, $x =$ _____

_____ $12 - x = 3$, $x =$ _____

2	A	8	P
3	E	9	S
4	G	10	T
5	H		
6	L		
7	N		

Solve one-step equations using addition or subtraction

Algebra

EMC 3019 • Basic Math Skills, Grade 6 • ©2003 by Evan-Moor Corp.

Solve It with Addition and Subtraction

Name _____

Solve each of the following equations. Show all your work.

Add the same value to each side.	Or subtract the same value from each side.
$x - 6 = 3$	$x + 2 = 7$
$x - 6 + 6 = 3 + 6$	$x + 2 - 2 = 7 - 2$
$x = 9$	$x = 5$

1. $x + 4 = 5, x = $ _____

2. $x + 8 = 12, x = $ _____

3. $x + 5 = 5, x = $ _____

4. $x + 2 = 11, x = $ _____

5. $x + 6 = 21, x = $ _____

6. $5 + x = 8, x = $ _____

7. $4 + x = 13, x = $ _____

8. $9 + x = 13, x = $ _____

9. $5 + x = 26, x = $ _____

10. $6 + x = 19, x = $ _____

11. $x - 5 = 12, x = $ _____

12. $x - 4 = 7, x = $ _____

13. $x - 8 = 13, x = $ _____

14. $x - 3 = 14, x = $ _____

15. $x - 10 = 30, x = $ _____

16. $x + 45 = 75, x = $ _____

17. $x - 48 = 50, x = $ _____

18. $35 + x = 45, x = $ _____

19. $29 + x = 49, x = $ _____

20. $x - 23 = 50, x = $ _____

Solve one-step equations using addition or subtraction

Algebra

Solve It with Addition and Subtraction II

Name _____

Solve each of the following equations. Show all your work.

Add the same value to each side.	Or subtract the same value from each side.
$x - 6 = 3$	$x + 2 = 7$
$x - 6 + 6 = 3 + 6$	$x + 2 - 2 = 7 - 2$
$x = 9$	$x = 5$

1. $x + 5 = 9$, $x =$ _____

2. $x + 3 = 8$, $x =$ _____

3. $x + 8 = 12$, $x =$ _____

4. $x + 15 = 15$, $x =$ _____

5. $x + 36 = 41$, $x =$ _____

6. $7 + x = 15$, $x =$ _____

7. $23 + x = 35$, $x =$ _____

8. $46 + x = 98$, $x =$ _____

9. $25 + x = 34$, $x =$ _____

10. $35 + x = 42$, $x =$ _____

11. $x - 9 = 15$, $x =$ _____

12. $x - 15 = 15$, $x =$ _____

13. $x - 36 = 39$, $x =$ _____

14. $x - 56 = 0$, $x =$ _____

15. $x - 28 = 49$, $x =$ _____

16. $x + 16 = 45$, $x =$ _____

17. $x - 37 = 29$, $x =$ _____

18. $69 + x = 72$, $x =$ _____

19. $26 + x = 35$, $x =$ _____

20. $x - 64 = 16$, $x =$ _____

Solve one-step equations using addition or subtraction

Algebra

EMC 3019 • Basic Math Skills, Grade 6 • ©2003 by Evan-Moor Corp.

Toby's Quiz

Name _____

Toby completed the following quiz, and it needs to be checked. Write a *C* next to each item that he got correct. Write a √ next to any that he got incorrect, and then write Toby a hint about what he should have done differently.

Name Toby

1. $x + 4 = 8$

$x + 4 - 4 = 8 - 4$

$x = 4$

2. $x - 5 = 12$

$x - 5 - 5 = 12 - 5$

$x = 7$

3. $7 + x = 13$

$7 - 7 + x = 13 - 7$

$x = 6$

4. $x - 8 = 5$

$x - 8 + 8 = 5 + 8$

$x = 13$

5. $4 + 5 = x$

$9 = x$

6. $x = 5 - 2$

$x = 3$

7. $x + 5 = 17$

$x + 5 - 5 = 17 - 5$

$x = 12$

8. $x + 18 = 20$

$x + 18 + 18 = 20 + 18$

$x = 38$

9. $x + 33 = 49$

$x + 33 - 33 = 49 - 33$

$x = 16$

10. $x + 34 = 64$

$x + 34 - 34 = 64 - 34$

$x = 30$

Solve one-step equations using addition or subtraction

Mystery Number

Name _____

Use the following clues to determine the mystery number. For each one, write an equation and then solve the equation.

1. When 3 is added to my number, the sum is 38. What is my number?

   _____

2. When 15 is subtracted from my number, the difference is 45. What is my number?

   _____

3. When my number is added to 18, the sum is 30. What is my number?

   _____

4. When 36 is subtracted from my number, the difference is 85. What is my number?

   _____

5. When 62 is added to my number, the sum is 130. What is my number?

   _____

6. When 49 is subtracted from my number, the difference is 15. What is my number?

   _____

7. When 22 is subtracted from my number, the difference is 54. What is my number?

   _____

8. When 55 is added to my number, the sum is 108. What is my number?

   _____

9. When my number is subtracted from 25, the difference is 7. What is my number?

   _____

10. When my number is added to 653, the sum is 1,637. What is my number?

   _____

Solve one-step equations using addition or subtraction

Algebra   EMC 3019 • Basic Math Skills, Grade 6 • ©2003 by Evan-Moor Corp.

Math Test

Name _____

Solve each of the following equations for x. Fill in the circle next to the correct answer.

1. $x + 5 = 8$

  Ⓐ $x = 3$ Ⓒ $x = 8$

  Ⓑ $x = 5$ Ⓓ $x = 13$

2. $x + 7 = 15$

  Ⓐ $x = 7$ Ⓒ $x = 15$

  Ⓑ $x = 8$ Ⓓ $x = 22$

3. $9 + x = 23$

  Ⓐ $x = 9$ Ⓒ $x = 23$

  Ⓑ $x = 14$ Ⓓ $x = 32$

4. $x - 5 = 8$

  Ⓐ $x = 3$ Ⓒ $x = 8$

  Ⓑ $x = 5$ Ⓓ $x = 13$

5. $x - 7 = 23$

  Ⓐ $x = 7$ Ⓒ $x = 23$

  Ⓑ $x = 16$ Ⓓ $x = 30$

6. $x - 37 = 50$

  Ⓐ $x = 13$ Ⓒ $x = 50$

  Ⓑ $x = 37$ Ⓓ $x = 87$

7. $25 - x = 18$

  Ⓐ $x = 7$ Ⓒ $x = 25$

  Ⓑ $x = 18$ Ⓓ $x = 43$

8. $42 + x = 91$

  Ⓐ $x = 42$ Ⓒ $x = 91$

  Ⓑ $x = 49$ Ⓓ $x = 133$

---

9. Write the equation for the following sentence: If 15 is subtracted from a number, then the difference is equal to 8.

10. Solve the equation you have written in #9.

Solve one-step equations using addition or subtraction

What is Glue-Covered Aspirin Good For?

Name_____

Solve each equation given below. Then write the corresponding letter on the line above the solution. The letters will spell out the answer to the riddle.

Hint: 4y means 4 times y.

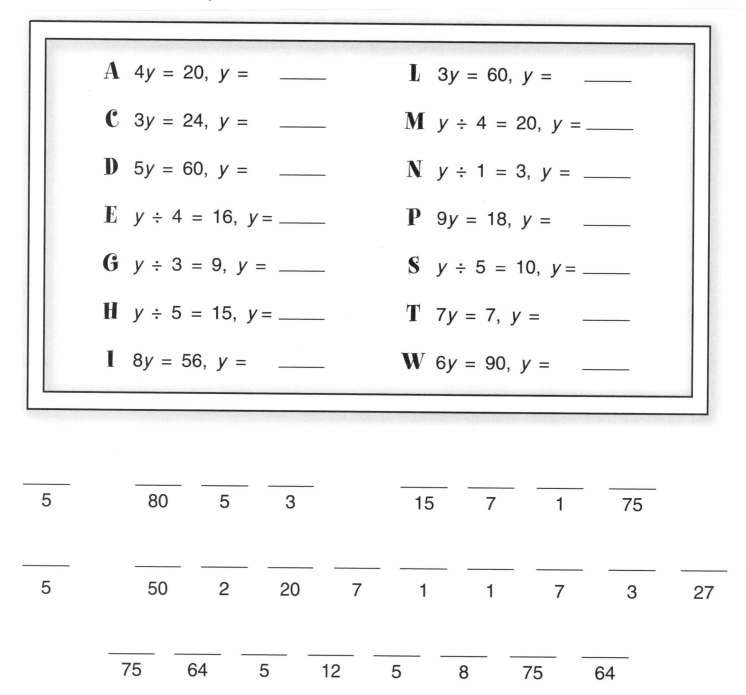

A $4y = 20$, $y =$ _____   L $3y = 60$, $y =$ _____

C $3y = 24$, $y =$ _____   M $y \div 4 = 20$, $y =$ _____

D $5y = 60$, $y =$ _____   N $y \div 1 = 3$, $y =$ _____

E $y \div 4 = 16$, $y =$ _____   P $9y = 18$, $y =$ _____

G $y \div 3 = 9$, $y =$ _____   S $y \div 5 = 10$, $y =$ _____

H $y \div 5 = 15$, $y =$ _____   T $7y = 7$, $y =$ _____

I $8y = 56$, $y =$ _____   W $6y = 90$, $y =$ _____

___ ___ ___ ___   ___ ___ ___ ___
 5   80   5   3   15   7   1   75

___ ___ ___ ___ ___ ___ ___ ___ ___
 5   50   2   20   7   1   1   7   3   27

___ ___ ___ ___ ___ ___ ___
75   64   5   12   5   8   75   64

Solve one-step equations using multiplication or division

EMC 3019 • Basic Math Skills, Grade 6 • ©2003 by Evan-Moor Corp.

Tongue Twister #11

Name _____

Solve each equation given below. Then write the corresponding letter on the line in front of the equation. The letters will spell out a tongue twister when read from top to bottom. How long does it take you to say it fast three times?

Hint: $4y$ means 4 times y.

_____ $3y = 18$, $y =$ _____

_____ $4y = 12$, $y =$ _____

_____ $7 \div y = 7$, $y =$ _____

_____ $12 \div y = 3$, $y =$ _____

_____ $4y = 36$, $y =$ _____

_____ $24 \div y = 4$, $y =$ _____

_____ $5y = 15$, $y =$ _____

_____ $6 \div 6 = y$, $y =$ _____

_____ $16 \div y = 4$, $y =$ _____

_____ $30 \div 5 = y$, $y =$ _____

_____ $45 \div y = 9$, $y =$ _____

_____ $7 \div y = 7$, $y =$ _____

_____ $28 \div y = 7$, $y =$ _____

_____ $4y = 8$, $y =$ _____

_____ $5y = 40$, $y =$ _____

_____ $49 \div y = 7$, $y =$ _____

1	**C**
2	**E**
3	**I**
4	**K**
5	**O**
6	**P**
7	**S**
8	**T**
9	**Y**

Solve one-step equations using multiplication or division

Solve It with Multiplication and Division

Name_____

Solve each of the following equations. Show all your work.

> Multiply both sides by the same number.   Or divide both sides by the same number.
> $$y \div 2 = 3$$
> $$y \div 2 \times 2 = 3 \times 2$$
> $$y = 6$$
>
> $$2y = 8$$
> $$2y \div 2 = 8 \div 2$$
> $$y = 4$$

1. $4y = 12$

2. $5y = 40$

3. $3y = 18$

4. $6y = 36$

5. $8y = 24$

6. $y \div 4 = 5$

7. $y \div 8 = 6$

8. $y \div 3 = 5$

9. $y \div 5 = 5$

10. $y \div 6 = 2$

11. $1y = 7$

12. $7y = 7$

13. $y \div 5 = 25$

14. $5y = 100$

15. $3y = 45$

16. $y \div 4 = 20$

17. $4y = 64$

18. $y \div 3 = 15$

19. $3y = 21$

20. $y \div 2 = 14$

21. $8y = 72$

Solve one-step equations using multiplication or division

Algebra   EMC 3019 • Basic Math Skills, Grade 6 • ©2003 by Evan-Moor Corp.

Solve It with Multiplication and Division II

Name _____

Solve each of the following equations. Show all your work.

Multiply both sides by the same number.	Or divide both sides by the same number.
$y \div 2 = 3$	$2y = 8$
$y \div 2 \times 2 = 3 \times 2$	$2y \div 2 = 8 \div 2$
$y = 6$	$y = 4$

1. $6y = 24$

2. $3y = 18$

3. $9y = 54$

4. $12y = 48$

5. $3y = 33$

6. $y \div 7 = 2$

7. $y \div 3 = 9$

8. $y \div 1 = 7$

9. $y \div 8 = 6$

10. $y \div 4 = 0$

11. $7y = 35$

12. $3y = 24$

13. $y \div 6 = 12$

14. $9y = 45$

15. $4y = 32$

16. $y \div 5 = 20$

17. $2y = 14$

18. $y \div 6 = 5$

19. $4y = 160$

20. $y \div 9 = 18$

21. $y \div 5 = 200$

Solve one-step equations using multiplication or division

©2003 by Evan-Moor Corp. • Basic Math Skills, Grade 6 • EMC 3019

Jessica's Quiz

Jessica completed the following quiz, and it needs to be checked. Write a *C* next to each item that she got correct. Write a ✓ next to any that she got incorrect, and then write a hint about what she should have done differently.

Name Jessica _____

1.
$$4y = 20$$
$$4y \div 4 = 20 \div 4$$
$$y = 5$$

6.
$$y \div 5 = 2$$
$$y \div 5(5) = 2(5)$$
$$y = 10$$

2.
$$5y = 45$$
$$5y \div 5 = 45 \div 5$$
$$y = 9$$

7.
$$7y = 35$$
$$7(7)y = 35(7)$$
$$y = 245$$

3.
$$y \div 6 = 24$$
$$y \div 6 \div 6 = 24 \div 6$$
$$y = 4$$

8.
$$12y = 48$$
$$12y \div 12 = 48 \div 12$$
$$y = 4$$

4.
$$7y = 7$$
$$7y \div 7 = 7 \div 7$$
$$y = 1$$

9.
$$y \div 8 = 4$$
$$y \div 8(8) = 4(8)$$
$$y = 32$$

5.
$$y \div 3 = 18$$
$$y \div 3(3) = 18(3)$$
$$y = 54$$

10.
$$y \div 4 = 28$$
$$y \div 4 \div 4 = 28 \div 4$$
$$y = 7$$

Solve one-step equations using multiplication or division

Mystery Number
(with One-Step Equations)

Name _____

Use the following clues to determine the mystery number. For each one, write the equation for each sentence and then solve the equation.

1. When 3 is multiplied by my number, the product is 36. What is my number?

   _____

2. When my number is divided by 8, the quotient is 3. What is my number?

   _____

3. When my number is multiplied by 8, the product is 48. What is my number?

   _____

4. When 30 is multiplied by my number, the product is 90. What is my number?

   _____

5. When my number is divided by 3, the quotient is 5. What is my number?

   _____

6. When my number is multiplied by 12, the product is 108. What is my number?

   _____

7. When my number is divided by 15, the quotient is 5. What is my number?

   _____

8. When 15 is multiplied by my number, the product is 345. What is my number?

   _____

9. When my number is divided by 25, the quotient is 12. What is my number?

   _____

10. When my number is multiplied by 8, the product is 208. What is my number?

    _____

Solve one-step equations using multiplication or division

Algebra

Math Test

Name_____

Solve each of the following equations for x. Fill in the circle next to the correct answer.

1. $6x = 18$

   Ⓐ 2   Ⓒ 6

   Ⓑ 3   Ⓓ 108

2. $5x = 20$

   Ⓐ 4   Ⓒ 20

   Ⓑ 5   Ⓓ 120

3. $x \div 4 = 8$

   Ⓐ 2   Ⓒ 40

   Ⓑ 32   Ⓓ 48

4. $x \div 3 = 12$

   Ⓐ 1   Ⓒ 12

   Ⓑ 4   Ⓓ 36

5. $8x = 24$

   Ⓐ 2   Ⓒ 24

   Ⓑ 3   Ⓓ 192

6. $5x = 0$

   Ⓐ 0   Ⓒ 5

   Ⓑ 1   Ⓓ 10

7. $x \div 6 = 48$

   Ⓐ 1   Ⓒ 7

   Ⓑ 6   Ⓓ 288

8. $x \div 1 = 9$

   Ⓐ 0   Ⓒ 9

   Ⓑ 1   Ⓓ 10

---

9. Write the equation for the following sentence: If 5 is multiplied by an unknown number, then the product is equal to 80.

10. Solve the equation you wrote in #9.

Solve one-step equations using multiplication or division

Algebra

EMC 3019 • Basic Math Skills, Grade 6 • ©2003 by Evan-Moor Corp.

Geometry

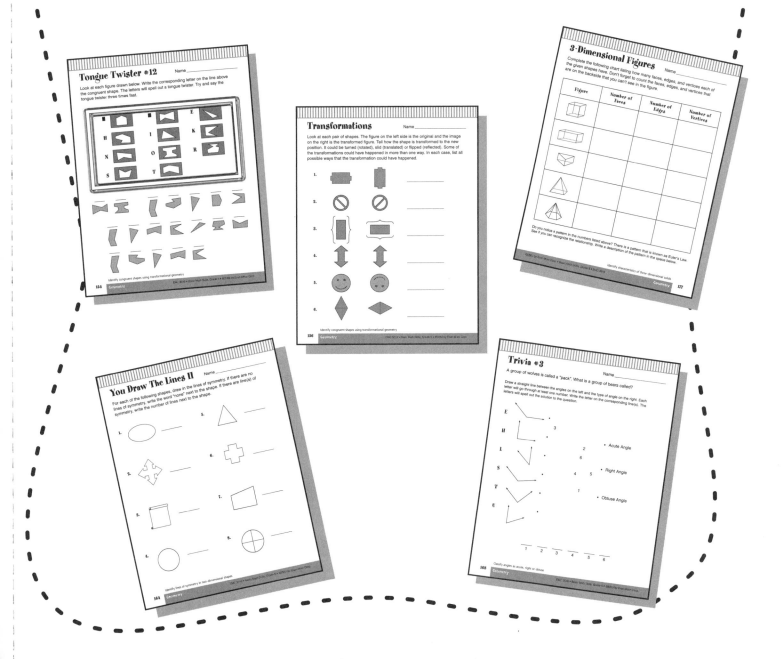

Tongue Twister #12

Look at each figure in the box. Find the shape at the bottom of the page that is congruent to the white region. Write the corresponding letter on the line above the congruent shape. The letters will spell out a tongue twister. Try to say it fast three times.

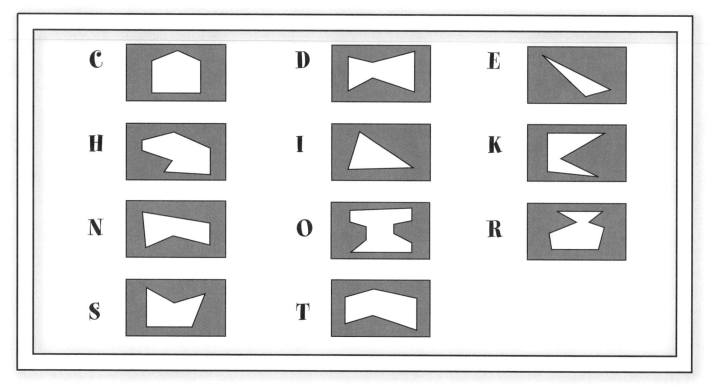

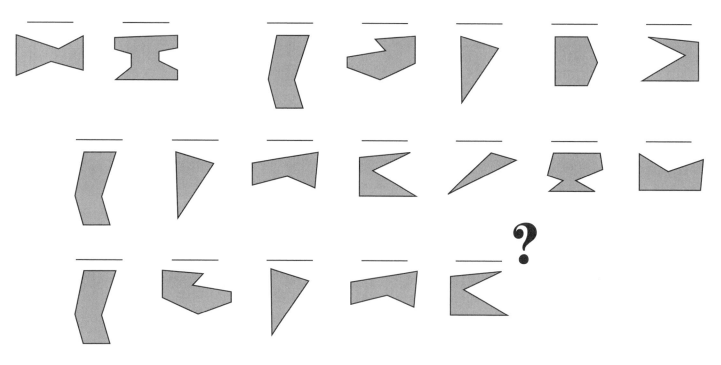

Identify congruent shapes using transformational geometry

EMC 3019 • Basic Math Skills, Grade 6 • ©2003 by Evan-Moor Corp.

What's a Cat's Favorite Television Show?

Name_____

Look at each figure in the box. Find the shape at the bottom of the page that is congruent to the white region. Write the corresponding letter on the line above the congruent shape. The letters will spell out the solution to the riddle.

Identify congruent shapes using transformational geometry

Transformations

Look at each pair of shapes. Determine how the shape is transformed from the one on the left to the one on the right. It could be *turned* (rotated), *slid* (translated), or *flipped* (reflected). Some of the transformations could have happened in more than one way. In each case, list all possible ways that the transformation could have happened.

1.

2.

3.

4.

5.

6.

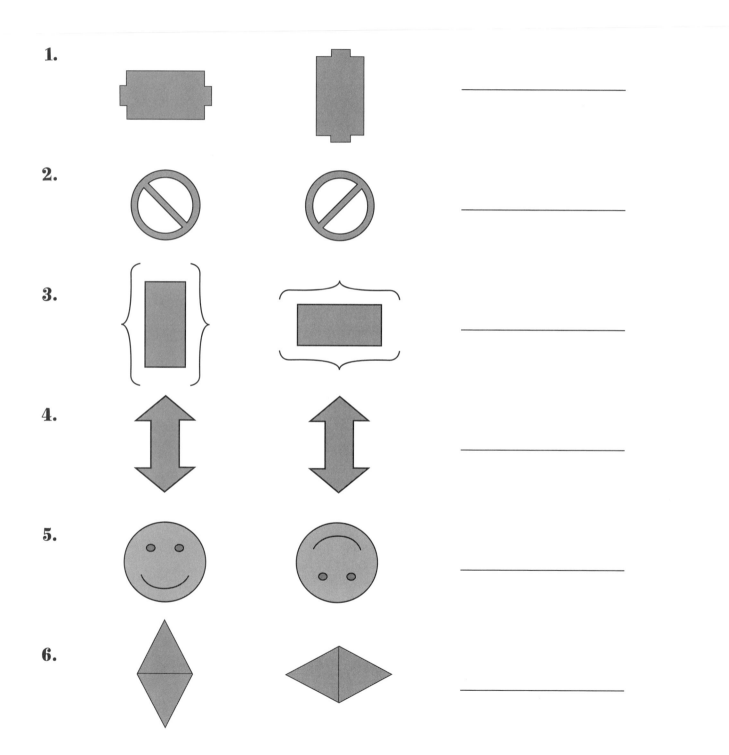

Identify congruent shapes using transformational geometry

EMC 3019 • Basic Math Skills, Grade 6 • ©2003 by Evan-Moor Corp.

Transform Me

Name _____

For each of the following figures, sketch what the figure will be after the given transformation.

1. Translate to the right.

2. Rotate to the left 90 degrees.

3. Reflect about the dashed line.

4. Translate to the right.

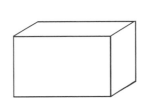

5. Reflect about the dashed line.

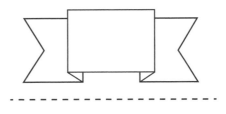

Identify congruent shapes using transformational geometry

Quilts

Name_____

1. Shelley made this quilt. Her friend, Julie, wants to make a quilt that is identical to Shelley's quilt. If they both start with the same first square in the top left corner, describe to Julie how all the other pieces are changed from the original square. Use the words *rotated* (turned), *translated* (slid), or *reflected* (flipped).

Original _____   _____

_____   _____

_____   _____

2. Timothy is making a cool quilt that can only be read by reading the message using a mirror. He would like the message to read, "Here lies Timothy, the world's best basketball player!" Write the message for him in the space below. The first two words are written for you to get you started.

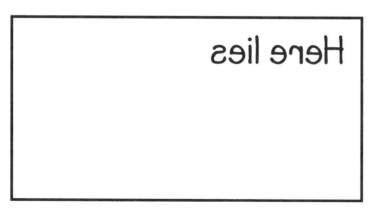

Identify congruent shapes using transformational geometry

EMC 3019 • Basic Math Skills, Grade 6 • ©2003 by Evan-Moor Corp.

Pair Me Up

Name _____

Draw a line connecting the congruent shapes. The shapes might be flipped or turned in their orientation. For each shape that doesn't have a partner, draw a congruent shape that is rotated 90 degrees.

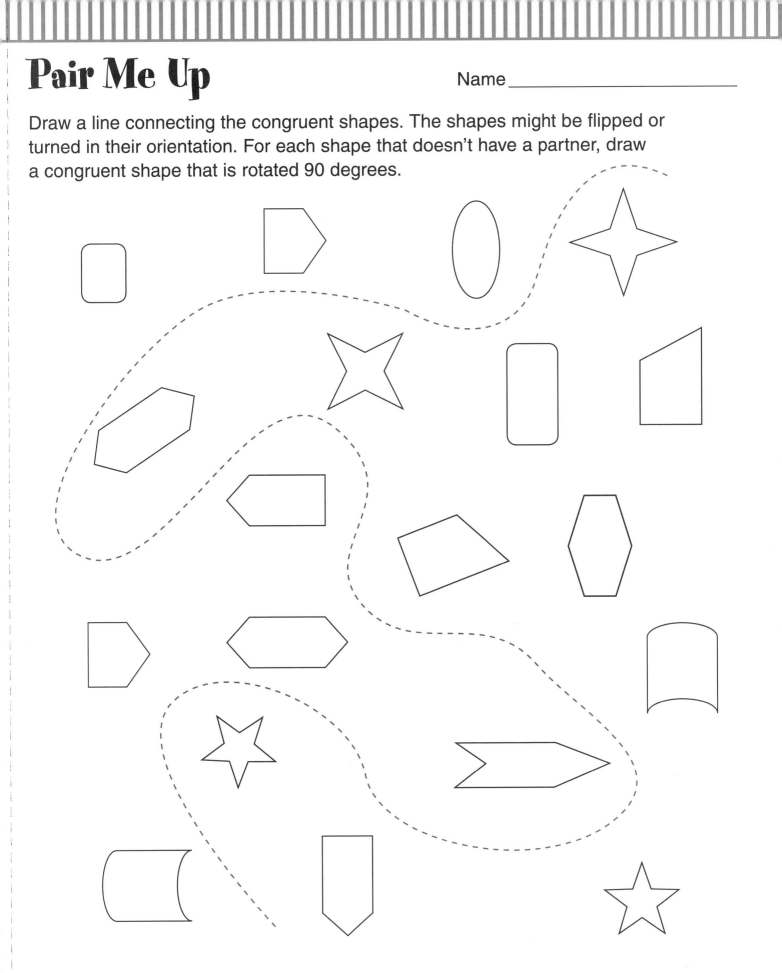

Identify congruent shapes using transformational geometry

Math Test

Fill in the circle next to the correct answer.

For Numbers 1 through 4, use these figures.

1. Which figure is congruent to the white region?

Ⓐ   figure A
Ⓑ   figure B
Ⓒ   figure C
Ⓓ   figure D

2. Which figure is congruent to the white region?

Ⓐ   figure A
Ⓑ   figure B
Ⓒ   figure C
Ⓓ   figure D

3. Which figure is congruent to the white region?

Ⓐ   figure A
Ⓑ   figure B
Ⓒ   figure C
Ⓓ   figure D

4. Which figure is congruent to the white region?

Ⓐ   figure A
Ⓑ   figure B
Ⓒ   figure C
Ⓓ   figure D

For Numbers 5 through 8, tell how the shapes are transformed.

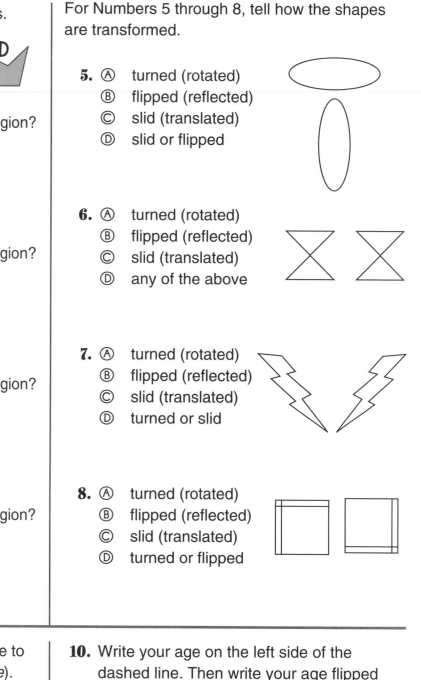

5. Ⓐ   turned (rotated)
   Ⓑ   flipped (reflected)
   Ⓒ   slid (translated)
   Ⓓ   slid or flipped

6. Ⓐ   turned (rotated)
   Ⓑ   flipped (reflected)
   Ⓒ   slid (translated)
   Ⓓ   any of the above

7. Ⓐ   turned (rotated)
   Ⓑ   flipped (reflected)
   Ⓒ   slid (translated)
   Ⓓ   turned or slid

8. Ⓐ   turned (rotated)
   Ⓑ   flipped (reflected)
   Ⓒ   slid (translated)
   Ⓓ   turned or flipped

9. Write your name. Then slide your name to the right and write it again (label it *slide*).

10. Write your age on the left side of the dashed line. Then write your age flipped across the line.

Identify congruent shapes using transformational geometry

What Is a Kangaroo's Favorite Year?

Name _____

Draw the lines of symmetry in each of the figures. (For one figure, watch the shading and make sure that your line is still a line of symmetry). Then draw a straight line between the figure on the left and the number of lines of symmetry on the right. The line will go through one letter. Write that letter on the line in front of the figure. The letters will spell out the solution to the riddle when read from top to bottom.

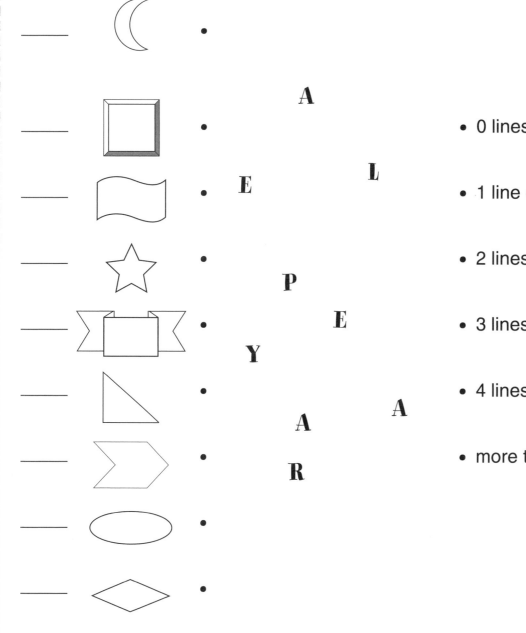

• 0 lines of symmetry

• 1 line of symmetry

• 2 lines of symmetry

• 3 lines of symmetry

• 4 lines of symmetry

• more than 4 lines of symmetry

Identify lines of symmetry in two-dimensional shapes

What Happened to the Cowardly Human Cannonball?

Draw the lines of symmetry in each of the figures. Then draw a straight line between the figure on the left and the number of lines of symmetry on the right. The line will go through one letter. Write that letter on the line in front of the figure. The letters will spell out the solution to the riddle when read from top to bottom.

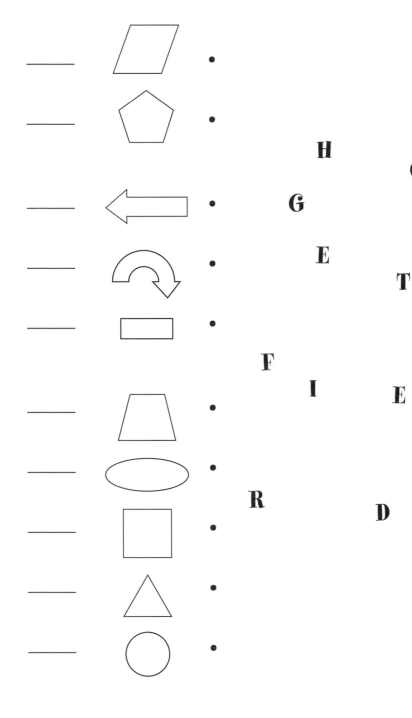

H

O

G

• 0 lines of symmetry

E

• 1 line of symmetry

T

• 2 lines of symmetry

• 3 lines of symmetry

F

I

E

• 4 lines of symmetry

• more than 4 lines of symmetry

R

D

Identify lines of symmetry in two-dimensional shapes

EMC 3019 • Basic Math Skills, Grade 6 • ©2003 by Evan-Moor Corp.

You Draw the Lines

For each of the following figures, draw the lines of symmetry. If there are no lines of symmetry, write the word *none* next to the figure. If there are line(s) of symmetry, write the number of lines next to the figure.

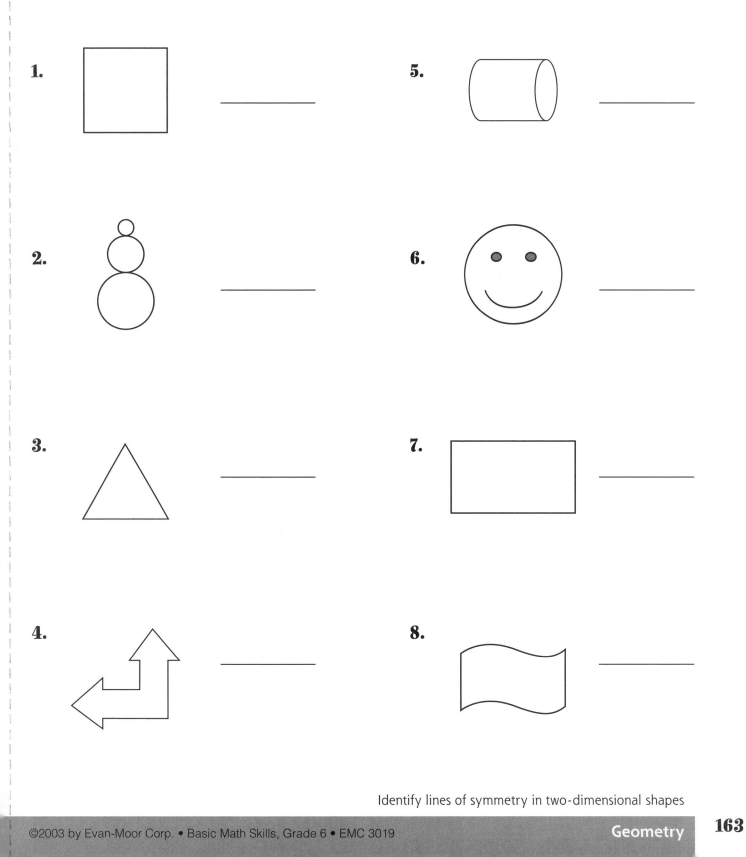

1. _____

2. _____

3. _____

4. _____

5. _____

6. _____

7. _____

8. _____

Identify lines of symmetry in two-dimensional shapes

You Draw the Lines II

Name _____

For each of the following figures, draw in the lines of symmetry. If there are no lines of symmetry, write the word *none* next to the figure. If there are line(s) of symmetry, write the number of lines next to the figure.

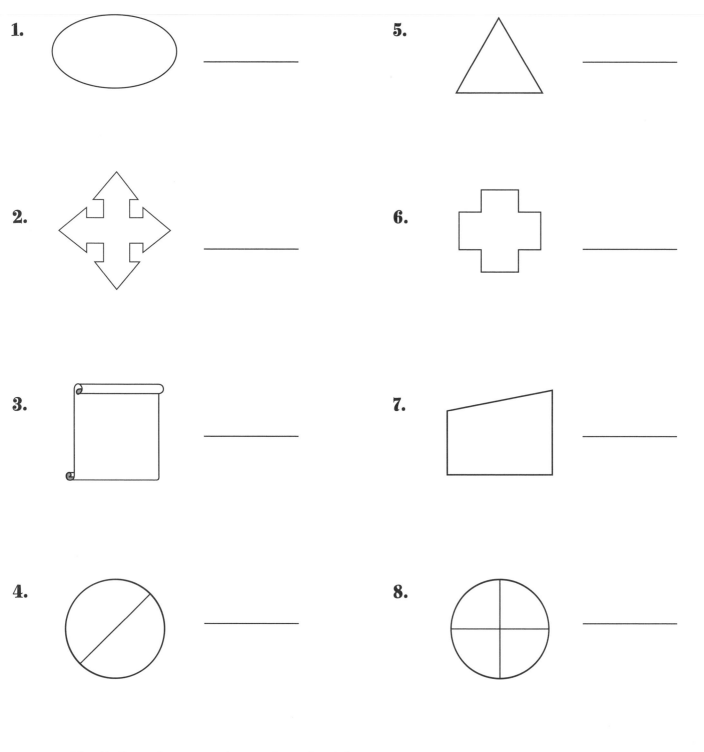

1. _____

2. _____

3. _____

4. _____

5. _____

6. _____

7. _____

8. _____

Identify lines of symmetry in two-dimensional shapes

EMC 3019 • Basic Math Skills, Grade 6 • ©2003 by Evan-Moor Corp.

Symmetry Around Us

Name_____

Look around you and find objects that have lines of symmetry. Complete the chart below, sketching and describing one object in each row.

Characteristics	Sketch of Object	Description of Object
Exactly 1 line of symmetry		
Exactly 2 lines of symmetry		
Exactly 3 lines of symmetry		
Exactly 4 lines of symmetry		
More than 4 lines of symmetry		
No lines of symmetry		

Identify lines of symmetry in two-dimensional shapes

Symmetric Words and Numbers

Name_____

Lisa was helping her younger sister with some reading and math flash cards.
She noticed that some of the cards have a line of symmetry.

Draw a line of symmetry on all the word cards that are symmetric. Circle the word cards that
are **not** symmetric.

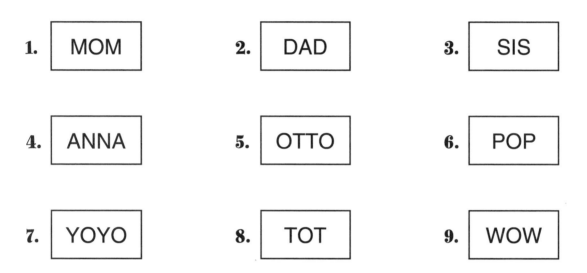

1. MOM   2. DAD   3. SIS

4. ANNA   5. OTTO   6. POP

7. YOYO   8. TOT   9. WOW

Draw a line of symmetry on all the math cards that are symmetric. Circle the math cards that
are **not** symmetric.

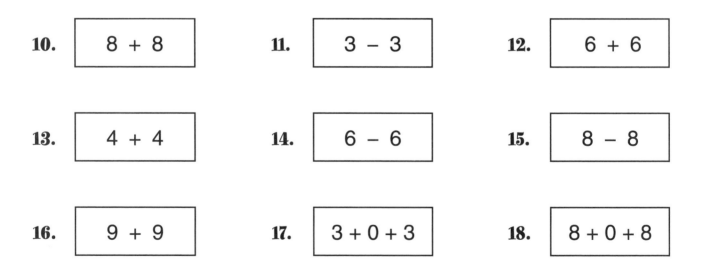

10. 8 + 8   11. 3 – 3   12. 6 + 6

13. 4 + 4   14. 6 – 6   15. 8 – 8

16. 9 + 9   17. 3 + 0 + 3   18. 8 + 0 + 8

Identify lines of symmetry in two-dimensional shapes

EMC 3019 • Basic Math Skills, Grade 6 • ©2003 by Evan-Moor Corp.

Math Test

Name_____

Fill in the circle next to the correct answer.
For Numbers 1 through 8, identify how many lines of symmetry each figure has.

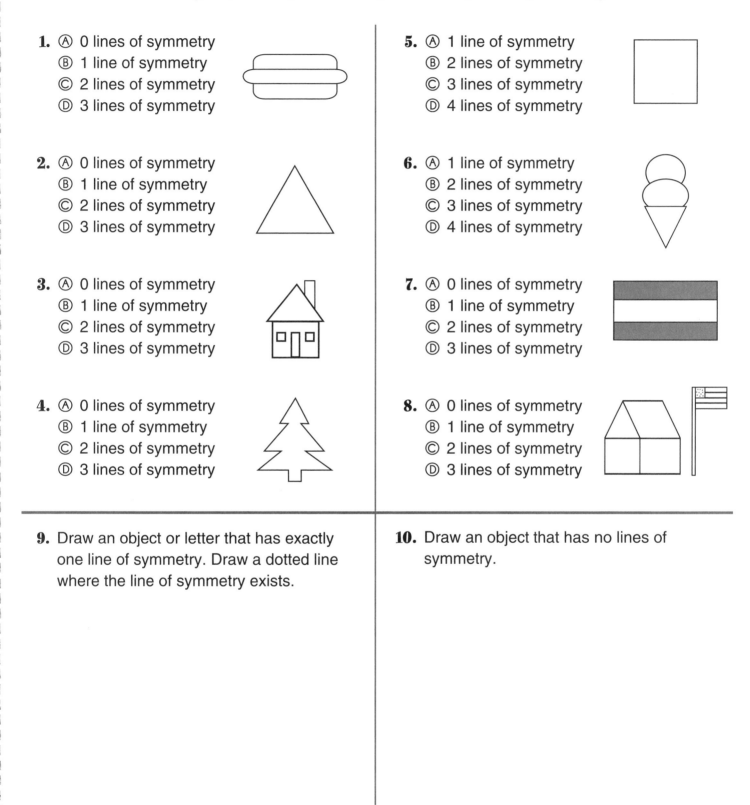

1. Ⓐ 0 lines of symmetry
   Ⓑ 1 line of symmetry
   Ⓒ 2 lines of symmetry
   Ⓓ 3 lines of symmetry

2. Ⓐ 0 lines of symmetry
   Ⓑ 1 line of symmetry
   Ⓒ 2 lines of symmetry
   Ⓓ 3 lines of symmetry

3. Ⓐ 0 lines of symmetry
   Ⓑ 1 line of symmetry
   Ⓒ 2 lines of symmetry
   Ⓓ 3 lines of symmetry

4. Ⓐ 0 lines of symmetry
   Ⓑ 1 line of symmetry
   Ⓒ 2 lines of symmetry
   Ⓓ 3 lines of symmetry

5. Ⓐ 1 line of symmetry
   Ⓑ 2 lines of symmetry
   Ⓒ 3 lines of symmetry
   Ⓓ 4 lines of symmetry

6. Ⓐ 1 line of symmetry
   Ⓑ 2 lines of symmetry
   Ⓒ 3 lines of symmetry
   Ⓓ 4 lines of symmetry

7. Ⓐ 0 lines of symmetry
   Ⓑ 1 line of symmetry
   Ⓒ 2 lines of symmetry
   Ⓓ 3 lines of symmetry

8. Ⓐ 0 lines of symmetry
   Ⓑ 1 line of symmetry
   Ⓒ 2 lines of symmetry
   Ⓓ 3 lines of symmetry

9. Draw an object or letter that has exactly one line of symmetry. Draw a dotted line where the line of symmetry exists.

10. Draw an object that has no lines of symmetry.

Identify lines of symmetry in two-dimensional shapes

Trivia #3

A group of wolves is called a *pack*. What is a group of bears called?

Draw a straight line between the angles on the left and the type of angle on the right. Each letter will go through at least one number. Write the letter on the corresponding line(s). The letters will spell out the solution to the question.

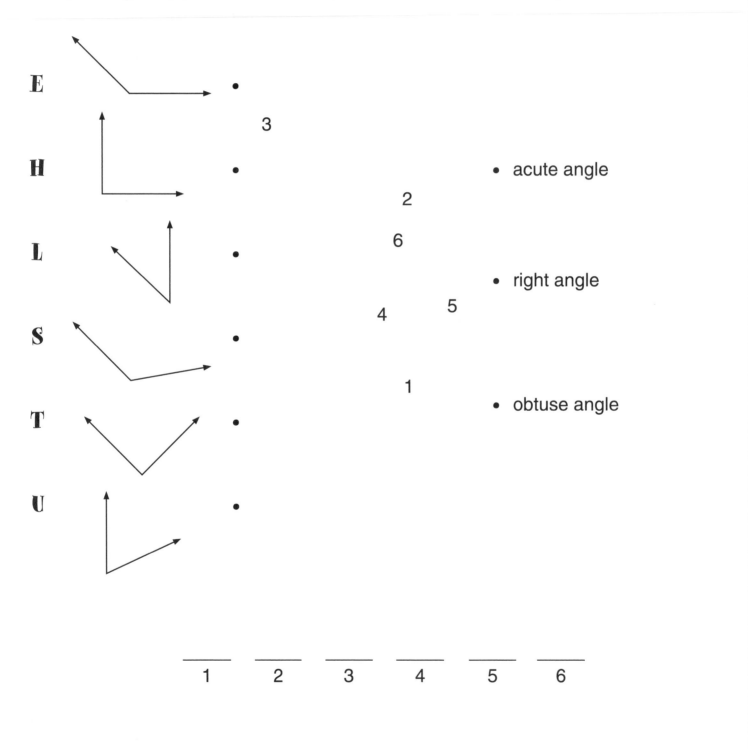

E

H   • acute angle

          3

              2

              6

L   • right angle

                4   5

S

              1

                        • obtuse angle

T

U

___ ___ ___ ___ ___ ___
 1   2   3   4   5   6

Classify angles as acute, right, or obtuse

EMC 3019 • Basic Math Skills, Grade 6 • ©2003 by Evan-Moor Corp.

What Is Green and Makes a Loud Noise?

Name _____

Draw a straight line between the angles on the left and the type of angle on the right. Each letter will go through at least one number. Write the letter on the corresponding line(s). The letters will spell out the solution to the riddle.

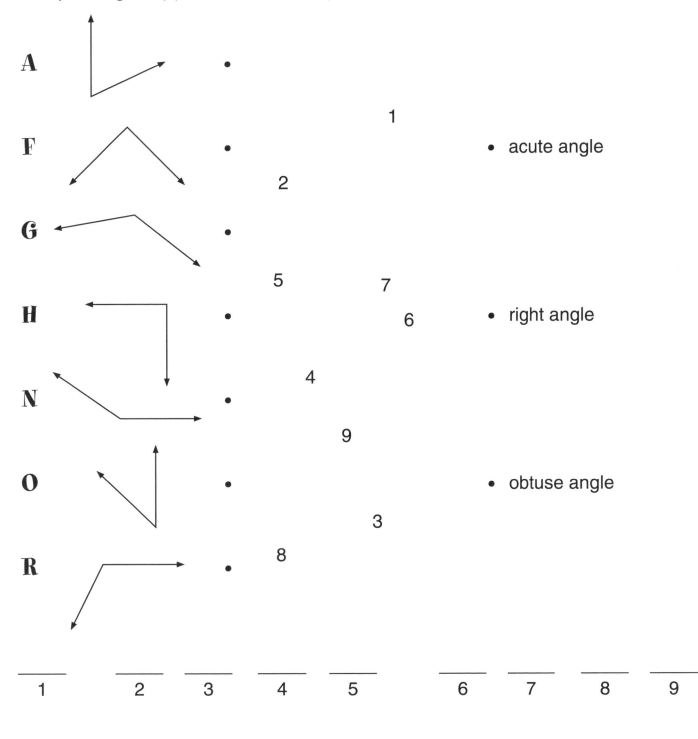

A

F   • 1

          • 2

G   •

          5   7

H   •   6   • right angle

          • acute angle

          4

N   •

          9

O   •   • obtuse angle

          3

R   8   •

___ ___ ___ ___ ___   ___ ___ ___ ___
 1   2   3   4   5   6   7   8   9

Classify angles as acute, right, or obtuse

Am I Right?

Name_____

Classify each of the following angles as *right, acute,* or *obtuse.*

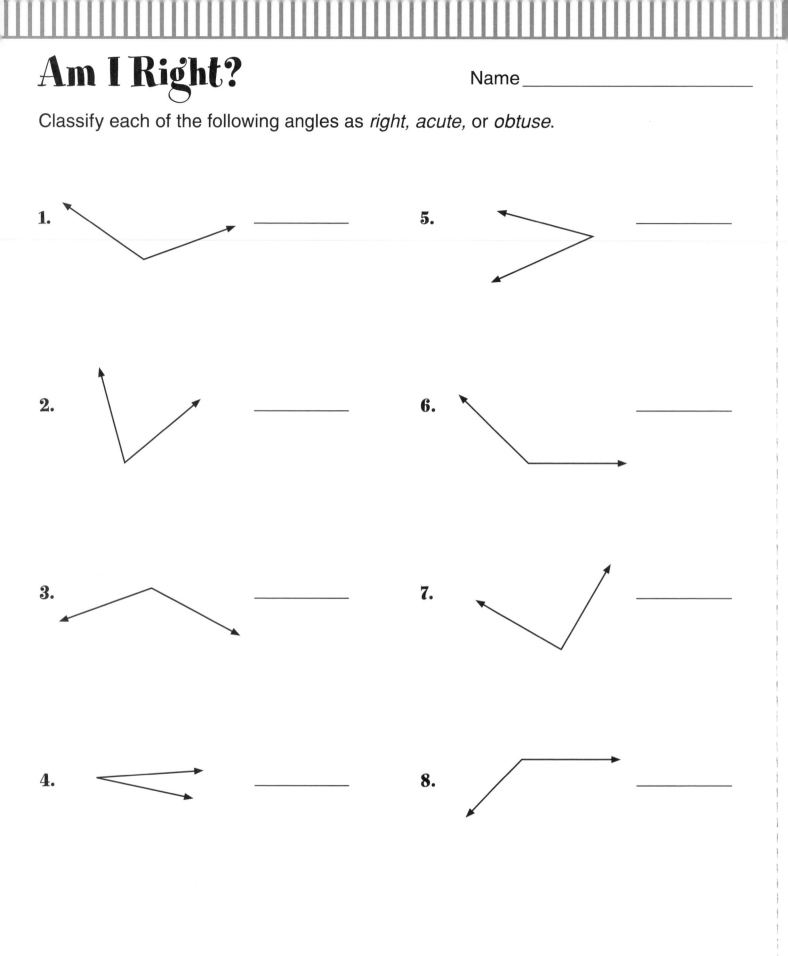

1. _____

2. _____

3. _____

4. _____

5. _____

6. _____

7. _____

8. _____

Classify angles as acute, right, or obtuse

EMC 3019 • Basic Math Skills, Grade 6 • ©2003 by Evan-Moor Corp.

Am I a Cute Angle?

Name_____

Classify each of the following angles as *right, acute,* or *obtuse.*

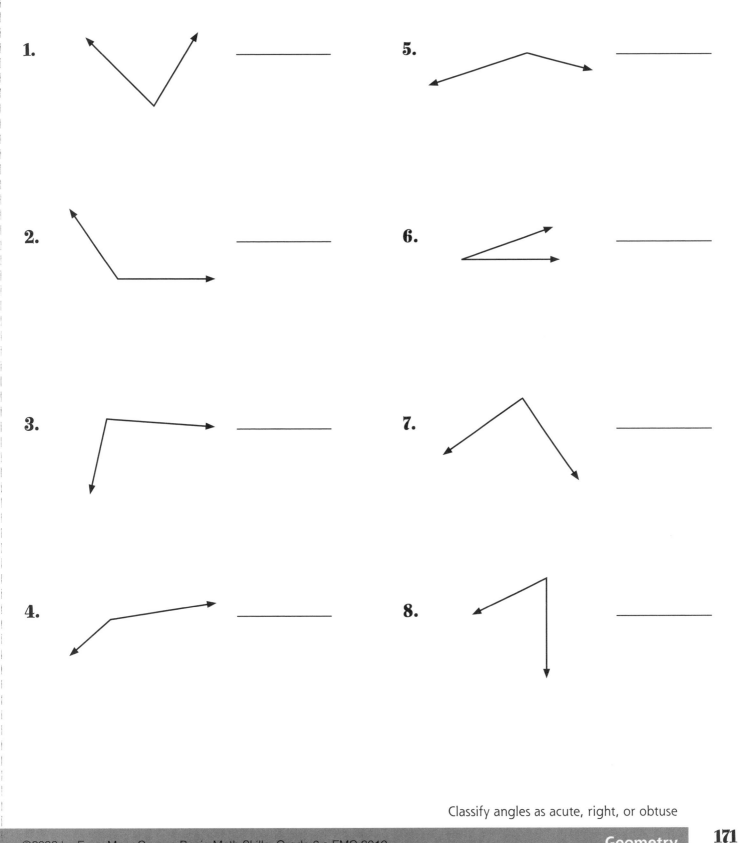

1. _____

2. _____

3. _____

4. _____

5. _____

6. _____

7. _____

8. _____

Classify angles as acute, right, or obtuse

The Angles Around Us

Name_____

Look around you and find examples of angles. To list just a few examples, think of the angle the wall in your classroom makes with the floor, or the angle that the edges of your desk or table make, or the angles that the legs on an easel make. On the chart, describe the angle and then draw a sketch of it.

Description of Angle	Description of Object	Sketch of Object
right		
right		
right		
acute		
acute		
acute		
obtuse		
obtuse		
obtuse		

Classify angles as acute, right, or obtuse

EMC 3019 • Basic Math Skills, Grade 6 • ©2003 by Evan-Moor Corp.

Large Angles in the World of Ice Skating

Name _____

Richard has heard of angles being used with ice-skating, and he has some questions for you to figure out.

1. He has heard of people doing "a 180." What does that mean in relation to a person ice-skating? What does that mean in terms of angle measurement?

   _____

2. Another thing he heard someone do was "a 360." What does that mean in relation to ice-skating? What does that mean in terms of angle measurement?

   _____

3. Keeping those concepts in mind, what do you think "a 270" would look like? Draw a sketch of someone ice-skating, looking down on him or her from above. Draw what direction this person would be facing initially, and then what direction he or she would be facing after turning 270 degrees. Does it matter if the skater turns to the right or the left?

   _____

4. Keeping those concepts in mind, what do you think "a 540" would look like? Draw a sketch of someone ice-skating, looking down on him or her from above. Draw what direction the skater would be facing initially, and then what direction he or she would be facing after turning 540 degrees. Does it matter if the skater turns to the right or the left?

   _____

5. If a person does a triple turn, how many degrees has he or she rotated?

   _____

Classify angles as acute, right, or obtuse

Math Test

Fill in the circle next to the correct answer.

1. An angle that measures 78 degrees is _____.

   Ⓐ an acute angle   Ⓒ a right angle
   Ⓑ an obtuse angle   Ⓓ a straight angle

2. An angle that measures 125 degrees is _____.

   Ⓐ an acute angle   Ⓒ a right angle
   Ⓑ an obtuse angle   Ⓓ a straight angle

3. An angle that measures 90 degrees is _____.

   Ⓐ an acute angle   Ⓒ a right angle
   Ⓑ an obtuse angle   Ⓓ a straight angle

4. An angle that measures 100 degrees is _____.

   Ⓐ an acute angle   Ⓒ a right angle
   Ⓑ an obtuse angle   Ⓓ a straight angle

5. What type of angle is this?
   Ⓐ an acute angle
   Ⓑ an obtuse angle
   Ⓒ a right angle
   Ⓓ a straight angle

6. What type of angle is this?
   Ⓐ an acute angle
   Ⓑ an obtuse angle
   Ⓒ a right angle
   Ⓓ a straight angle

7. What type of angle is this?
   Ⓐ an acute angle
   Ⓑ an obtuse angle
   Ⓒ a right angle
   Ⓓ a straight angle

8. What type of angle is this?
   Ⓐ an acute angle
   Ⓑ an obtuse angle
   Ⓒ a right angle
   Ⓓ a straight angle

9. Draw a simple picture of a house with a front door and two windows. Identify all the angles in the picture and label them as *acute, obtuse,* or *right* angles.

10. Write your name. Identify any angles in each letter of your name and label them as *acute, obtuse,* or *right* angles.

Classify angles as acute, right, or obtuse

What's Full of Holes and Holds Water?

Name _____

Draw a straight line from each term on the left with its definition on the right. Each line will go through at least one number. Write the corresponding letter on the line above the number. The letters will spell out the solution to the riddle.

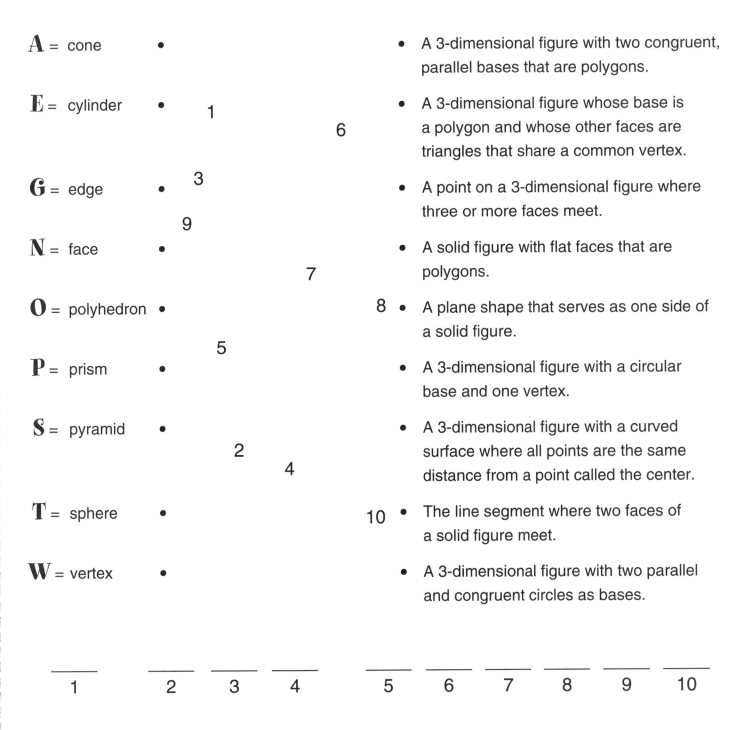

A = cone •

E = cylinder •
    1
            6

G = edge •
  3
  9

N = face •
      7

O = polyhedron •
        8 •

  5

P = prism •

S = pyramid •
  2
   4

T = sphere •
     10 •

W = vertex •

- A 3-dimensional figure with two congruent, parallel bases that are polygons.
- A 3-dimensional figure whose base is a polygon and whose other faces are triangles that share a common vertex.
- A point on a 3-dimensional figure where three or more faces meet.
- A solid figure with flat faces that are polygons.
- A plane shape that serves as one side of a solid figure.
- A 3-dimensional figure with a circular base and one vertex.
- A 3-dimensional figure with a curved surface where all points are the same distance from a point called the center.
- The line segment where two faces of a solid figure meet.
- A 3-dimensional figure with two parallel and congruent circles as bases.

___ ___ ___ ___   ___ ___ ___ ___ ___ ___
1   2   3   4   5   6   7   8   9   10

Identify characteristics of three-dimensional solids

What Stays Hot in the Refrigerator?

Name _____

Draw a straight line from each figure on the left with the correct number of faces that figure has. Each line will go through a number. Write the corresponding letter on the line above the number. The letters will spell out the solution to the riddle.

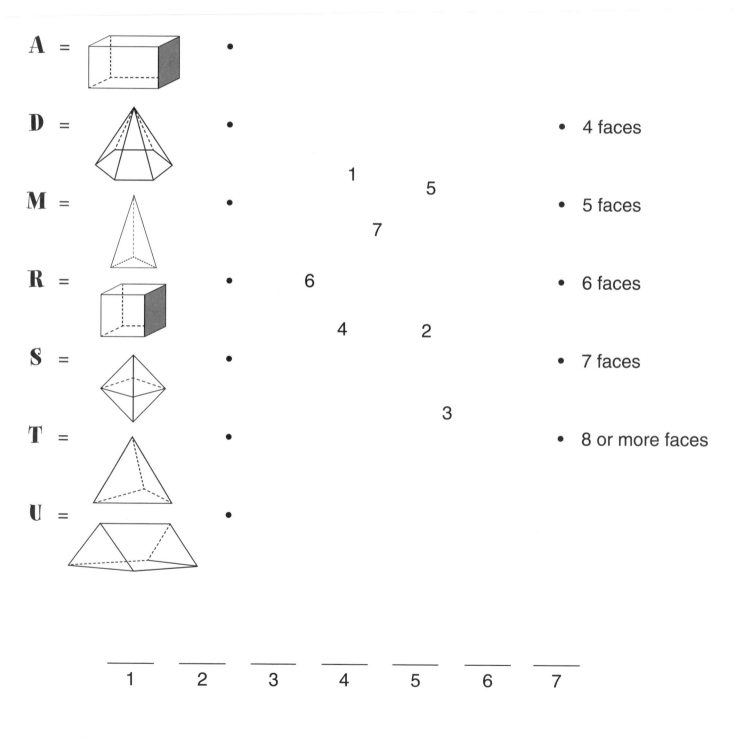

A =

D =

M =

R =

S =

T =

U =

1

5

7

6

4   2

3

• 4 faces

• 5 faces

• 6 faces

• 7 faces

• 8 or more faces

___ ___ ___ ___ ___ ___ ___
 1   2   3   4   5   6   7

Identify characteristics of three-dimensional solids

176 **Geometry**

EMC 3019 • Basic Math Skills, Grade 6 • ©2003 by Evan-Moor Corp.

3-Dimensional Figures

Complete the following chart by listing how many faces, edges, and vertices each of the given shapes have. Don't forget to count the faces, edges, and vertices on the backside that you can't see in the figure.

Figure	Number of Faces	Number of Edges	Number of Vertices
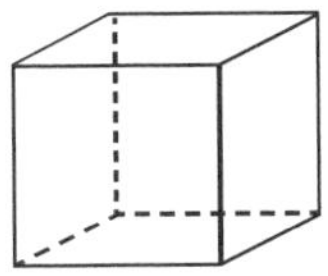			
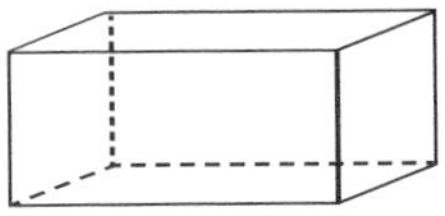			
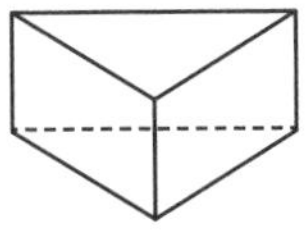			
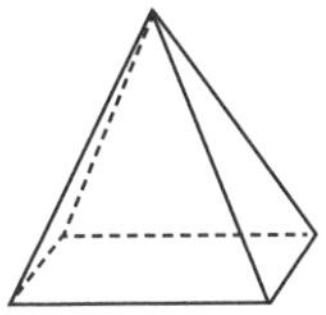			
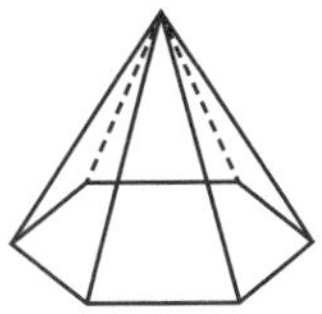			

Do you notice a pattern in the numbers listed above? There is a pattern known as Euler's Law. See if you can recognize the relationship. Write a description of the pattern below.

Identify characteristics of three-dimensional solids

Nets

For each of the following figures, draw the net. Remember that a net is the flat drawing as if you were to cut along the edges of the figure and lay the faces out flat. The first one has been drawn for you as an example. Also notice that there are many different ways to draw a net.

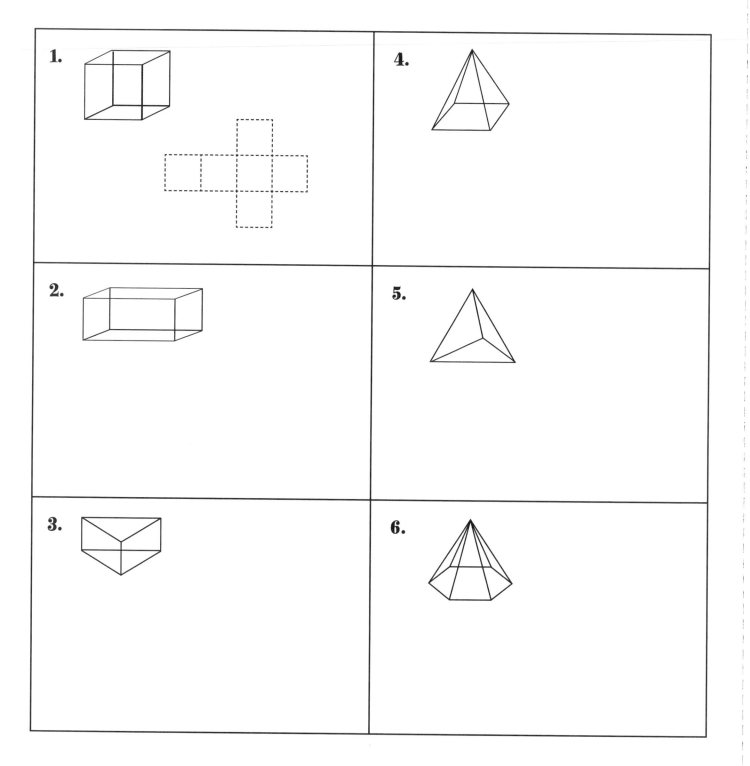

1.

2.

3.

4.

5.

6.

Identify characteristics of three-dimensional solids

Tetrahedrons and Octahedrons

Name _____

The tetrahedron and the octahedron are special three-dimensional figures.
Cut out each net below to make the figures. Then complete the chart to find out
what makes them special.

	Tetrahedron	Octahedron
Number of faces		
Shape of faces		
Number of vertices		
Number of faces that meet at each vertex		

Tetrahedron   **Octahedron**

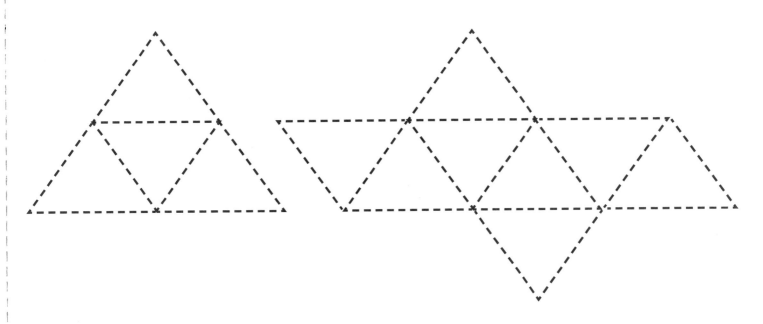

Identify characteristics of three-dimensional solids

Structures

Name _____

1. Look around your classroom. What three-dimensional figure do the walls, the ceiling, and the floor make? How many faces does it have (how many walls, ceilings, and floors are there)? How many edges does it have (look for the lines where the wall and ceiling meet, for example)? How many vertices does it have (look for the corners)?

_____

2. Look at the Egyptian pyramid. How many faces does it have? How many edges? How many vertices?

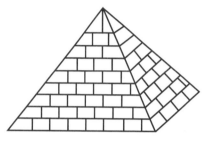

_____

3. Look at the picture of a school with one floor across the whole building and then a second floor on just one end. How many faces does it have? How many edges? How many vertices?

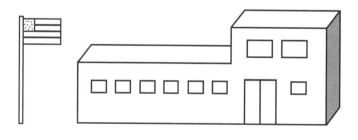

_____

Identify characteristics of three-dimensional solids

EMC 3019 • Basic Math Skills, Grade 6 • ©2003 by Evan-Moor Corp.

Math Test

Name _____

Fill in the circle next to the correct answer.

For Numbers 1 through 4, select the appropriate term for each definition of a three-dimensional figure.

1. One base that is a circle and one vertex

Ⓐ pyramid   Ⓒ cone

Ⓑ prism   Ⓓ cylinder

2. Two bases that are parallel and congruent polygons and sides that are parallelograms

Ⓐ pyramid   Ⓒ cone

Ⓑ prism   Ⓓ cylinder

3. Two parallel and congruent circles as bases

Ⓐ pyramid   Ⓒ cone

Ⓑ prism   Ⓓ cylinder

4. One base that is a polygon, with triangular sides that meet at a common vertex

Ⓐ pyramid   Ⓒ cone

Ⓑ prism   Ⓓ cylinder

Use the following figure to answer Numbers 5 through 9.

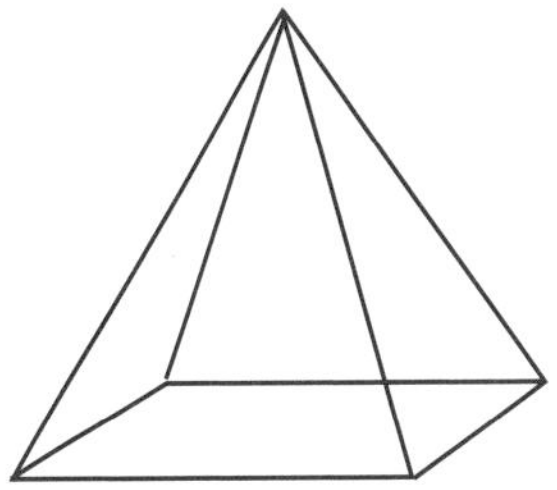

5. How many faces does this solid have?

Ⓐ 3   Ⓒ 5

Ⓑ 4   Ⓓ 6

6. How many edges does this solid have?

Ⓐ 4   Ⓒ 8

Ⓑ 6   Ⓓ 10

7. How many vertices does this solid have?

Ⓐ 3   Ⓒ 5

Ⓑ 4   Ⓓ 6

8. What is the shape of the base?

Ⓐ triangle   Ⓒ circle

Ⓑ square   Ⓓ hexagon

---

9. Draw a picture of what the net would look like for this solid if each of the faces were laid out flat.

10. Sketch a picture of a rectangular prism.

Identify characteristics of three-dimensional solids

Measurement

Customary and metric measurement

Perimeter, area, and volume

EMC 3019 • Basic Math Skills, Grade 6 • ©2003 by Evan-Moor Corp.

What Animal Doesn't Play Fair?

Name _____

To solve the riddle, measure each of the following pencils to the nearest quarter inch. Then write the corresponding letter on the line above the measurement. The letters will spell out the solution to the riddle.

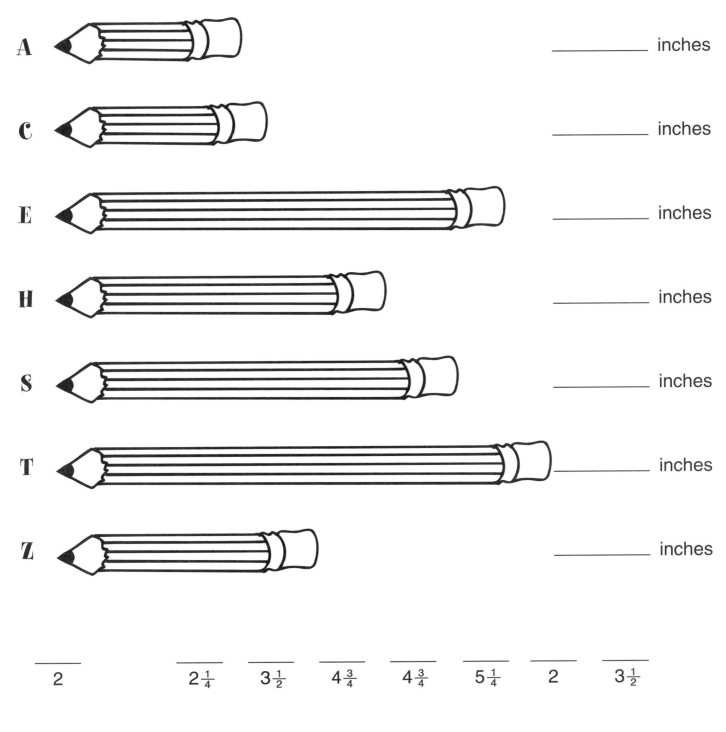

A _____ inches

C _____ inches

E _____ inches

H _____ inches

S _____ inches

T _____ inches

Z _____ inches

___ ___ ___ ___ ___ ___ ___ ___
 2   $2\frac{1}{4}$ $3\frac{1}{2}$ $4\frac{3}{4}$ $4\frac{3}{4}$ $5\frac{1}{4}$ 2 $3\frac{1}{2}$

Utilize customary and metric units of linear measurement

What's the Best Thing to Put into a Cake?

Name_____

To solve the riddle, measure each of the following straws to the nearest half centimeter. Then write the corresponding letter on the line above the measurement. The letters will spell out the solution to the riddle.

E _____ centimeters

H _____ centimeters

O _____ centimeters

R _____ centimeters

T _____ centimeters

U _____ centimeters

Y _____ centimeters

$$\frac{\quad}{3\frac{1}{2}} \quad \frac{\quad}{8} \quad \frac{\quad}{7\frac{1}{2}} \quad \frac{\quad}{9}$$

$$\frac{\quad}{8\frac{1}{2}} \quad \frac{\quad}{5\frac{1}{2}} \quad \frac{\quad}{5\frac{1}{2}} \quad \frac{\quad}{8\frac{1}{2}} \quad \frac{\quad}{10\frac{1}{2}}$$

Utilize customary and metric units of linear measurement

Measurement

EMC 3019 • Basic Math Skills, Grade 6 • ©2003 by Evan-Moor Corp.

Art Supplies

Measure the length of each of the following objects to the nearest quarter inch.

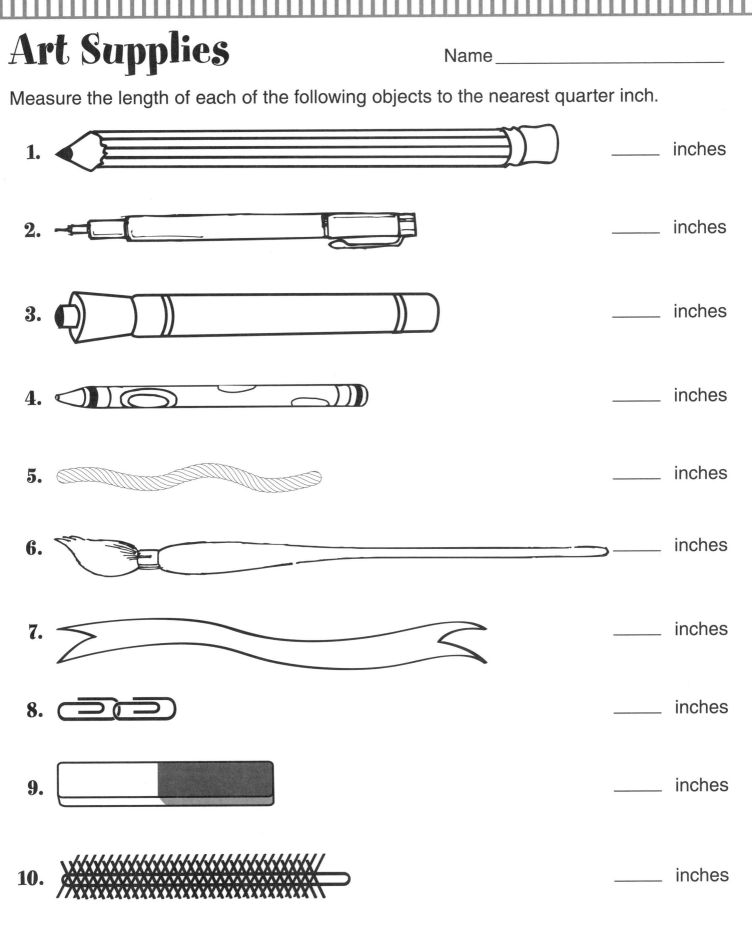

1. _____ inches

2. _____ inches

3. _____ inches

4. _____ inches

5. _____ inches

6. _____ inches

7. _____ inches

8. _____ inches

9. _____ inches

10. _____ inches

Utilize customary and metric units of linear measurement

Candy Store

Name_____

Measure the length of the pepermint sticks to the nearest half centimeter.

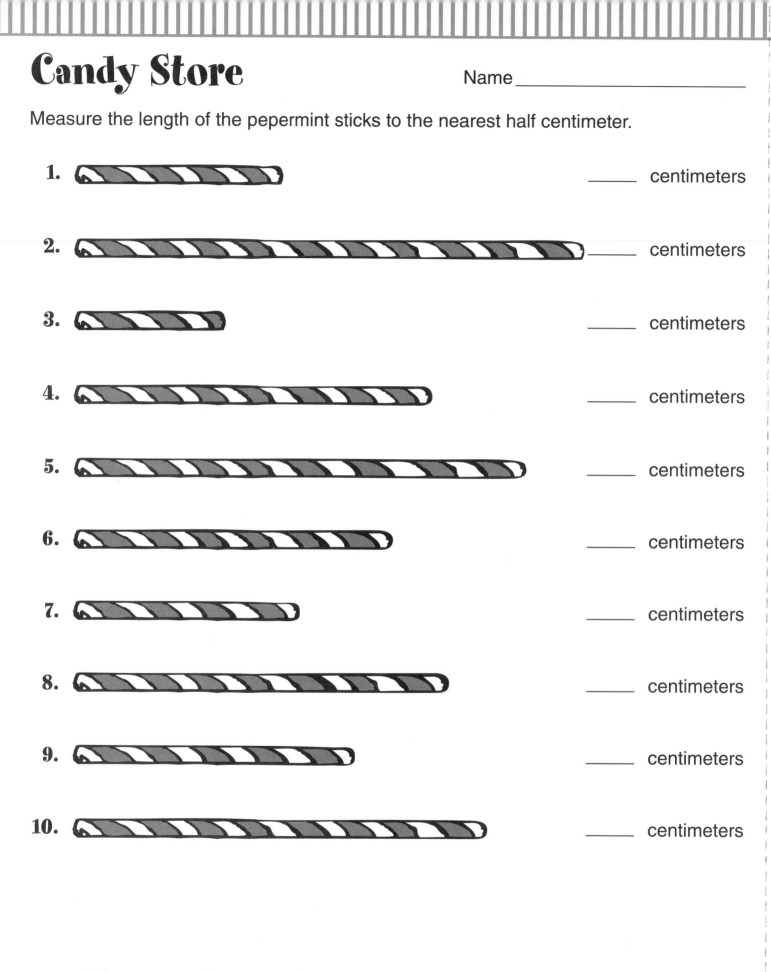

1. _____ centimeters

2. _____ centimeters

3. _____ centimeters

4. _____ centimeters

5. _____ centimeters

6. _____ centimeters

7. _____ centimeters

8. _____ centimeters

9. _____ centimeters

10. _____ centimeters

Utilize customary and metric units of linear measurement

EMC 3019 • Basic Math Skills, Grade 6 • ©2003 by Evan-Moor Corp.

Standard Measurement Around Us

Name_____

Find the objects listed below and first estimate their lengths in standard measurement. After you have written all the estimates, go back with a ruler and measure the actual lengths of the items to the nearest quarter inch. Good luck with your estimation.

Object	Estimation of the object's length	Actual measurement of the object's length
Length of your math book		
Length of your desk from the left side to the right side		
Length of your pencil		
Diagonal length of this paper		
Length of your pinky finger		
Length of your shoe		
Height of your chair from the floor to the top of the back		
Length of your arm from your elbow to your wrist		

Utilize customary and metric units of linear measurement

Metric Measurement Around Us

Name _____

Find the objects listed below and first estimate their lengths in metric measurement. After you have written all the estimates, go back with a ruler and measure the actual lengths of the items to the nearest millimeter. Good luck with your estimation.

Object	Estimation of the object's length	Actual measurement of the object's length
Length of your math book		
Length of your desk from the left side to the right side		
Length of your pencil		
Diagonal length of this paper		
Length of your pinky finger		
Length of your shoe		
Height of your chair from the floor to the top of the back		
Length of your arm from your elbow to your wrist		

Utilize customary and metric units of linear measurement

Measurement

EMC 3019 • Basic Math Skills, Grade 6 • ©2003 by Evan-Moor Corp.

Math Test

Name _____

Fill in the circle next to the correct answer.

1. Which of the following is the best estimate for the width of this paper from left to right?

   Ⓐ 3 inches
   Ⓑ 30 inches
   Ⓒ 20 centimeters
   Ⓓ 200 centimeters

2. Which of the following is the best estimate for the height of the door to your classroom?

   Ⓐ 6 yards   Ⓒ 48 inches
   Ⓑ 15 feet   Ⓓ 7 feet

3. What is the length of the nail, measured to the nearest quarter inch?

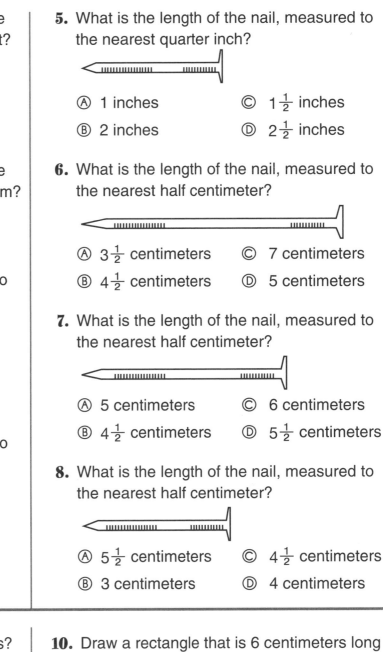

   Ⓐ $3\frac{1}{4}$ inches   Ⓒ $1\frac{3}{4}$ inches
   Ⓑ $2\frac{3}{4}$ inches   Ⓓ $2\frac{1}{4}$ inches

4. What is the length of the nail, measured to the nearest quarter inch?

   Ⓐ $2\frac{1}{4}$ inches   Ⓒ $1\frac{3}{4}$ inches
   Ⓑ 2 inches   Ⓓ $2\frac{1}{2}$ inches

5. What is the length of the nail, measured to the nearest quarter inch?

   Ⓐ 1 inches   Ⓒ $1\frac{1}{2}$ inches
   Ⓑ 2 inches   Ⓓ $2\frac{1}{2}$ inches

6. What is the length of the nail, measured to the nearest half centimeter?

   Ⓐ $3\frac{1}{2}$ centimeters   Ⓒ 7 centimeters
   Ⓑ $4\frac{1}{2}$ centimeters   Ⓓ 5 centimeters

7. What is the length of the nail, measured to the nearest half centimeter?

   Ⓐ 5 centimeters   Ⓒ 6 centimeters
   Ⓑ $4\frac{1}{2}$ centimeters   Ⓓ $5\frac{1}{2}$ centimeters

8. What is the length of the nail, measured to the nearest half centimeter?

   Ⓐ $5\frac{1}{2}$ centimeters   Ⓒ $4\frac{1}{2}$ centimeters
   Ⓑ 3 centimeters   Ⓓ 4 centimeters

---

9. Which is shorter, 2 inches or 3 centimeters?

   _____

10. Draw a rectangle that is 6 centimeters long and 3 centimeters wide.

Utilize customary and metric units of linear measurement

Tongue Twister #13

Name _____

Complete each math sentence below with a value that makes the sentence true. Then write the corresponding letter in front of the math sentence. The letters will spell out a tongue twister when read from **bottom to top**, starting from the right. Try to say it fast three times.

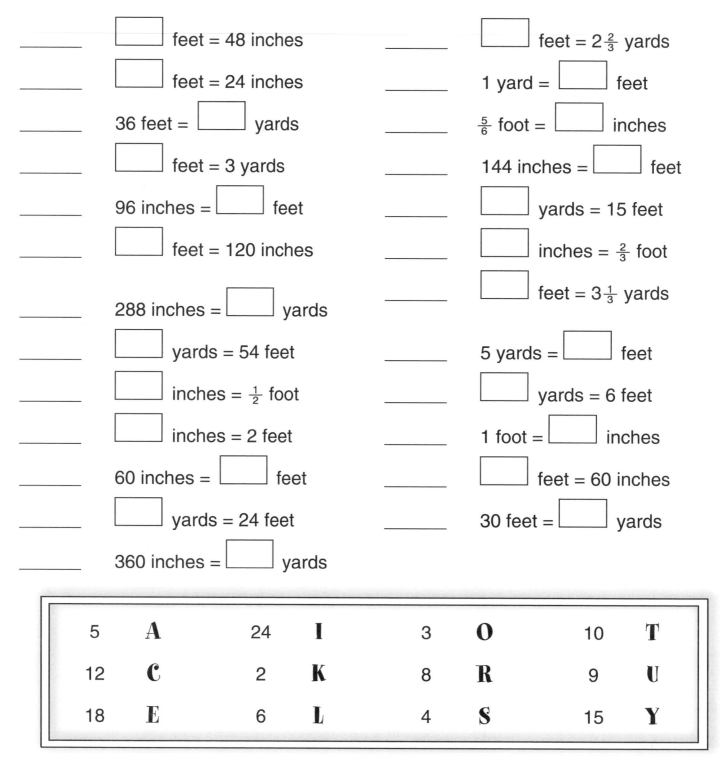

_____ [ ] feet = 48 inches

_____ [ ] feet = 24 inches

_____ 36 feet = [ ] yards

_____ [ ] feet = 3 yards

_____ 96 inches = [ ] feet

_____ [ ] feet = 120 inches

_____ 288 inches = [ ] yards

_____ [ ] yards = 54 feet

_____ [ ] inches = $\frac{1}{2}$ foot

_____ [ ] inches = 2 feet

_____ 60 inches = [ ] feet

_____ [ ] yards = 24 feet

_____ 360 inches = [ ] yards

_____ [ ] feet = 2$\frac{2}{3}$ yards

_____ 1 yard = [ ] feet

_____ $\frac{5}{6}$ foot = [ ] inches

_____ 144 inches = [ ] feet

_____ [ ] yards = 15 feet

_____ [ ] inches = $\frac{2}{3}$ foot

_____ [ ] feet = 3$\frac{1}{3}$ yards

_____ 5 yards = [ ] feet

_____ [ ] yards = 6 feet

_____ 1 foot = [ ] inches

_____ [ ] feet = 60 inches

_____ 30 feet = [ ] yards

5	**A**	24	**I**	3	**O**	10	**T**
12	**C**	2	**K**	8	**R**	9	**U**
18	**E**	6	**L**	4	**S**	15	**Y**

Find conversions between units within a system of linear measurement

Riddle

Name_____

What's plastic, runs on batteries, and counts cattle?

Complete each math sentence below with a value that makes the sentence true. Then write the corresponding letter in front of the math sentence. The letters will spell out the solution to the riddle when read from top to bottom.

_____ [ ] centimeters = 400 millimeters

_____ 1 decimeter = [ ] centimeters

_____ [ ] meters = 200 centimeters

_____ 40 meters = [ ] dekameters

_____ [ ] dekameters = 1 hectometer

_____ 30 millimeters = [ ] centimeters

_____ [ ] centimeters = 2 decimeters

_____ 400 millimeters = [ ] centimeters

_____ 3 hectometers = [ ] dekameters

_____ [ ] kilometers = 2,000 meters

_____ [ ] dekameters = 100 decimeters

40	A
10	C
20	L
2	O
1	R
30	T
3	U
4	W

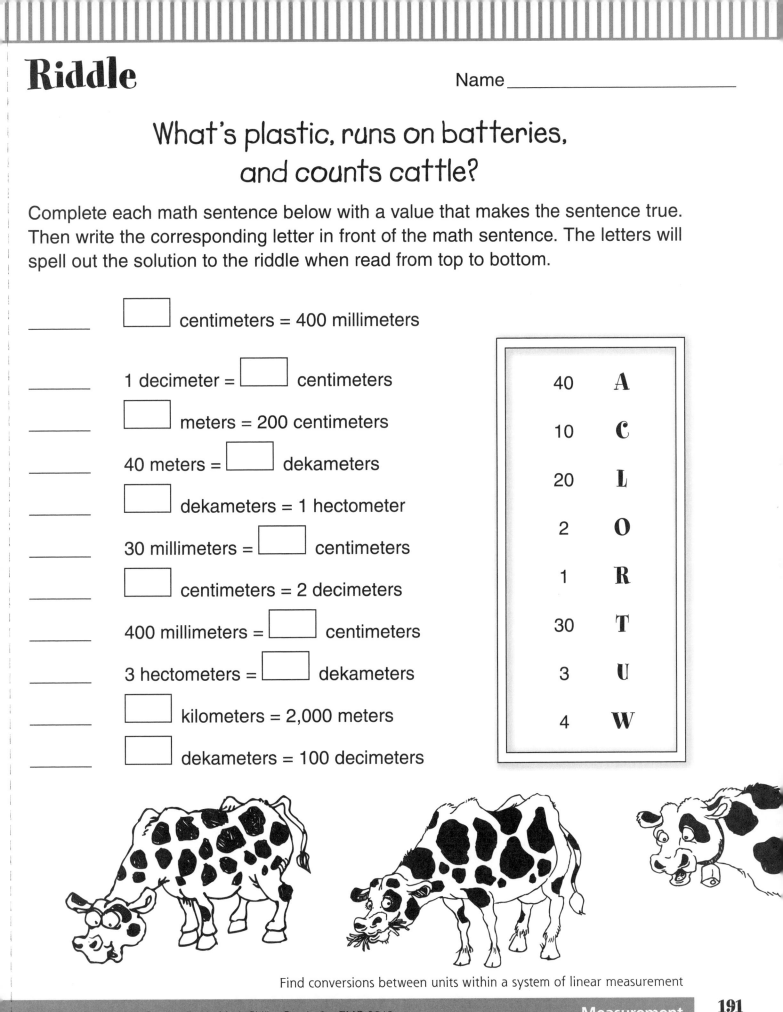

Find conversions between units within a system of linear measurement

Convert My Standards

Name_____

Complete each of the following to make a true math sentence.

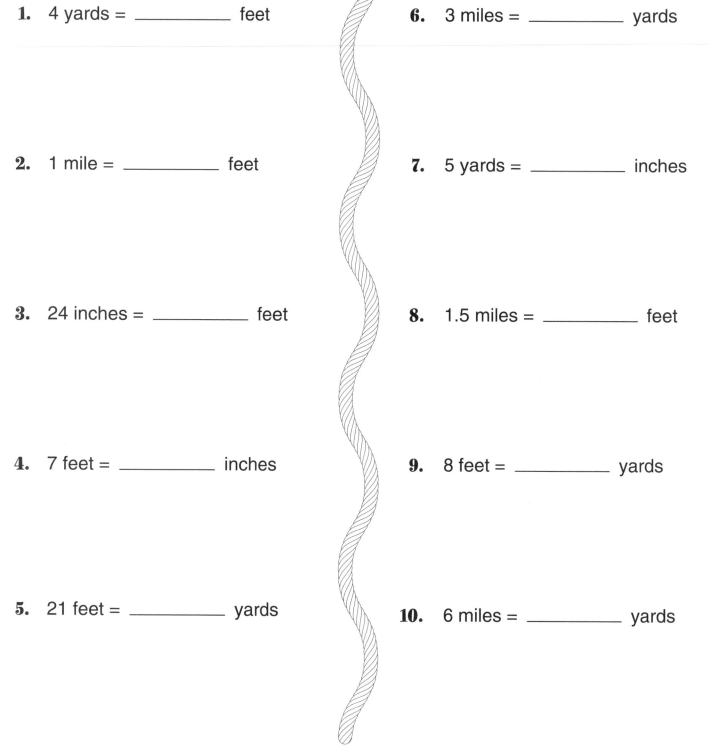

1. 4 yards = _____ feet

2. 1 mile = _____ feet

3. 24 inches = _____ feet

4. 7 feet = _____ inches

5. 21 feet = _____ yards

6. 3 miles = _____ yards

7. 5 yards = _____ inches

8. 1.5 miles = _____ feet

9. 8 feet = _____ yards

10. 6 miles = _____ yards

Find conversions between units within a system of linear measurement

EMC 3019 • Basic Math Skills, Grade 6 • ©2003 by Evan-Moor Corp.

Convert My Metrics

Name _____

Complete each of the following to make a true math sentence.

1. 1 meter = _____ centimeters

2. 2 kilometers = _____ meters

3. 6 centimeters = _____ millimeters

4. 150 centimeters = _____ meters

5. 6 hectometers = _____ meters

6. 8 decimeters = _____ centimeters

7. $1\frac{3}{4}$ meters = _____ centimeters

8. 0.5 hectometers = _____ meters

9. 3 kilometers = _____ centimeters

10. 5.2 centimeters = _____ millimeters

Find conversions between units within a system of linear measurement

Races

Name _____

1. Timothy ran 100 yards in 21 seconds and Juan ran 25 feet in 8 seconds.
   Who was running faster and why?

   _____

2. Harold ran 100 meters in 25 seconds. Gerald ran 1 kilometer in 4 minutes
   15 seconds. Who was the faster runner? Justify your response.

   _____

3. Frances walked 10 meters while Darcy walked 1,200 centimeters. Who
   walked farther? Why?

   _____

4. Rachel and her brother Mark were running in the 10-kilometer race. When
   Rachel crossed the finish line, Mark was 120 meters behind her. How much
   of the race had Mark already completed?

   _____

5. Marcos was running in a race that started at one goal line on a football
   field and ended at the other end, 100 yards away. Marcos came in second.
   When the first place runner crossed the finish line, Marcos had 8 feet left to
   go in the race. How far had Marcos already run?

   _____

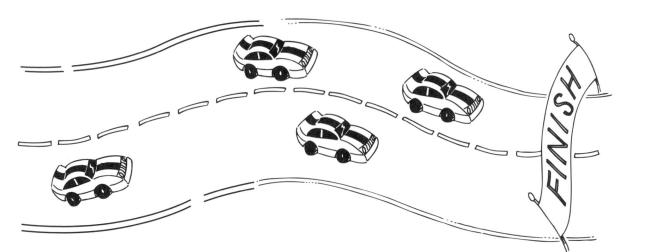

Find conversions between units within a system of linear measurement

EMC 3019 • Basic Math Skills, Grade 6 • ©2003 by Evan-Moor Corp.

Sewing

Name _____

1. Tom and his brother are sewing a pirate costume for a play that Tom is in. They have $3\frac{1}{2}$ yards of fabric, and the pattern calls for 10 feet. Do they have enough fabric? Why or why not?

   _____

2. Patricia made six square pillows to give to her grandmother for her birthday. She would like to put a ribbon around the perimeter of each pillow. The pillows are each 2 feet by 2 feet. If the ribbon comes in packages containing 2 yards, how many packages of ribbon does she need?

   _____

3. Melanie is making a bedspread and is going to trim the edges with fringe. She wants fringe around the two sides and the foot of the bed, but not up by her pillows. The bedspread is 8 feet by 8 feet. In addition, she wants to put fringe around all four sides of the two shams she has made. The shams are 24 inches by 40 inches. The fringe comes in packages that contain 4 yards. How many packages of fringe does she need?

   _____

4. Brandon is making curtains for his room. The window is 150 centimeters across and 75 centimeters high. The fabric available is 1 meter wide and as long as needed. How much fabric do you think Brandon should order and why?

   _____

5. Julie is making a miniature couch for her grandfather's dollhouse. The couch is 13 millimeters by 28 millimeters. She is going to put a thin gold trim around the perimeter of the couch after putting on the new fabric. How many centimeters of gold trim does she need?

   _____

Find conversions between units within a system of linear measurement

Math Test

Fill in the circle next to the correct answer.

1. Which of the following is equivalent to 3 yards?

   Ⓐ 3 feet
   Ⓑ 6 feet
   Ⓒ 72 inches
   Ⓓ 9 feet

2. Which of the following is equivalent to 1 mile?

   Ⓐ 1,000 yards
   Ⓑ 500 feet
   Ⓒ 5,280 feet
   Ⓓ 100 yards

3. Which of the following is equivalent to 48 inches?

   Ⓐ 3 feet
   Ⓑ 4 feet
   Ⓒ 2 yards
   Ⓓ 3 yards

4. Which of the following is equivalent to 12 feet?

   Ⓐ 60 inches
   Ⓑ 108 inches
   Ⓒ 3 yards
   Ⓓ 4 yards

5. Which of the following is equivalent to 100 centimeters?

   Ⓐ 1 meter
   Ⓑ 1 kilometer
   Ⓒ 1 decimeter
   Ⓓ 1 hectometer

6. Which of the following is equivalent to 10 decimeters?

   Ⓐ 1 centimeter
   Ⓑ 1 meter
   Ⓒ 1 hectometer
   Ⓓ 100 meters

7. Which of the following is equivalent to 100 dekameters?

   Ⓐ 1 kilometer
   Ⓑ 1 hectometer
   Ⓒ 1 meter
   Ⓓ 1 centimeter

8. Which of the following is equivalent to 10 millimeters?

   Ⓐ 1 meter
   Ⓑ 1 centimeter
   Ⓒ 1 decimeter
   Ⓓ 1 dekameter

---

9. List two lengths that are equivalent to 36 inches.

   _____

   _____

10. List two lengths that are equivalent to 100 centimeters.

   _____

   _____

Find conversions between units within a system of linear measurement

Measurements

EMC 3019 • Basic Math Skills, Grade 6 • ©2003 by Evan-Moor Corp.

Riddle

Name _____

What would you get if all the cars in the United States were painted red?

To solve the riddle, calculate the elapsed time using the given starting and ending times. Then write the corresponding letter on the line. The letters will spell out the solution when read from **bottom to top**.

_____ starting time of 6:07 A.M. and ending time of 9:54 A.M.

_____ starting time of 8:19 P.M. and ending time of 12:26 A.M.

_____ starting time of 10:12 A.M. and ending time of 1:29 P.M.

_____ starting time of 4:59 P.M. and ending time of 9:56 P.M.

_____ starting time of 7:27 P.M. and ending time of 9:27 P.M.

_____ starting time of 11:10 A.M. and ending time of 2:57 P.M.

_____ starting time of 4:09 A.M. and ending time of 8:26 A.M.

_____ starting time of 3:15 A.M. and ending time of 5:15 A.M.

_____ starting time of 8:52 P.M. and ending time of 10:59 P.M.

_____ starting time of 8:38 P.M. and ending time of 11:05 P.M.

_____ starting time of 6:34 A.M. and ending time of 9:21 A.M.

_____ starting time of 4:42 P.M. and ending time of 8:59 P.M.

_____ starting time of 5:17 A.M. and ending time of 7:17 A.M.

A	2 hours
C	2 hours 7 minutes
D	2 hours 27 minutes
E	2 hours 47 minutes
I	3 hours 17 minutes
N	3 hours 47 minutes
O	4 hours 7 minutes
R	4 hours 17 minutes
T	4 hours 57 minutes

Calculate elapsed time

Riddle

Name _____

What lies on the ground one hundred feet in the air?

To solve the riddle, calculate the elapsed time using the starting and ending times. Then write the corresponding letter on the line. The letters will spell out the solution when read from **bottom to top**.

_____ starting time of 7:07 A.M. and ending time of 10:45 A.M.

_____ starting time of 8:29 P.M. and ending time of 11:47 P.M.

_____ starting time of 10:17 A.M. and ending time of 1:55 P.M.

_____ starting time of 4:53 P.M. and ending time of 9:41 P.M.

_____ starting time of 8:13 P.M. and ending time of 12:41 A.M.

_____ starting time of 12:10 A.M. and ending time of 5:28 A.M.

_____ starting time of 8:53 A.M. and ending time of 1:31 P.M.

_____ starting time of 3:21 A.M. and ending time of 6:59 A.M.

_____ starting time of 8:42 P.M. and ending time of 11:50 P.M.

_____ starting time of 6:32 P.M. and ending time of 9:50 P.M.

_____ starting time of 9:03 A.M. and ending time of 12:03 P.M.

_____ starting time of 7:53 P.M. and ending time of 11:31 P.M.

_____ starting time of 3:25 P.M. and ending time of 6:43 P.M.

_____ starting time of 9:27 A.M. and ending time of 12:27 P.M.

A	3 hours
C	3 hours 8 minutes
D	3 hours 18 minutes
E	3 hours 38 minutes
I	4 hours 28 minutes
N	4 hours 38 minutes
P	4 hours 48 minutes
T	5 hours 18 minutes

Calculate elapsed time

EMC 3019 • Basic Math Skills, Grade 6 • ©2003 by Evan-Moor Corp.

Elapsed Time 1

Name _____

Complete the following chart by calculating the elapsed time for each row.

	Starting Time	Ending Time	Elapsed Time
1.	5:15 A.M.	5:55 A.M.	
2.	6:30 P.M.	7:15 P.M.	
3.	3:15 P.M.	4:20 P.M.	
4.	6:07 A.M.	8:32 A.M.	
5.	4:15 A.M.	8:07 A.M.	
6.	7:15 A.M.	8:00 P.M.	
7.	5:15 P.M.	6:09 P.M.	
8.	9:06 A.M.	3:16 P.M.	
9.	10:10 A.M.	2:15 P.M.	
10.	4:40 P.M.	9:02 A.M.	

Calculate elapsed time

Elapsed Time II

Name _____

Complete the following chart by filling in all empty spaces.

	Starting Time	Ending Time	Elapsed Time
1.	7:15 A.M.	9:00 A.M.	
2.	5:20 P.M.	6:15 P.M.	
3.	11:00 A.M.	3:08 P.M.	
4.	5:45 A.M.		2 hours 20 minutes
5.	8:42 P.M.		1 hour 8 minutes
6.	5:14 A.M.		5 hours 55 minutes
7.		7:19 P.M.	2 hours 7 minutes
8.		9:15 A.M.	1 hour 47 minutes
9.	5:19 A.M.	9:17 P.M.	
10.		8:15 P.M.	14 hours 42 minutes

Calculate elapsed time

EMC 3019 • Basic Math Skills, Grade 6 • ©2003 by Evan-Moor Corp.

Finish Times

Name _____

Answer the questions below.

1. Ian started reading a book at 3:45 P.M. He finished reading at
5:15 P.M. How long did he read his book?   _____

2. Jackie started walking to school at 7:20 A.M. She arrived at school
at 8:10 A.M. On the way, she stopped for 3 minutes to pet a dog.
How long was she walking?   _____

3. Harry began his exercises at 5:40 A.M. He jogged for 30 minutes
and then did push-ups and sit-ups for another 14 minutes.
At what time did he finish?   _____

4. Angel went out to walk her three dogs. She left her house 20
minutes after her favorite TV show ended. The show ended at
4:00 P.M. She walked for 42 minutes and then returned to her
house. At what time did she return?   _____

5. Aaron was told to do 30 minutes of his homework before he went
outside to play basketball. He started his homework at
3:42 P.M. and ended at 4:10 P.M. Did he complete the 30 minutes
of homework that he was supposd to? Explain your answer.   _____

6. Luke left his house to play at a friend's house at 9:35 A.M.
He played football and video games with his friend most of the
day. He finally returned home at 4:28 P.M. How long had Luke
been gone?   _____

7. Matthew was baking some cupcakes. He was supposed to bake
them for 20 to 22 minutes. He put them into the oven at 3:52 P.M.
and pulled them out at 4:14 P.M. Did they cook long enough? _____

8. Marsadie went on a bike ride. She was keeping track of her
exercise and got to color in a star on her chart for every
15 minutes of exercise. She left at 4:20 P.M. and returned home
from her bike ride at 5:10 P.M. How many stars did she color in? _____

Calculate elapsed time

Baking

Name _____

Answer the questions below.

1. Wes made a cake that needed to bake for 23 minutes. He put the cake in the oven at 4:48 P.M. At what time did he take the cake out of the oven? _____

2. Julie is making some cookies. Each batch of cookies bakes for 12 minutes, and she can put 12 cookies in the oven at a time. If the recipe makes 72 cookies and she starts baking the cookies at 5:15 P.M., at what time will she finish baking the last batch of cookies? (Assume that there is no lag time between each batch of cookies since she has two cookie sheets and can prepare one while the other one is baking.) _____

3. Raymond put 24 brownies into the oven at 8:08 P.M. and took them out of the oven at 8:32 P.M. They were perfect! His mother wanted to bake the same brownies and asked Raymond how long he baked the brownies. How long did Raymond bake them? _____

4. Jessica made a casserole for dinner that she wants to serve hot out of the oven at 6:15 P.M. when her father gets home from work. The casserole needs to bake for 40 minutes. At what time should she put the casserole into the oven? _____

5. Naomi is baking some bread for her family and wants it to be done 45 minutes before they have dinner so that it can cool down before slicing it. They want to eat dinner at 5:30 P.M. The bread needs to bake for 55 minutes. At what time should she put the bread into the oven? _____

6. J.D. is making cookies to take to his school tomorrow. The recipe makes 84 cookies, and he can put 12 cookies on a cookie sheet. He only has one cookie sheet, so after baking each batch, he needs about 2 minutes to get the next pan ready before it goes into the oven. If each batch of cookies bakes for 14 minutes and he starts baking at 7:17 P.M., at what time will the last batch of cookies finish baking? _____

Calculate elapsed time

EMC 3019 • Basic Math Skills, Grade 6 • ©2003 by Evan-Moor Corp.

Math Test

Fill in the circle next to the correct answer.

1. How much time elapses between 5:15 A.M. and 5:45 A.M.?

   Ⓐ 30 minutes
   Ⓑ 5 hours
   Ⓒ 15 minutes
   Ⓓ 1 hour

2. How much time elapses between 4:45 A.M. and 6:17 A.M.?

   Ⓐ 2 hours 32 minutes
   Ⓑ 1 hour 28 minutes
   Ⓒ 1 hour 32 minutes
   Ⓓ 32 minutes

3. How much time elapses between 11:50 A.M. and 1:10 P.M.?

   Ⓐ 2 hours 20 minutes
   Ⓑ 1 hour 10 minutes
   Ⓒ 2 hours 10 minutes
   Ⓓ 1 hour 20 minutes

4. How much time elapses between 9:15 A.M. and 10:45 P.M.?

   Ⓐ 1 hour 30 minutes
   Ⓑ 13 hours 30 minutes
   Ⓒ 30 minutes
   Ⓓ 1 hour 15 minutes

5. Tim is baking cookies for 13 minutes. If he puts them into the oven at 5:48 P.M., at what time should he take them out of the oven?

   Ⓐ 6:00 P.M.
   Ⓑ 6:01 P.M.
   Ⓒ 5:13 P.M.
   Ⓓ 5:51 P.M.

6. Julie is baking a cake for 55 minutes. If she put the pan into the oven at 9:10 A.M., at what time should she take it out of the oven?

   Ⓐ 9:55 A.M.
   Ⓑ 10:00 A.M.
   Ⓒ 10:10 A.M.
   Ⓓ 10:05 A.M.

7. Juanita is baking some rolls and wants them to be served hot out of the oven at 6:15 P.M. The rolls take 22 minutes to bake, so when should she put them into the oven?

   Ⓐ 5:53 P.M.
   Ⓑ 6:37 P.M.
   Ⓒ 6:35 P.M.
   Ⓓ 6:22 P.M.

8. Kendra took her dog for a walk. She left at 6:15 A.M. and returned home at 7:05 A.M. How long did she walk her dog?

   Ⓐ 50 minutes
   Ⓑ 10 minutes
   Ⓒ 45 minutes
   Ⓓ 1 hour 10 minutes

9. Glenn is making shortbread and it needs to bake for 42 minutes. He wants to take it out of the oven at 7:15 P.M. At what time should he put the shortbread into the oven?

   _____

10. Seth started playing basketball at 9:15 A.M. and played until 3:45 P.M. How long did he play basketball?

   _____

Calculate elapsed time

Riddle

What is smashing and comes between morning and afternoon?

To solve the riddle, measure each of the following angles with a protractor (to the nearest 5°). Then write the corresponding letter on the line above the angle measure. The letters will spell out the solution to the riddle.

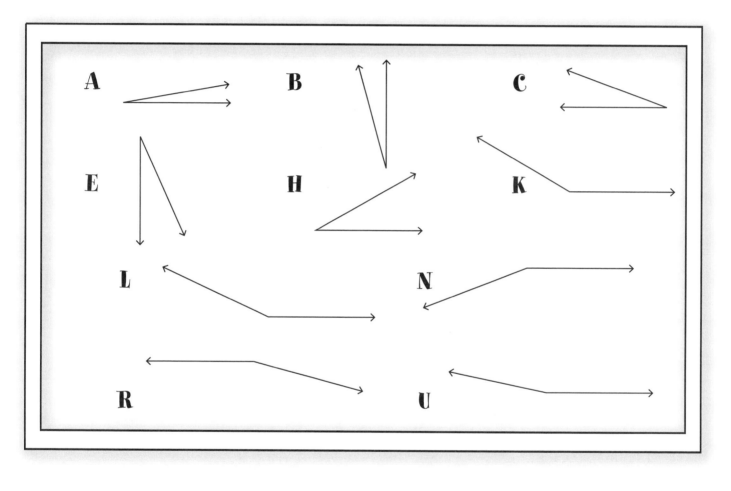

___ 10°   ___ 155°   ___ 170°   ___ 160°   ___ 20°   ___ 30°

    ___ 15°   ___ 165°   ___ 25°   ___ 10°   ___ 150°

Measure angles using a protractor

EMC 3019 • Basic Math Skills, Grade 6 • ©2003 by Evan-Moor Corp.

What Can Be Right but Never Wrong?

Name_____

To solve the riddle, measure each of the following angles with a protractor (to the nearest 10°). Then write the corresponding letter on the line above the angle measure. The letters will spell out the solution to the riddle.

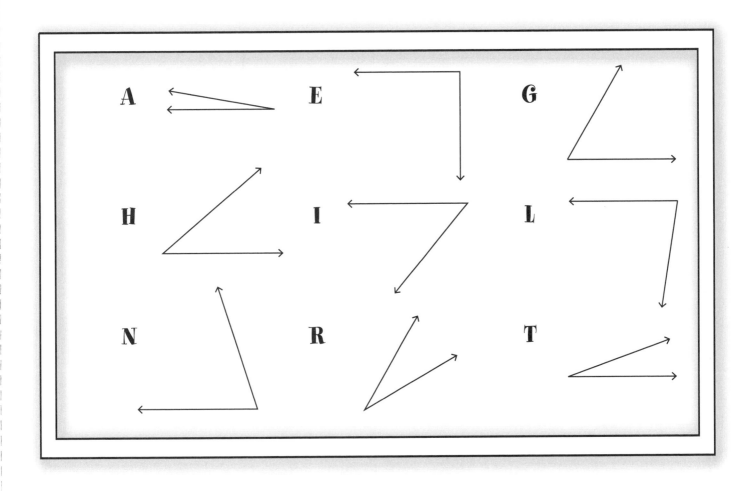

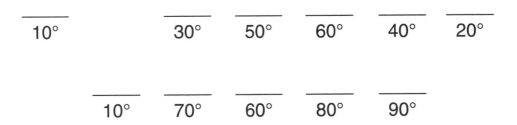

10°	30°	50°	60°	40°	20°

10°	70°	60°	80°	90°

Measure angles using a protractor

What's My Angle Measure 1?

Name_____

Using a protractor, measure each of the following angles to the nearest 5°.

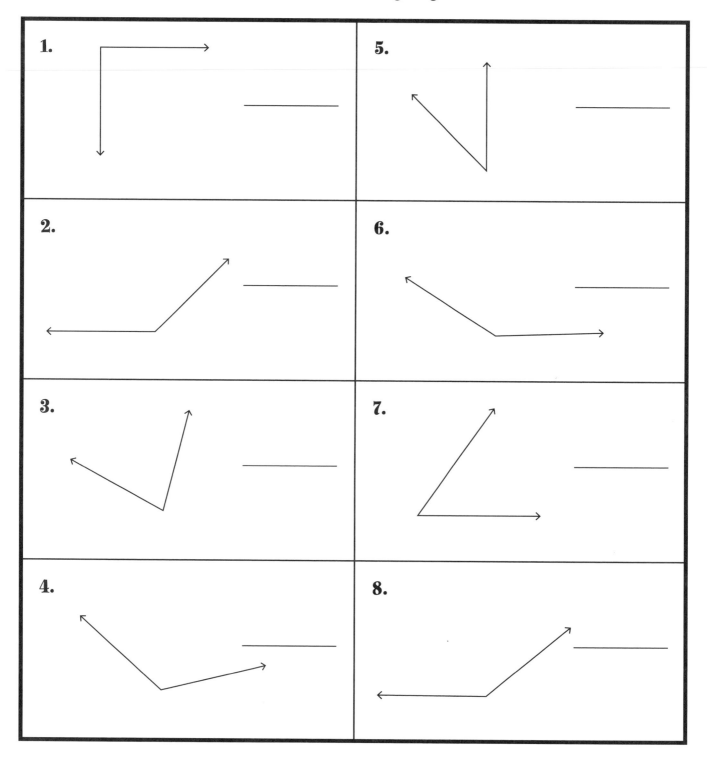

1. _____

2. _____

3. _____

4. _____

5. _____

6. _____

7. _____

8. _____

Measure angles using a protractor

EMC 3019 • Basic Math Skills, Grade 6 • ©2003 by Evan-Moor Corp.

What's My Angle Measure II?

Name _____

Using a protractor, measure each of the following angles to the nearest 5°.

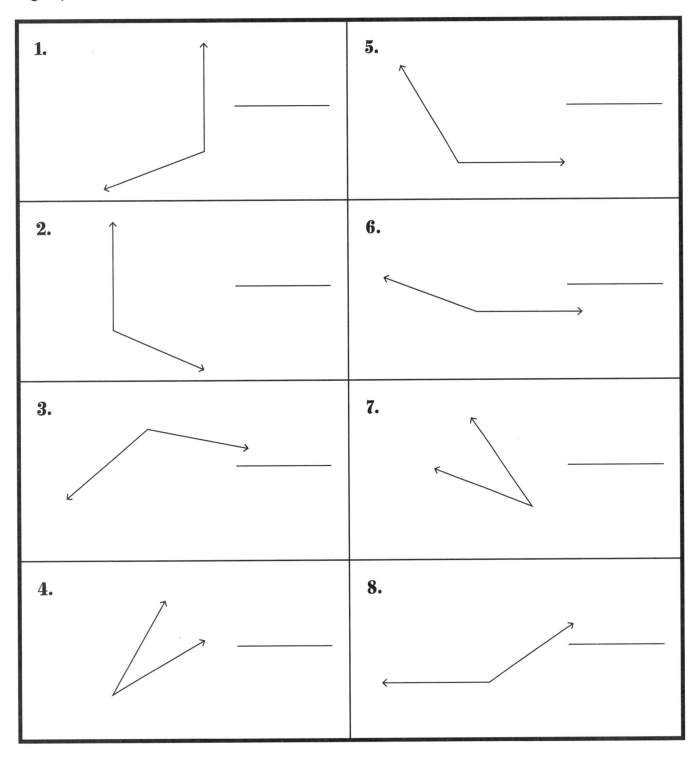

1. _____

2. _____

3. _____

4. _____

5. _____

6. _____

7. _____

8. _____

Measure angles using a protractor

The Angles Around Us

Name_____

Look around you and find examples of angles listed in the chart below. Think about the angle where two walls meet, or the edges of your desk, or the angle between the wall and the floor, etc. Write a description of each given angle, and then sketch it.

Angle	Description of the Object	Sketch of the Object
30°		
45°		
60°		
90°		
120°		
135°		
150°		

Measure angles using a protractor

EMC 3019 • Basic Math Skills, Grade 6 • ©2003 by Evan-Moor Corp.

Magnification

Name _____

The figure below is a model, and you need to create a copy of it that is twice as large. In order to do this, start out by labeling each side a different letter of alphabet. Then measure the length of each side. Double each length and draw a straight line on another piece of paper that is the doubled length and label it with the corresponding letter. Continue doing this until all sides have been measured and a new line twice as long has been drawn and labeled.

Now cut out each line segment with scissors and lay them out roughly in the same pattern as they were below. The last step is to measure each angle in the original figure and arrange the new lines with the same angle measurement. After you have completed this, tape your new figure down so it won't shift anymore.

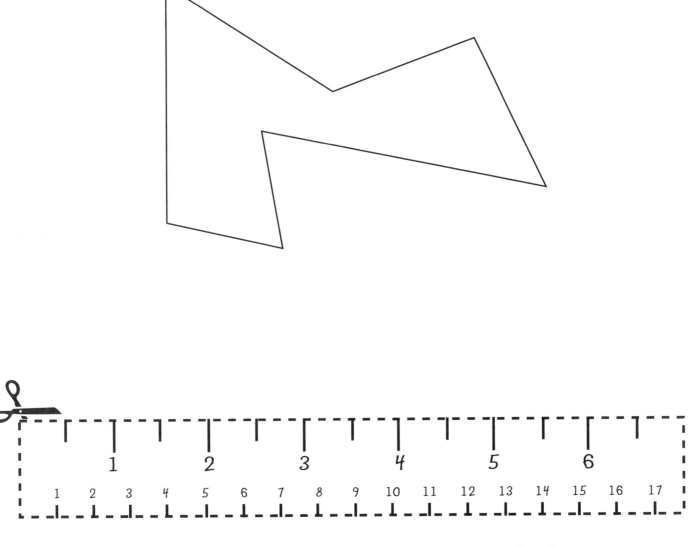

Measure angles using a protractor

Math Test

Name_____

Fill in the circle next to the correct answer.

1. What is the measure of this angle?

  Ⓐ   45°
  Ⓑ   55°
  Ⓒ 135°
  Ⓓ 120°

2. What is the measure of this angle?

  Ⓐ   80°
  Ⓑ   85°
  Ⓒ   95°
  Ⓓ 145°

3. What is the measure of this angle?

  Ⓐ 185°
  Ⓑ 175°
  Ⓒ   35°
  Ⓓ   5°

4. What is the measure of this angle?

  Ⓐ   25°
  Ⓑ 160°
  Ⓒ 155°
  Ⓓ 175°

5. What is the measure of this angle?

  Ⓐ 150°
  Ⓑ 145°
  Ⓒ   30°
  Ⓓ   90°

6. What is the measure of this angle?

  Ⓐ 115°
  Ⓑ 105°
  Ⓒ 125°
  Ⓓ   75°

7. What is the measure of this angle?

  Ⓐ 150°
  Ⓑ 140°
  Ⓒ 145°
  Ⓓ   40°

8. What is the measure of this angle?

  Ⓐ 105°
  Ⓑ   85°
  Ⓒ   75°
  Ⓓ   95°

9. Draw an angle that measures 45°.

10. Draw an angle that measures 120°.

Measure angles using a protractor

EMC 3019 • Basic Math Skills, Grade 6 • ©2003 by Evan-Moor Corp.

What Is the Most Slippery Country in the World?

Name _____

Find the perimeter of each of the following polygons. Then write the letter that corresponds to the perimeter on the line next to the figure. The letters will spell out the answer to the riddle.

16	C	34	R
24	E	36	S
28	G	42	T
32	M		

Find the perimeter of polygons

Tongue Twister #14

Name_____

Find the perimeter of each of the following polygons. Then write the letter that corresponds to the perimeter on the line below the figure. The letters will spell out a tongue twister. Try to say it fast three times.

8	**A**	16	**D**	26	**L**
9	**B**	18	**E**	27	**N**
10	**C**	24	**K**	28	**R**

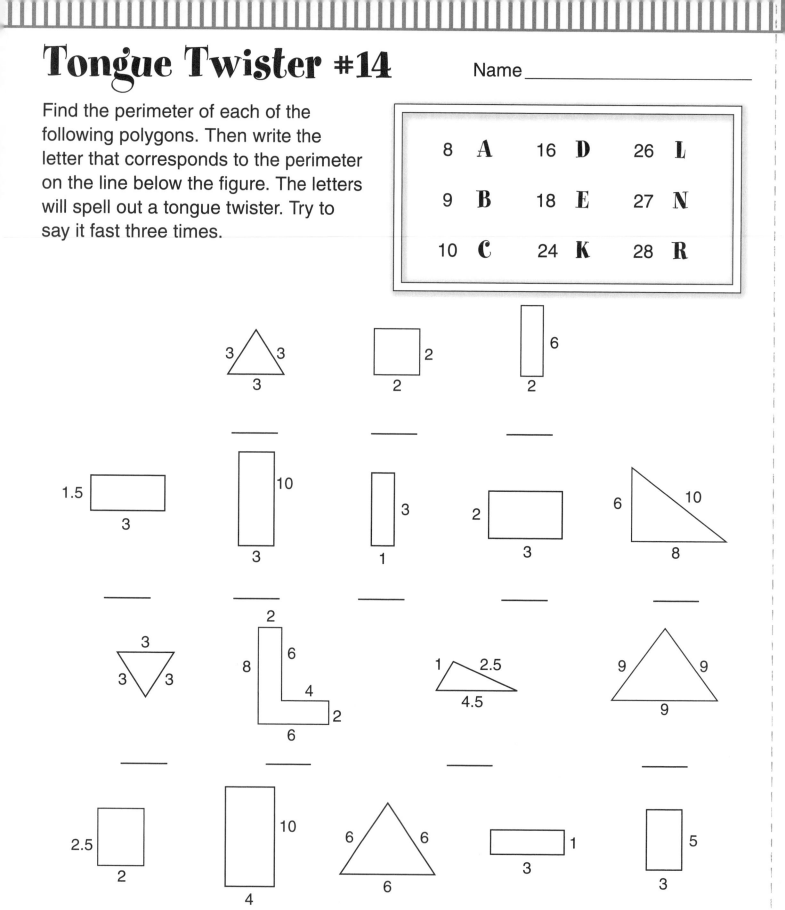

Find the perimeter of polygons

EMC 3019 • Basic Math Skills, Grade 6 • ©2003 by Evan-Moor Corp.

Perimeters, Please

Name _____

Determine the perimeter of each of the following figures.

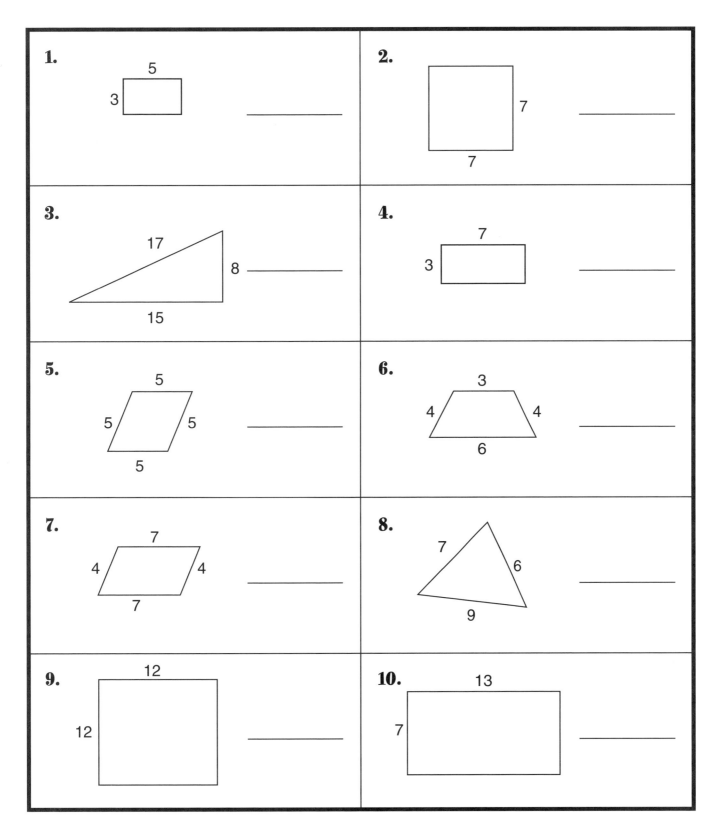

1. 5 / 3 _____

2. 7 / 7 _____

3. 17 / 8 / 15 _____

4. 7 / 3 _____

5. 5 / 5 / 5 / 5 _____

6. 3 / 4 / 4 / 6 _____

7. 7 / 4 / 4 / 7 _____

8. 7 / 6 / 9 _____

9. 12 / 12 _____

10. 13 / 7 _____

Find the perimeter of polygons

More Perimeters

Determine the perimeter of each of the following figures.

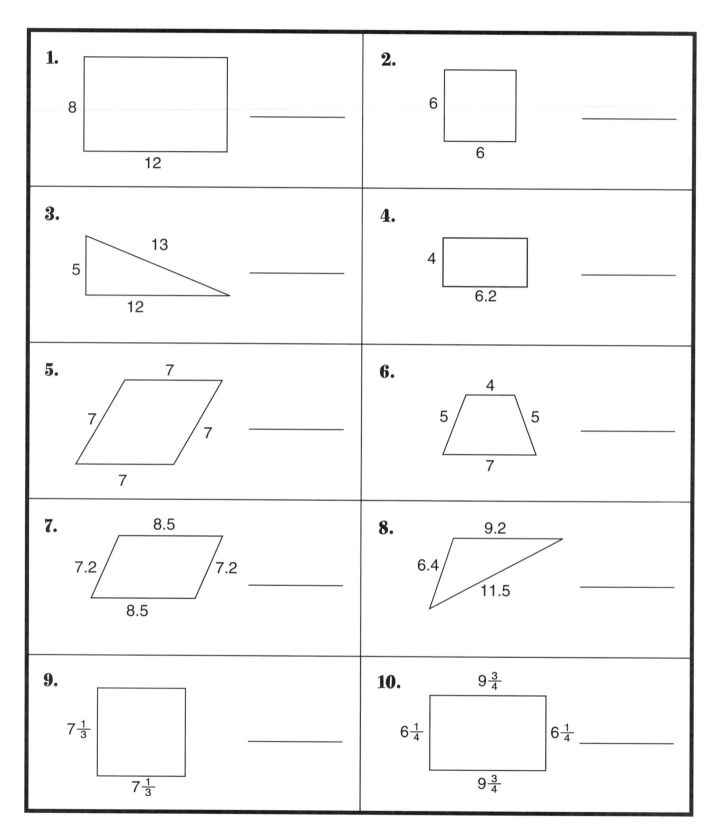

1.

8

12

_____

2.

6

6

_____

3.

13

5

12

_____

4.

4

6.2

_____

5.

7

7

7

7

_____

6.

4

5   5

7

_____

7.

8.5

7.2   7.2

8.5

_____

8.

9.2

6.4

11.5

_____

9.

$7\frac{1}{3}$

$7\frac{1}{3}$

_____

10.

$9\frac{3}{4}$

$6\frac{1}{4}$ $6\frac{1}{4}$

$9\frac{3}{4}$

_____

Find the perimeter of polygons

EMC 3019 • Basic Math Skills, Grade 6 • ©2003 by Evan-Moor Corp.

Polygon My World

Name _____

Look around you to find an example of each of the following polygons in your classroom, at home, on the playground, or somewhere in the world around you. You may only use any one object once in the chart. Complete the chart by sketching the object, measuring each side of the polygon, and then computing its perimeter.

Polygon	Sketch and Measurements	Perimeter
right triangle		
acute triangle		
obtuse triangle		
rectangle		
parallelogram		
square		
quadrilateral		
rhombus		
trapezoid		

Find the perimeter of polygons

Perimeter Puzzles

Name _____

Draw a sketch of each of the following polygons using the given clues. Label the length of each side on your drawing.

1. The first polygon has the following characteristics:
   - It has a perimeter of 16 inches.
   - It has four right angles.
   - The length is 2 more than the width.

2. The second polygon has the following characteristics:
   - It has a perimeter of 14 centimeters.
   - It has four sides.
   - Three sides are congruent.
   - One side is 2 centimeters longer than each of the other three sides.

3. The third polygon has the following characteristics:
   - It has a perimeter of 16 inches.
   - It has more than 4 right angles.
   - It has six sides.
   - The lengths of all the sides are even numbers.
   - All sides are either 2 inches or 4 inches long.
   - Two of the sides are congruent, while the other four sides are also congruent.

4. The fourth polygon has the following characteristics:
   - It has a perimeter of 20 centimeters.
   - It has five sides.
   - It has two pairs of congruent sides that are consecutive numbers in their lengths.
   - The side that isn't congruent to any other side is 6 centimeters long.
   - The shortest sides are adjacent to the side that is 6 centimeters in length.

5. The fifth polygon has the following characteristics:
   - It has a perimeter of 14 centimeters.
   - It has three sides.
   - Two of the sides are congruent.
   - One side is 2 more than each of the other two congruent sides.

Find the perimeter of polygons

EMC 3019 • Basic Math Skills, Grade 6 • ©2003 by Evan-Moor Corp.

Math Test

Name _____

Fill in the circle next to the correct answer.

Use the following four figures to answer Numbers 1 through 3.

Figure A

Figure B

Figure C

Figure D

1. Which figure has a perimeter of 26 inches?

Ⓐ Figure A   Ⓒ Figure C
Ⓑ Figure B   Ⓓ Figure D

2. Which figure has a perimeter of 24 inches?

Ⓐ Figure A   Ⓒ Figure C
Ⓑ Figure B   Ⓓ Figure D

3. Which figure has a perimeter of 20 inches?

Ⓐ Figure A   Ⓒ Figure C
Ⓑ Figure B   Ⓓ Figure D

4. What is the perimeter of this figure?

Ⓐ 20 units
Ⓑ 24 units
Ⓒ 10 units
Ⓓ 14 units

5. What is the perimeter of this figure?

Ⓐ 81 units
Ⓑ 36 units
Ⓒ 9 units
Ⓓ 18 units

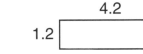

6. What is the perimeter this figure?

Ⓐ 5.4 units
Ⓑ 5.04 units
Ⓒ 10.8 units
Ⓓ 50.4 units

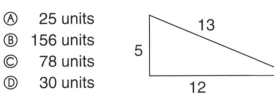

7. What is the perimeter of this figure?

Ⓐ 25 units
Ⓑ 156 units
Ⓒ 78 units
Ⓓ 30 units

8. What is the perimeter of this figure?

Ⓐ 35 units
Ⓑ 42 units
Ⓒ 39 units
Ⓓ 46 units

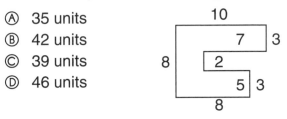

9. Draw a figure with a perimeter of 20 units.

10. Draw a figure with a perimeter of 15 units.

Find the perimeter of polygons

©2003 by Evan-Moor Corp. • Basic Math Skills, Grade 6 • EMC 3019

Tongue Twister #15

Name _____

Find the area of each of the following polygons. Then write the corresponding letter on the line below the figure. The letters will spell out a tongue twister. Try to say it fast three times.

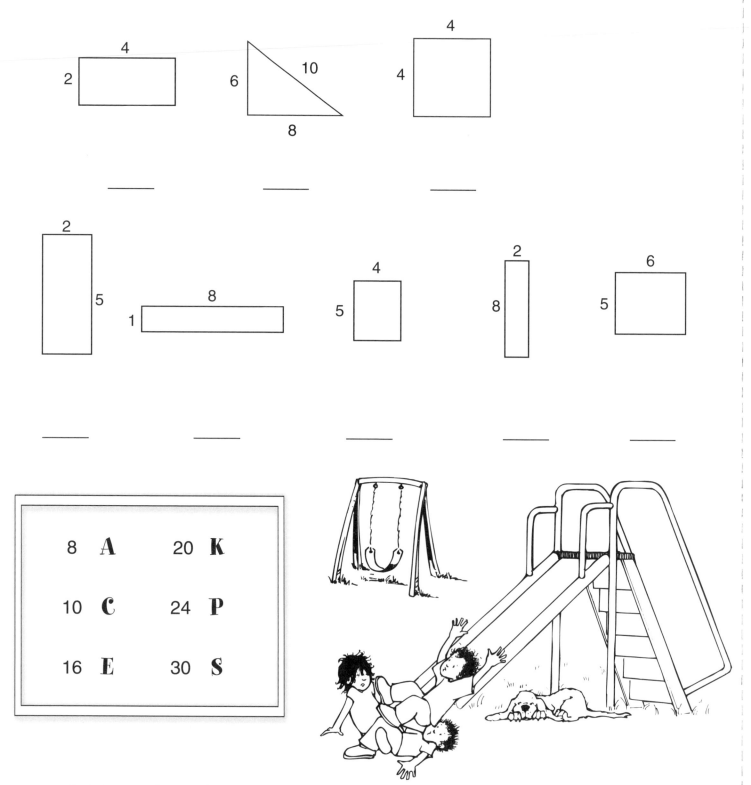

What's Worse Than a Giraffe with a Sore Throat?

Name _____

Find the area of each of the following figures. Then write the corresponding letter on the line above the area. The letters will spell out the answer to the riddle.

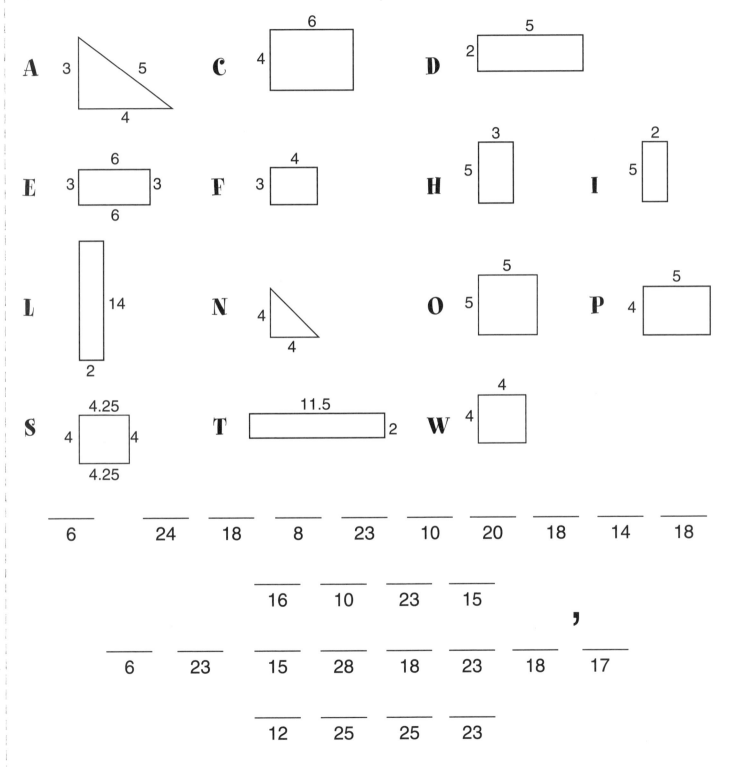

___ ___ ___ ___ ___ ___ ___ ___ ___ ___
6   24   18   8   23   10   20   18   14   18

___ ___ ___ ___
16   10   23   15
                             ,

___ ___ ___ ___ ___ ___ ___ ___
6   23   15   28   18   23   18   17

___ ___ ___ ___
12   25   25   23

Find the area of rectangles, squares, and triangles

Give Me Your Area

Name_____

Determine the area of each of the following figures.

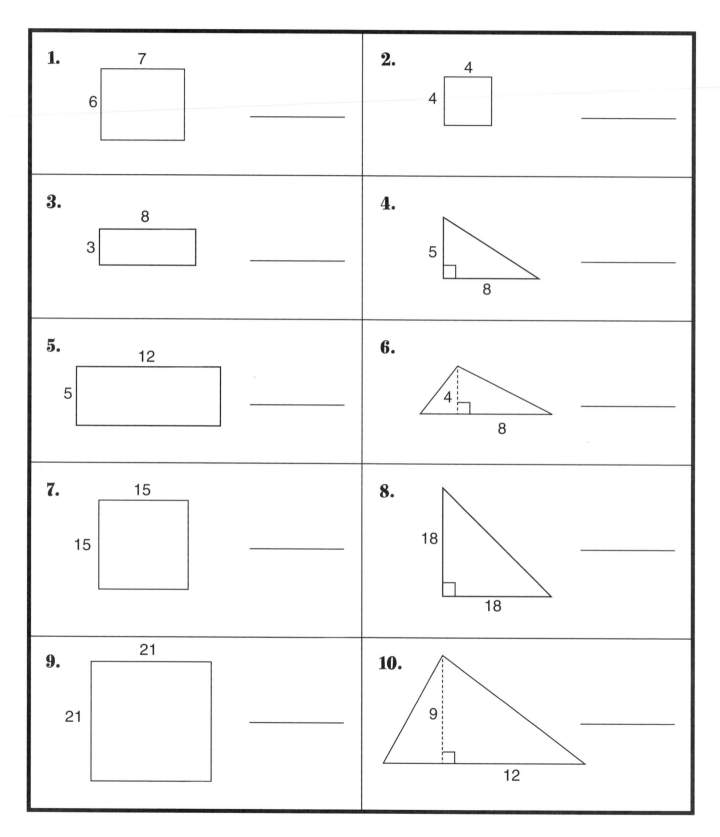

Find the area of rectangles, squares, and triangles

EMC 3019 • Basic Math Skills, Grade 6 • ©2003 by Evan-Moor Corp.

Give Me Your Area II

Name _____

Determine the area of each of the following figures.

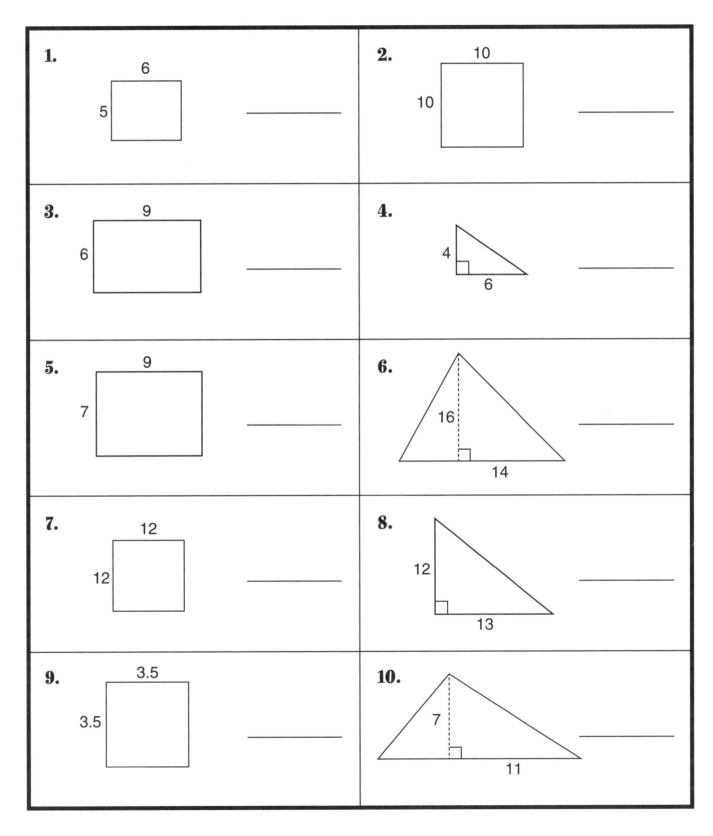

1.

6

5

_____

2.

10

10

_____

3.

9

6

_____

4.

4

6

_____

5.

9

7

_____

6.

16

14

_____

7.

12

12

_____

8.

12

13

_____

9.

3.5

3.5

_____

10.

7

11

_____

Find the area of rectangles, squares, and triangles

Tile the Room

Name _____

The figure below is a scale drawing of Jim's bedroom. His parents are installing tile on the floor and want to know how many square feet of tile they need. How many square feet do they need? Write your answer and explain how you solved the problem.

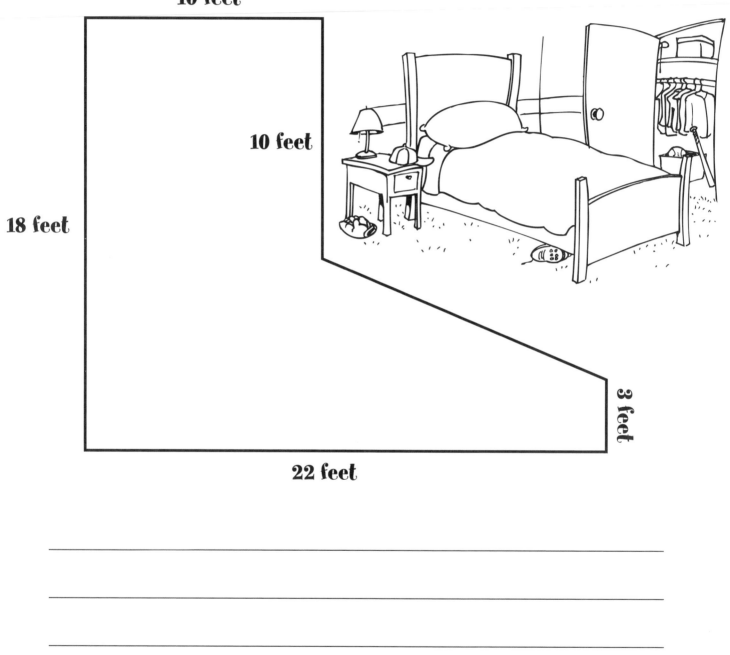

_____

_____

_____

_____

Find the area of rectangles, squares, and triangles

EMC 3019 • Basic Math Skills, Grade 6 • ©2003 by Evan-Moor Corp.

Carpet the Room

Name_____

The figure below is a scale drawing of the TV room at Cindy's house. Her family is installing new carpet and wants to know how much carpet they need, but they also know that carpet is sold by the square yard. How many square yards do they need? Write your answer and explain how you solved the problem.

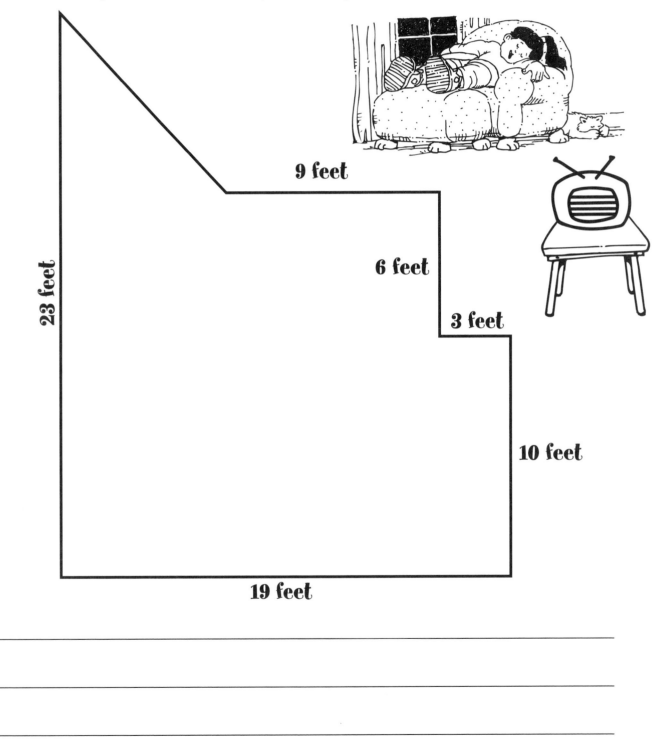

23 feet

9 feet

6 feet

3 feet

10 feet

19 feet

_____

_____

_____

Find the area of rectangles, squares, and triangles

Math Test

Name_____

Fill in the circle next to the correct answer.

Use the following four figures to answer Numbers 1 through 3.

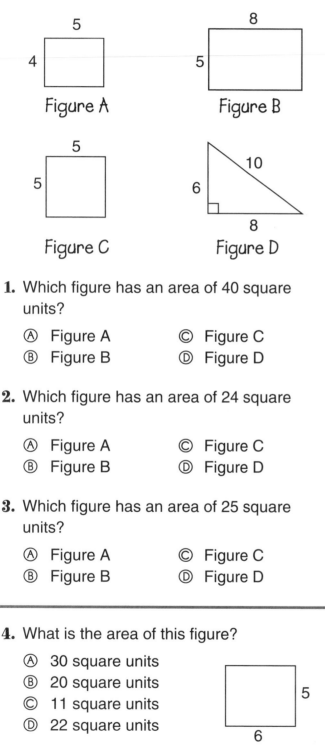

Figure A

Figure B

Figure C

Figure D

1. Which figure has an area of 40 square units?

Ⓐ Figure A   Ⓒ Figure C
Ⓑ Figure B   Ⓓ Figure D

2. Which figure has an area of 24 square units?

Ⓐ Figure A   Ⓒ Figure C
Ⓑ Figure B   Ⓓ Figure D

3. Which figure has an area of 25 square units?

Ⓐ Figure A   Ⓒ Figure C
Ⓑ Figure B   Ⓓ Figure D

4. What is the area of this figure?

Ⓐ 30 square units
Ⓑ 20 square units
Ⓒ 11 square units
Ⓓ 22 square units

5. What is the area of this figure?

Ⓐ 8.1 square units
Ⓑ 4.3 square units
Ⓒ 4.2 square units
Ⓓ 8.2 square units

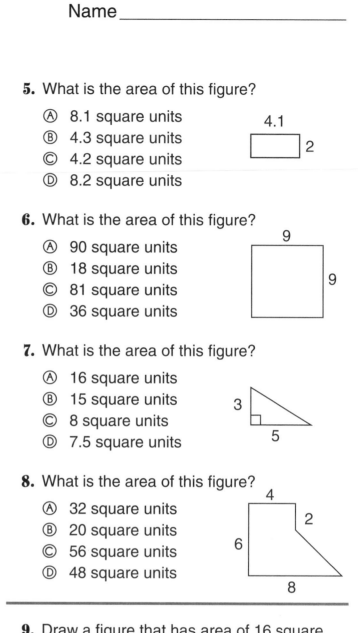

6. What is the area of this figure?

Ⓐ 90 square units
Ⓑ 18 square units
Ⓒ 81 square units
Ⓓ 36 square units

7. What is the area of this figure?

Ⓐ 16 square units
Ⓑ 15 square units
Ⓒ 8 square units
Ⓓ 7.5 square units

8. What is the area of this figure?

Ⓐ 32 square units
Ⓑ 20 square units
Ⓒ 56 square units
Ⓓ 48 square units

9. Draw a figure that has area of 16 square units.

10. Draw two different figures that each have an area of 15 square units.

Find the area of rectangles, squares, and triangles

EMC 3019 • Basic Math Skills, Grade 6 • ©2003 by Evan-Moor Corp.

What Is Always Flying and Never Goes Anywhere?

Name _____

To solve the riddle, find the area of each circle below. After you have computed each area, write the letter that corresponds to the area on the line below the figure. The letters will spell out the solution to the riddle.

Remember that you can use the following formula to find the area of a circle:

Area = pi times radius squared

$$A = \pi \times r^2$$

Use 3.14 as the value of pi for these problems.

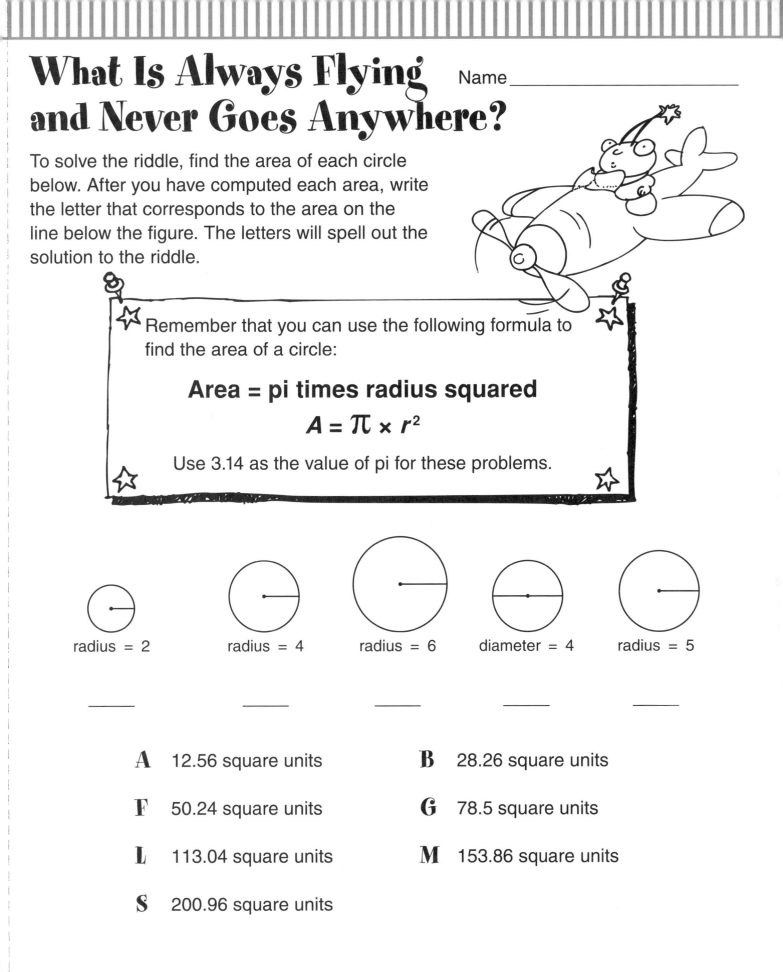

radius = 2   radius = 4   radius = 6   diameter = 4   radius = 5

____   ____   ____   ____   ____

A 12.56 square units		**B** 28.26 square units
F 50.24 square units		**G** 78.5 square units
L 113.04 square units		**M** 153.86 square units
S 200.96 square units		

Find the area and circumference of circles

©2003 by Evan-Moor Corp. • Basic Math Skills, Grade 6 • EMC 3019

What Do You Give a Seasick Elephant?

Name _____

To solve the riddle, find the circumference of each circle below. After you have computed each circumference, write the corresponding letter on the line below the figure. The letters will spell out the solution to the riddle.

Remember that you can use the following formula:

Circumference = pi times diameter **OR**
Circumference = 2 times pi times radius
$C = \pi \times d$ **OR** $C = 2 \times \pi \times r$

Use 3.14 as the value of pi for these problems.

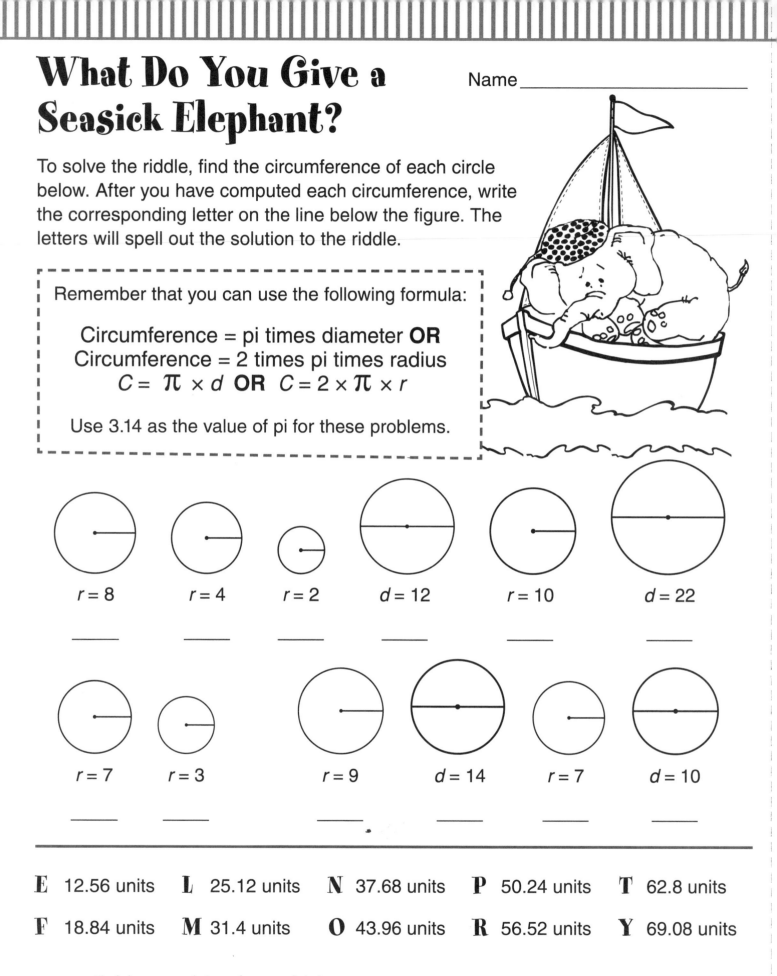

r = 8   r = 4   r = 2   d = 12   r = 10   d = 22

_____   _____   _____   _____   _____   _____

r = 7   r = 3   r = 9   d = 14   r = 7   d = 10

_____   _____   _____   _____   _____   _____

E 12.56 units   **L** 25.12 units   **N** 37.68 units   **P** 50.24 units   **T** 62.8 units

F 18.84 units   **M** 31.4 units   **O** 43.96 units   **R** 56.52 units   **Y** 69.08 units

Find the area and circumference of circles

Measurement   EMC 3019 • Basic Math Skills, Grade 6 • ©2003 by Evan-Moor Corp.

Areas of Circles

Name _____

Find the area of each of the following circles.

> Remember that you can use the following formula to find the area of a circle:
>
> ## Area = pi times radius squared
> ## $A = \pi \times r^2$
>
> Use 3.14 as the value of pi for these problems.

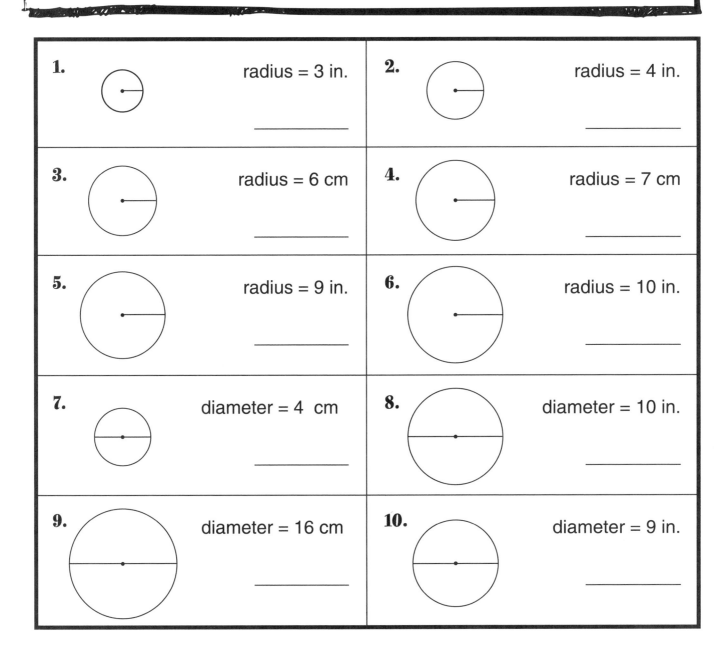

1. radius = 3 in.

_____

2. radius = 4 in.

_____

3. radius = 6 cm

_____

4. radius = 7 cm

_____

5. radius = 9 in.

_____

6. radius = 10 in.

_____

7. diameter = 4 cm

_____

8. diameter = 10 in.

_____

9. diameter = 16 cm

_____

10. diameter = 9 in.

_____

Find the area and circumference of circles

Circumference of Circles Name_____

Find the circumference of each of the following circles.

> Remember that you can use the following formula:
>
> ## Circumference = pi times diameter OR
> ## Circumference = 2 times pi times radius
> $$C = \pi \times d \quad \textbf{OR} \quad C = 2 \times \pi \times r$$
>
> Use 3.14 as the value of pi for these problems.

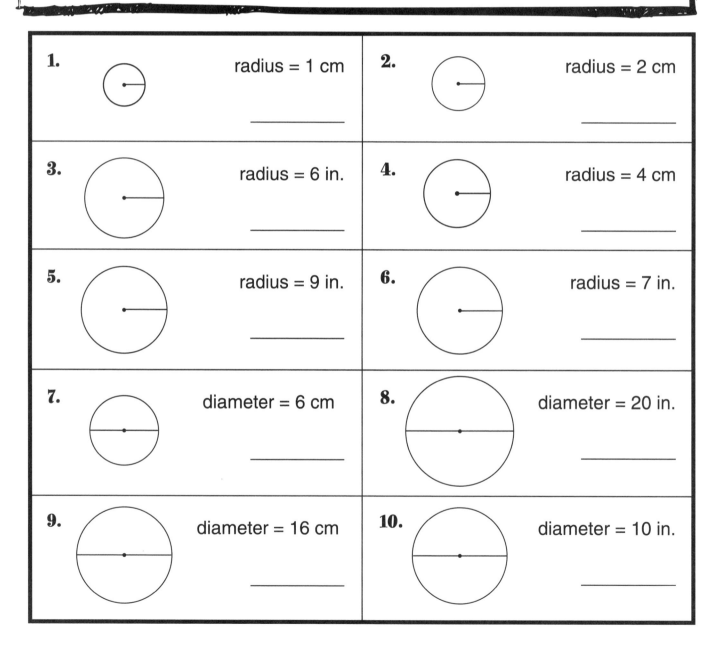

1. radius = 1 cm

_____

2. radius = 2 cm

_____

3. radius = 6 in.

_____

4. radius = 4 cm

_____

5. radius = 9 in.

_____

6. radius = 7 in.

_____

7. diameter = 6 cm

_____

8. diameter = 20 in.

_____

9. diameter = 16 cm

_____

10. diameter = 10 in.

_____

Find the area and circumference of circles

EMC 3019 • Basic Math Skills, Grade 6 • ©2003 by Evan-Moor Corp.

The Woodshop

For each of the following questions, write the answer and show your work. Use 3.14 as the value for pi in these problems.

1. Patricia is making 5 stools with circular seats that are each 12 inches in diameter. She wants to paint the tops of all the stools bright red, but needs to know the area she will paint. What is the total area of the tops of all 5 stools?

   _____

2. Heather made a round picture frame that is 20 inches in diameter. She wants to wrap a gold ribbon around the outside of the frame one time and needs to know how long the ribbon should be. How long does the ribbon need to be?

   _____

3. Troy made some blocks for his younger brother to play with. Eight of the blocks are cylinders, and he would like to glue a yellow ribbon around the top and bottom of each cylinder to decorate them. The radius of each block is 3 centimeters. How much ribbon does he need to complete his project?

   _____

4. Robert completed a plant stand that has a round top. The top is 24 centimeters in diameter and is painted gold. He wants to glue a silver trim around the outer edge of the top and needs to know how long the trim should be. How much silver trim does Robert need?

   _____

5. Ian is using 15 washers to create a collage for his art class. He is making the collage in his woodshop class, and he wants to cover each of the washers with some gold leaf, but because of the cost of gold leaf, he doesn't want to buy extra. He wants to cover the entire washer, including the center hole. He measures one of the washers and finds the diameter to be 14 millimeters. What is the total area of all the washers that needs to be covered with gold leaf?

   _____

Find the area and circumference of circles

Baking

For each of the following questions, give your answer with some justification or reasoning for why it is correct. Use 3.14 as the value for pi in these problems.

1. Jelena has two cakes that she is getting ready to frost. She has two tubs of frosting: butter cream and chocolate. The tub of chocolate has more frosting, so she wants to use the chocolate on the cake that has the larger surface area on top. One cake is a 16 inch by 8 inch rectangular cake. The other cake is a circular cake with a diameter of 10 inches. Which cake should she frost with chocolate?

   _____

2. Jimmy made a cake that he just finished frosting. It is a round cake with a radius of 8 inches. He would like to run a strand of red licorice around the circumference of the cake and wonders if the 3 feet of licorice that he has is enough. Is the licorice long enough?

   _____

3. Tara made 36 cookies that are each 4 inches in diameter. She would like to pair the cookies and put frosting in between to make cookie sandwiches. She needs to know the area that she will be frosting. What is the area of half of the cookies if she puts frosting on half and then sets the other cookies on top of them?

   _____

4. Larry is making a pizza that is 18 inches in diameter. He is using a recipe that calls for a $\frac{1}{4}$ pound of cheese for each 40 square inches of pizza. How much cheese does he need to cover the 18-inch pizza?

   _____

Find the area and circumference of circles

Math Test

Name _____

Fill in the circle next to the correct answer.

Use the following four figures to answer Numbers 1 through 4.

Figure A   Figure B

Figure C   Figure D

1. Which figure has a circumference of 31.4 centimeters?

Ⓐ Figure A   Ⓒ Figure C
Ⓑ Figure B   Ⓓ Figure D

2. Which figure has a circumference of 37.68 centimeters?

Ⓐ Figure A   Ⓒ Figure C
Ⓑ Figure B   Ⓓ Figure D

3. Which figure has an area of 153.86 square centimeters?

Ⓐ Figure A   Ⓒ Figure C
Ⓑ Figure B   Ⓓ Figure D

4. Which figure has an area of 113.04 square centimeters?

Ⓐ Figure A   Ⓒ Figure C
Ⓑ Figure B   Ⓓ Figure D

5. If a circle has a diameter of 6 inches, what is its area?

Ⓐ 18.84 square inches
Ⓑ 37.68 square inches
Ⓒ 28.26 square inches
Ⓓ 9.42 square inches

6. If a circle has a radius of 5 inches, what is its area?

Ⓐ 78.5 square inches
Ⓑ 15.7 square inches
Ⓒ 31.4 square inches
Ⓓ 69 square inches

7. If a circle has a diameter of 8 inches, what is its circumference?

Ⓐ 12.56 inches
Ⓑ 200.96 inches
Ⓒ 50.24 inches
Ⓓ 25.12 inches

8. If a circle has a radius of 7 inches, what is its circumference?

Ⓐ 153.86 inches
Ⓑ 43.96 inches
Ⓒ 21.98 inches
Ⓓ 149.27 inches

9. Theodore is baking a round cake. He wants to put a licorice rope around the outside of the cake and needs to know how long it should be. If the cake has a diameter of 12 inches, how long should the licorice rope be?

_____

10. Denise has a stool with a circular seat on top. The diameter of the seat is 14 inches, and she wants to know the area of the top in order to cover the seat. What is the area of the seat top?

_____

Find the area and circumference of circles

What Does a Skunk Do When It Gets Angry?

Name_____

Determine the volume of each figure. Then write the corresponding letter on the line above the appropriate volume. (Only the number is listed, but remember that all units for volume are cubic units.) The letters will spell out the answer to the riddle.

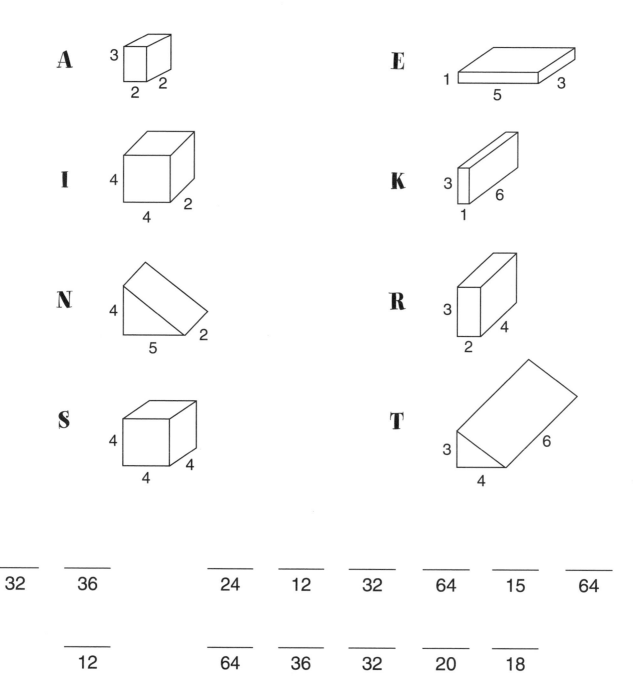

A 3, 2, 2

E 1, 5, 3

I 4, 4, 2

K 3, 6, 1

N 4, 5, 2

R 3, 2, 4

S 4, 4, 4

T 3, 4, 6

___ ___   ___ ___ ___ ___ ___ ___
32   36   24   12   32   64   15   64

___   ___ ___ ___ ___ ___
12   64   36   32   20   18

Calculate the volume of rectangular and triangular prisms

EMC 3019 • Basic Math Skills, Grade 6 • ©2003 by Evan-Moor Corp.

What Are Gegs?

Name_____

Determine the volume of each figure. Then write the corresponding letter on the line above the appropriate volume. (Only the number is listed, but remember that all units for volume are cubic units.) The letters will spell out the answer to the riddle.

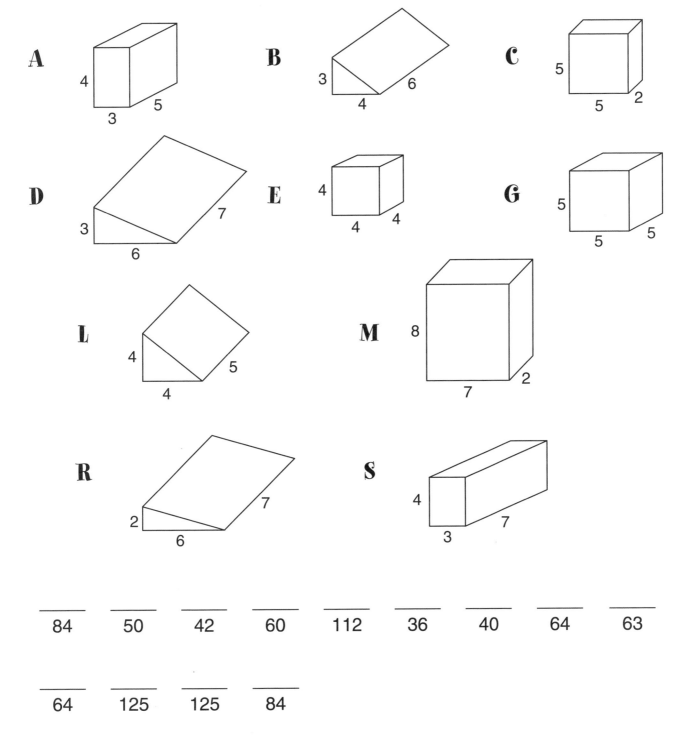

‾‾‾	‾‾‾	‾‾‾	‾‾‾	‾‾‾	‾‾‾	‾‾‾	‾‾‾	‾‾‾
84	50	42	60	112	36	40	64	63

‾‾‾	‾‾‾	‾‾‾	‾‾‾
64	125	125	84

Calculate the volume of rectangular and triangular prisms

Turn Up the Volume
a Centimeter

Name_____

Determine the volume of each of the following prisms.

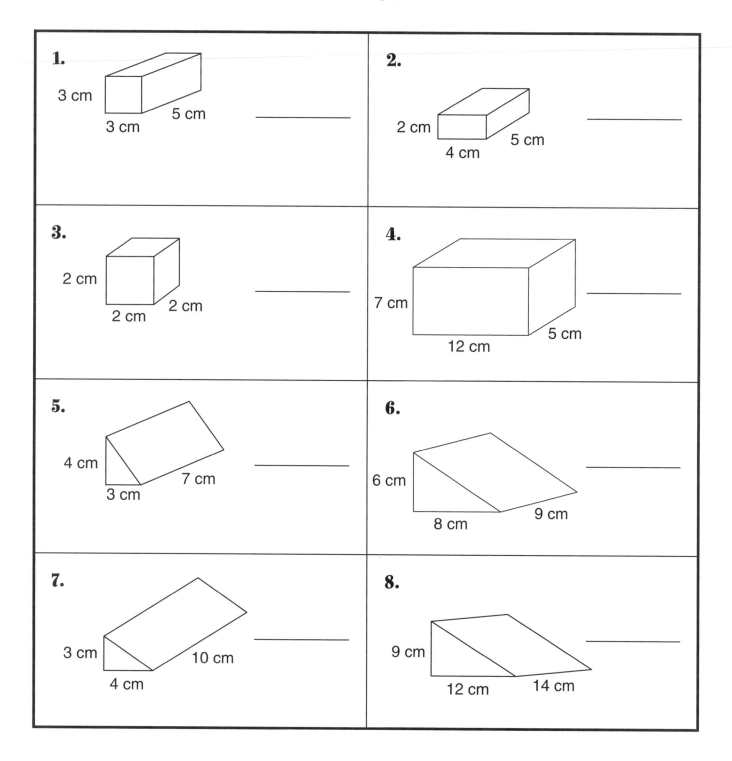

1. 3 cm, 3 cm, 5 cm _____

2. 2 cm, 4 cm, 5 cm _____

3. 2 cm, 2 cm, 2 cm _____

4. 7 cm, 12 cm, 5 cm _____

5. 4 cm, 3 cm, 7 cm _____

6. 6 cm, 8 cm, 9 cm _____

7. 3 cm, 4 cm, 10 cm _____

8. 9 cm, 12 cm, 14 cm _____

Calculate the volume of rectangular and triangular prisms

EMC 3019 • Basic Math Skills, Grade 6 • ©2003 by Evan-Moor Corp.

Turn Up the Volume an Inch

Name _____

Determine the volume of each of the following prisms.

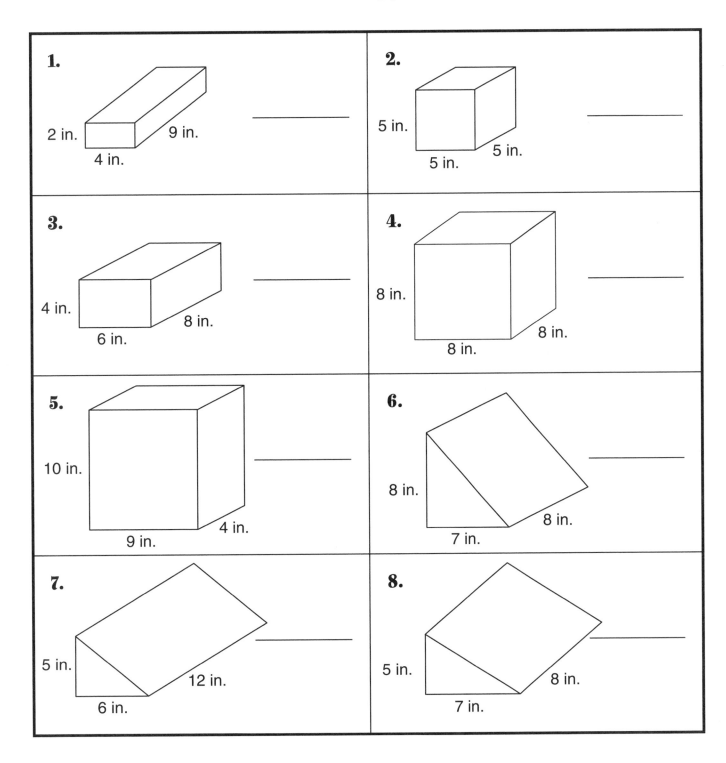

1.

2 in.   4 in.   9 in.   _____

2.

5 in.   5 in.   5 in.   5 in.   _____

3.

4 in.   6 in.   8 in.   _____

4.

8 in.   8 in.   8 in.   _____

5.

10 in.   9 in.   4 in.   _____

6.

8 in.   7 in.   8 in.   _____

7.

5 in.   6 in.   12 in.   _____

8.

5 in.   7 in.   8 in.   _____

Calculate the volume of rectangular and triangular prisms

Shipping Boxes

Name_____

1. Super Buy is getting ready to ship out several boxes of candles. The candles are each in a box that is 4 inches by 4 inches and 10 inches tall. The clerks will fit as many boxes as possible into each shipping crate. The shipping crate is 24 inches by 32 inches by 20 inches. What is the maximum number of candles that will fit into the shipping crate?

_____

2. Super Buy also has a shipment of snow globes to go out. They are in a box shaped like a cube that is 1 inch on each side. How many snow globes will fit into a shipping box that is 20 inches by 36 inches by 12 inches?

_____

3. Super Buy has many shipping boxes like the one pictured. The triangle has a base of 8 inches and a height of 7 inches. The distance between the two triangles is 20 inches. They would like to ship popcorn in this box and are wondering if a bag that contains 550 cubic inches of popcorn will fit inside. Will it all fit inside this box? Why or why not?

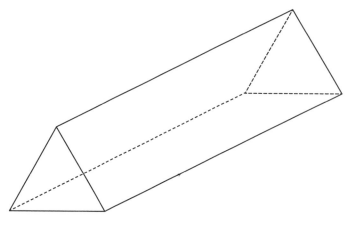

_____

4. Super Buy has another shipping box that is shaped like a cube, with 8 inches on each side. Will this box hold the 550 cubic inches of popcorn? Why or why not?

_____

Calculate the volume of rectangular and triangular prisms

236

EMC 3019 • Basic Math Skills, Grade 6 • ©2003 by Evan-Moor Corp.

Here's the Volume, Give Me the Dimensions

Name _____

Use the following clues to figure out the dimensions of each prism.

1. The first rectangular prism has the following characteristics:

   - It has a volume of 108 cubic inches.
   - The length and width of the base are identical.
   - The height is half of the length.

   What are the dimensions of this rectangular prism? _____

2. The second rectangular prism has the following characteristics:

   - It has a volume of 70 cubic inches.
   - The sum of the three lengths is 14.
   - The width is 2 less than the length.
   - The length is 5 more than the height.

   What are the dimensions of this rectangular prism? _____

3. The third prism is a triangular prism and has the following characteristics:

   - It has a volume of 360 cubic inches.
   - The base of the triangle is twice the height of the triangle.
   - The difference between the height of the prism and the height of the triangle is 4 inches.
   - The height of the prism is 10 inches.

   What are the dimensions of this triangular prism? _____

4. The fourth prism is a triangular prism and has the following characteristics:

   - It has a volume of 900 cubic inches.
   - Two of the dimensions are consecutive even numbers.
   - Two of the dimensions are multiples of 5.
   - All the dimensions are less than 16, but greater than 6.
   - All the lengths are different.
   - The base of the triangle is five more than the height of the triangle.

   What are the dimensions of this triangular prism? _____

Calculate the volume of rectangular and triangular prisms

Math Test

Name _____

Fill in the circle next to the correct answer.

Use the following four figures to answer Numbers 1 through 4.

8
8
8
Figure A

10
9
4
Figure B

8
8
7
Figure C

6
8
5
Figure D

1. Which figure has a volume of 240 cubic inches?

  Ⓐ Figure A   Ⓒ Figure C
  Ⓑ Figure B   Ⓓ Figure D

2. Which figure has a volume of 360 cubic inches?

  Ⓐ Figure A   Ⓒ Figure C
  Ⓑ Figure B   Ⓓ Figure D

3. Which figure has a volume of 224 cubic inches?

  Ⓐ Figure A   Ⓒ Figure C
  Ⓑ Figure B   Ⓓ Figure D

4. Which figure has a volume of 512 cubic inches?

  Ⓐ Figure A   Ⓒ Figure C
  Ⓑ Figure B   Ⓓ Figure D

5. What is the volume of a cube that is 5 centimeters on each edge?

  Ⓐ   25 cubic centimeters
  Ⓑ 125 cubic centimeters
  Ⓒ 100 cubic centimeters
  Ⓓ   30 cubic centimeters

6. What is the volume of a rectangular prism that is 4 inches by 3 inches by 8 inches?

  Ⓐ 15 cubic inches   Ⓒ 32 cubic inches
  Ⓑ 12 cubic inches   Ⓓ 96 cubic inches

7. What is the volume of a rectangular prism that is 5 inches by 5 inches by 7 inches?

  Ⓐ 25 cubic inches   Ⓒ   17 cubic inches
  Ⓑ 35 cubic inches   Ⓓ 175 cubic inches

8. What is the volume of a triangular prism where the base of the triangle is 4 inches, the height of the triangle is 5 inches, and the height of the prism is 8 inches?

  Ⓐ 80 cubic inches   Ⓒ   40 cubic inches
  Ⓑ 20 cubic inches   Ⓓ 160 cubic inches

9. Draw a solid that has a volume of 32 cubic inches and label the dimensions.

10. Given these two boxes, tell which has a larger volume and why. Box 1 is a rectangular prism that is 5 inches by 7 inches by 9 inches. Box 2 is a cube that is 7 inches on each side.

Box 1
5
9
7

Box 2
7
7
7

Calculate the volume of rectangular and triangular prisms

Data Analysis and Probability

Data and graphs

Probability

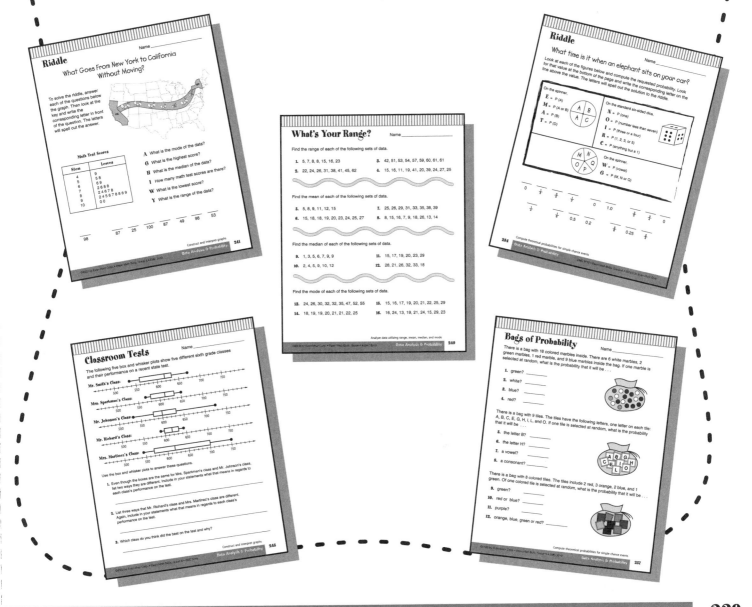

Riddle

Name_____

What is bought by the yard and worn by the foot?

To find the answer to this riddle, follow the steps below.

1. This table represents the sports students like to watch on TV. Use it to draw a double bar graph that represents the information on the empty graph below.

	Football	Basketball	Soccer	Baseball
Boys	10	4	11	3
Girls	5	9	12	1

2. Each line below has a sport and a gender listed under it. This corresponds to one of the bars you drew on the graph. Go to the top of each bar and look horizontally to the right and you will see a letter. Write this letter on the corresponding line and it will spell out the answer to the riddle.

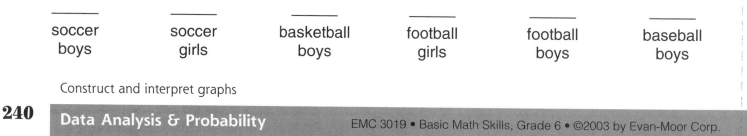

____	____	____	____	____	____
soccer boys	soccer girls	basketball boys	football girls	football boys	baseball boys

Construct and interpret graphs

Data Analysis & Probability   EMC 3019 • Basic Math Skills, Grade 6 • ©2003 by Evan-Moor Corp.

Riddle

What goes from New York to California without moving?

To solve the riddle, answer each of the questions below. Then write the corresponding letter above the answer to the question. The letters will spell out the answer to the riddle.

Math Test Scores

Stem	Leaves
4	9
5	5 8
6	6 9
7	2 6 8 8
8	2 4 6 7 8
9	2 4 5 6 7 8 8 8 9
10	0 0

A What is the mode of this data? _____

G What is the highest score? _____

H What is the median of this data? _____

I How many math test scores are there? _____

W What is the lowest score? _____

Y What is the range of this data? _____

_____   _____ _____ _____   _____ _____ _____ _____
98   87   25   100   87   49   98   51

Construct and interpret graphs

Circle Graph

Name_____

Mr. Call surveyed the 200 students in the sixth grade about their favorite flavor of soda. Here are the results:

Cola: 70 students   Root beer: 50 students

Lemon-Lime: 34 students   Grape: 16 students

Orange: 10 students   Cherry: 20 students

Use the information to complete the circle graph below. Make a key and color each section a different color. Be sure the colors on your key match the data and your graph.

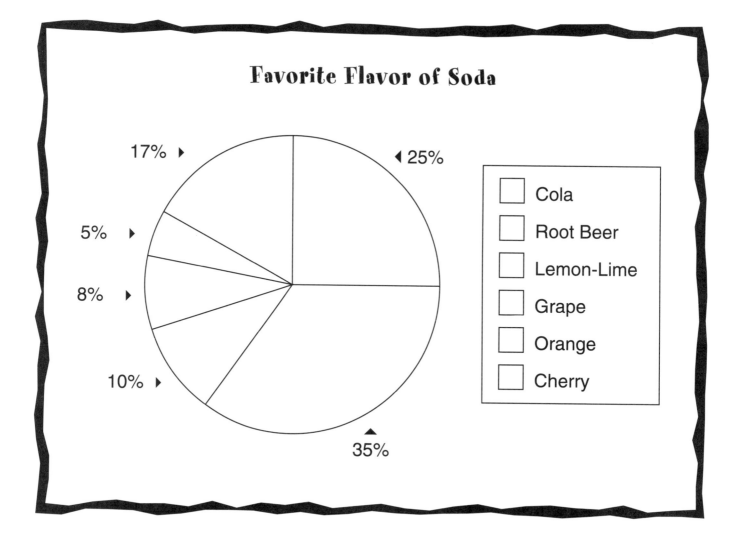

Favorite Flavor of Soda

17% ▸   ◂ 25%

5% ▸

8% ▸

10% ▸

▴ 35%

☐ Cola
☐ Root Beer
☐ Lemon-Lime
☐ Grape
☐ Orange
☐ Cherry

Construct and interpret graphs

Box and Whisker

Name _____

Olivia collected the following data about students in her class and their percents on the last spelling test.

64   76   78   85   85   85   86   88   94   100

She put the data into a Box and Whisker Plot by following these directions:

1. Order the data from least to greatest value.
2. Mark the lowest value and the greatest value.
3. Mark the median of the data.
4. Mark the median of the lower half of the data (the lower quartile).
5. Mark the median of the upper half of the data (the upper quartile).
6. Draw a box around the median values.

This is what her Box and Whisker Plot looked like:

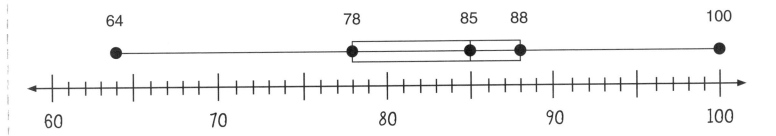

Now it's your turn. Follow the same directions to construct a Box and Whisker plot for this data about students in Olivia's class and their percents on the last math test.

80   72   100   80   70   84   88   90   98   78

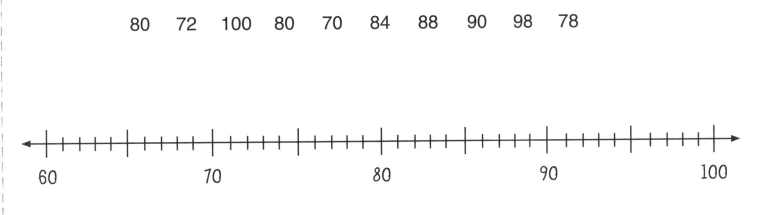

Construct and interpret graphs

Bathtub

Name_____

The following line graph represents the depth of water in a bathtub as it is filling up and then draining. At the bottom of the page, describe what happens at each interval on the graph. Then add the appropriate labels on each axis and number each axis according to your story.

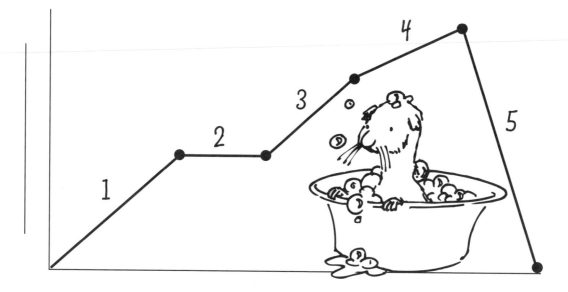

_____

1. _____

2. _____

3. _____

4. _____

5. _____

Construct and interpret graphs

Data Analysis & Probability   EMC 3019 • Basic Math Skills, Grade 6 • ©2003 by Evan-Moor Corp.

Classroom Tests

Name_____

The following five box and whisker plots show five different sixth-grade classes and their performance on a recent state test.

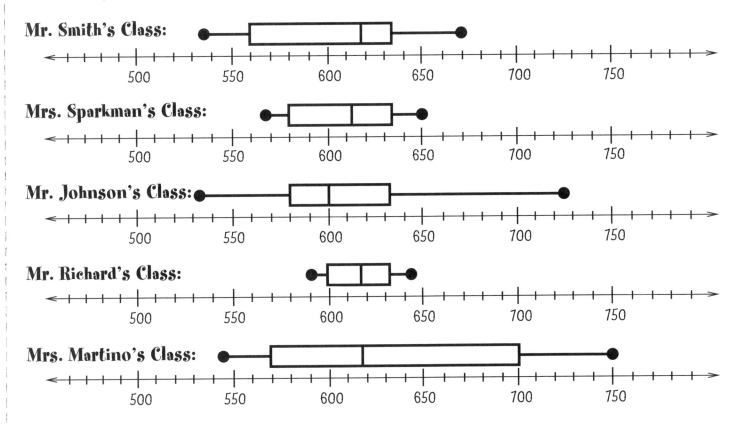

Use the box and whisker plots to answer the questions.

1. Even though the boxes are the same for Mrs. Sparkman's class and Mr. Johnson's class, list two ways they are different. Include in your statements what that means in regard to each class's performance on the test.

_____

2. List three ways that Mr. Richard's class and Mrs. Martino's class are different. Again, include in your statements what that means in regard to each class's performance on the test.

_____

3. Which class do you think did the best on the test, and why?

_____

Construct and interpret graphs

Math Test

Name_____

Fill in the circle next to the correct answer.

Use the circle graph to answer Numbers 1 through 3.

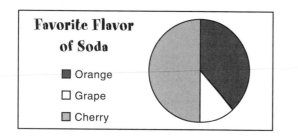

1. If there were 40 children surveyed, about how many liked cherry the best?

  Ⓐ 10   Ⓒ 20

  Ⓑ 15   Ⓓ 30

2. About how many children liked grape?

  Ⓐ 2   Ⓒ 10

  Ⓑ 5   Ⓓ 15

3. About how many more children liked orange compared to grape?

  Ⓐ 1   Ⓒ 10

  Ⓑ 5   Ⓓ 15

Use the stem and leaf plot to answer Numbers 4 and 5.

Math Test Scores

Stem	Leaves
4	9
5	
6	5 9
7	5 9 9
8	0 1 2 4 5 6 7 8 8
9	0 2 2 2 4 5 5 5 8 8 9
10	0 0 1

4. What is the median score on the math test?

  Ⓐ 87   Ⓑ 92   Ⓒ 88   Ⓓ 95

5. What was the lowest test score?

  Ⓐ 0   Ⓑ 1   Ⓒ 9   Ⓓ 49

Use the box and whisker plot to answer Numbers 6 through 8.

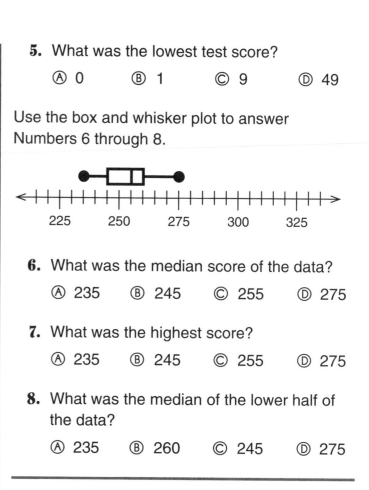

6. What was the median score of the data?

  Ⓐ 235   Ⓑ 245   Ⓒ 255   Ⓓ 275

7. What was the highest score?

  Ⓐ 235   Ⓑ 245   Ⓒ 255   Ⓓ 275

8. What was the median of the lower half of the data?

  Ⓐ 235   Ⓑ 260   Ⓒ 245   Ⓓ 275

9. Make a box and whisker plot to represent the following test scores:

20, 22, 23, 26, 27, 27, 28, 31, 34, 39

10. Make a stem and leaf plot to represent the following test scores:

72, 75, 80, 85, 89, 90, 95, 96, 96, 99, 99

Construct and interpret graphs

Data Analysis & Probability   EMC 3019 • Basic Math Skills, Grade 6 • ©2003 by Evan-Moor Corp.

Riddle

What did the banana do when the chimp chased it?

To solve the riddle, answer each of the following questions about the given data. Then write the corresponding letter on the line in front of the question. The letters will spell out the answer to the riddle when read from **top to bottom**.

Data Set 1: 41, 43, 43, 43, 44, 45, 49

Data Set 2: 15, 17, 18, 21, 24, 24, 28

Data Set 3: 15, 24, 36, 38, 38, 42, 45

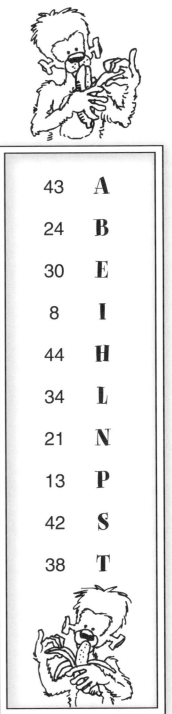

43	**A**
24	**B**
30	**E**
8	**I**
44	**H**
34	**L**
21	**N**
13	**P**
42	**S**
38	**T**

_____ What is the mode of the third data set?

_____ What is the mean of the first data set?

_____ What is the range of the third data set?

_____ What is the mode of the second data set?

_____ What is the median of the first data set?

_____ What is the median of the second data set?

_____ What is the second smallest value in the first data set?

_____ What is the mean of the second data set?

_____ What is the mode of the first data set?

_____ What is the second largest value in the third data set?

_____ What is the range of the second data set?

_____ What is the mean of the third data set?

_____ What is the range of the first data set?

_____ What is the median of the third data set?

Analyze data utilizing range, mean, median, and mode

What Is a Goose's Favorite Fruit?

To solve the riddle, answer each of the following questions about the given data. Then write the corresponding letter on the line in front of the question. The letters will spell out the answer to the riddle when read from **bottom to top**.

Data Set 1: 50, 57, 65, 75, 78, 78, 80, 82, 90, 95

Data Set 2: 22, 23, 23, 23, 25, 29, 33, 33, 35, 44

Data Set 3: 69, 69, 69, 69, 69, 73, 73, 73, 73, 83

____S____ What is the median of the first data set?

____E____ What is the mean of the first data set?

____I____ What is the range of the third data set?

____R____ What is the mode of the second data set?

____R____ What is the range of the first data set?

____E____ What is the mode of the third data set?

____B____ What is the median of the third data set?

____E____ What is the median of the second data set?

____S____ What is the mode of the first data set?

____O____ What is the mean of the second data set?

____O____ What is the range of the second data set?

____G____ What is the mean of the third data set?

B = 71

E = 27 or 69 or 75

G = 72

I = 14

O = 22 or 29

R = 23 or 45

S = 78

Analyze data utilizing range, mean, median, and mode

EMC 3019 • Basic Math Skills, Grade 6 • ©2003 by Evan-Moor Corp.

What's Your Range?

Name _____

Find the **range** of each set of data.

1. 5, 7, 8, 8, 15, 16, 23 _____

3. 42, 51, 53, 54, 57, 59, 60, 61, 61 _____

2. 22, 24, 26, 31, 38, 41, 45, 62 _____

4. 15, 16, 11, 19, 41, 20, 39, 24, 27, 25 _____

Find the **mean** of each set of data.

5. 5, 8, 9, 11, 12, 15 _____

7. 25, 26, 29, 31, 33, 35, 38, 39 _____

6. 15, 18, 18, 19, 20, 23, 24, 25, 27 _____

8. 8, 15, 16, 7, 9, 18, 26, 13, 14 _____

Find the **median** of each set of data.

9. 1, 3, 5, 6, 7, 9, 9 _____

11. 15, 17, 19, 20, 23, 29 _____

10. 2, 4, 5, 9, 10, 12 _____

12. 28, 21, 26, 32, 33, 18 _____

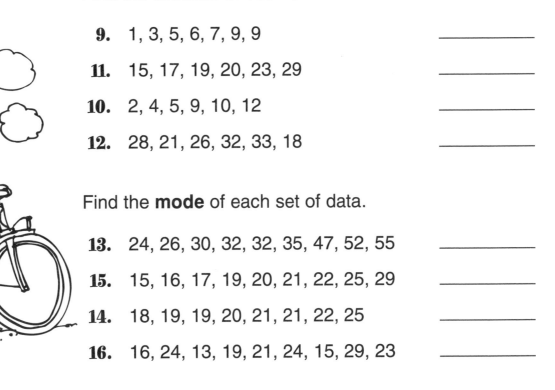

Find the **mode** of each set of data.

13. 24, 26, 30, 32, 32, 35, 47, 52, 55 _____

15. 15, 16, 17, 19, 20, 21, 22, 25, 29 _____

14. 18, 19, 19, 20, 21, 21, 22, 25 _____

16. 16, 24, 13, 19, 21, 24, 15, 29, 23 _____

Analyze data utilizing range, mean, median, and mode

Data Analysis & Probability

Compute My Data

Complete the following chart.

	Set of Data	Range	Mean	Median	Mode
1.	15, 23, 23, 24, 26				
2.	1, 2, 4, 4, 4, 5, 8, 9				
3.	6, 6, 6, 6, 6, 6, 6				
4.	21, 23, 25, 28, 32, 39				
5.	40, 45, 50, 55, 60, 65, 70				

Analyze data utilizing range, mean, median, and mode

Survey the Class

Name_____

1. Survey at least 20 of your classmates using one of the following questions:

   - How old is your mother?

   - How old is your father?

   - Think about all the drinks that you consume in a day. About how many times do you swallow?

   - How many people live on your block in all?

   - How much TV do you watch in an average month?

   - How many times does your heart beat in one minute?

   - Write your own question that has a numerical answer.

   _____

2. Calculate the range, mean, median, and mode for your data.

   _____

3. What does the range tell you about your data?

   _____

4. Considering the mean, median, and mode, which would you say is the best one to describe the "average" of your data? Why would you select that measure?

   _____

Analyze data utilizing range, mean, median, and mode

Change the Data

Name _____

The following data set represents scores on a recent spelling test out of a possible 50 points. Use the data set to answer the questions.

> **20, 22, 28, 30, 30, 30, 32, 35, 35, 38, 40, 44, 46, 46, 48, 48, 48, 48, 49, 50**

1. What value could you add to the data set to create two different modes?

_____

2. What value could you add to the data to create a range of 40? Is there another value that would also accomplish this task? If so, how many other values would accomplish this same task?

_____

3. What is the mean of the original data set?

_____

4. Is it possible to add one test score to the data and change the mean value to 40?

_____

5. What is the median of the original data set?

_____

6. What value could you add to the data to create a different median? Is there another value that would also accomplish this task? If so, how many other values would accomplish this same task?

_____

Analyze data utilizing range, mean, median, and mode

Data Analysis & Probability

EMC 3019 • Basic Math Skills, Grade 6 • ©2003 by Evan-Moor Corp.

Math Test

Fill in the circle next to the correct answer.

For Numbers 1 through 4, use the following data:

25, 27, 28, 29, 29, 30, 32, 35, 35

1. What is the mean of the data set?

   Ⓐ 29   Ⓒ 31
   Ⓑ 30   Ⓓ 32

2. What is the range of the data set?

   Ⓐ 25   Ⓒ 15
   Ⓑ 10   Ⓓ 35

3. What is the mode of the data set?

   Ⓐ 29   Ⓒ both 29 and 35
   Ⓑ 35   Ⓓ there is no mode

4. What is the median of the data set?

   Ⓐ 29   Ⓒ 32
   Ⓑ 30   Ⓓ 35

For Numbers 5 through 8, use the following data:

25, 30, 40, 50, 72, 83

5. What is the mean of the data set?

   Ⓐ 30   Ⓒ 50
   Ⓑ 40   Ⓓ 45

6. What is the range of the data set?

   Ⓐ 58   Ⓒ 25
   Ⓑ 62   Ⓓ 83

7. What is the mode of the data set?

   Ⓐ 25   Ⓒ 0
   Ⓑ 30   Ⓓ there is no mode

8. What is the median of the data set?

   Ⓐ 40   Ⓒ 45
   Ⓑ 50   Ⓓ 83

For Numbers 9 and 10, use the following data:

40, 42, 44, 44, 46, 48, 50

9. What value could you add to the data set to get a different median value? What is the new median after you add your new value?

   _____

   _____

   _____

10. What value could you add to get a mean of exactly 46? Explain how you solved this problem.

   _____

   _____

   _____

Data Analysis and Probability: Analyze data utilizing range, mean, median, and mode

Riddle

What time is it when an elephant sits on your car?

Look at each of the figures below and compute the requested probability. Look for that value at the bottom of the page and write the corresponding letter on the line above the value. The letters will spell out the solution to the riddle.

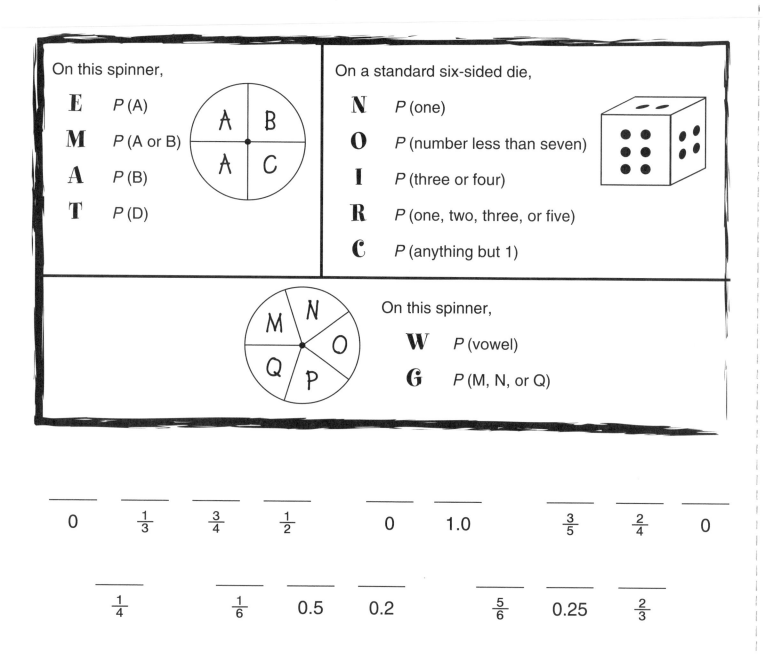

On this spinner,

E $P(A)$

M $P(A \text{ or } B)$

A $P(B)$

T $P(D)$

On a standard six-sided die,

N $P(\text{one})$

O $P(\text{number less than seven})$

I $P(\text{three or four})$

R $P(\text{one, two, three, or five})$

C $P(\text{anything but 1})$

On this spinner,

W $P(\text{vowel})$

G $P(M, N, \text{ or } Q)$

___	___	___	___		___	___		___	___	___
0	$\frac{1}{3}$	$\frac{3}{4}$	$\frac{1}{2}$		0	1.0		$\frac{3}{5}$	$\frac{2}{4}$	0

___		___	___	___		___	___	___
$\frac{1}{4}$		$\frac{1}{6}$	0.5	0.2		$\frac{5}{6}$	0.25	$\frac{2}{3}$

Compute theoretical probabilities for simple chance events

What is the difference between a bus driver and a cold?

To solve the riddle, look at each of the figures below and compute the requested probability. Look for that value at the bottom of the page and write the corresponding letter on the line above the value. The letters will spell out the answer to the riddle.

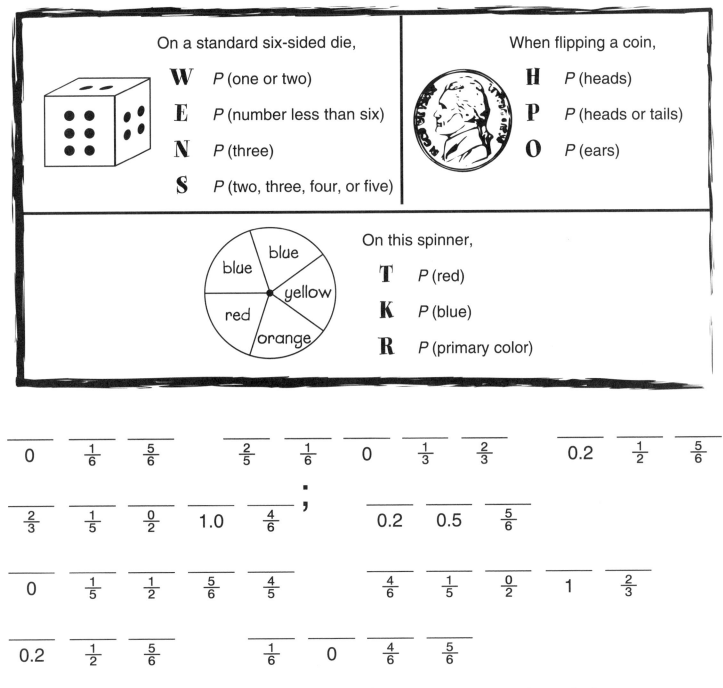

On a standard six-sided die,

W P (one or two)

E P (number less than six)

N P (three)

S P (two, three, four, or five)

When flipping a coin,

H P (heads)

P P (heads or tails)

O P (ears)

On this spinner,

T P (red)

K P (blue)

R P (primary color)

___ ___ ___   ___ ___ ___ ___ ___ ___   ___ ___ ___
0   $\frac{1}{6}$ $\frac{5}{6}$ $\frac{2}{5}$ $\frac{1}{6}$ 0 $\frac{1}{3}$ $\frac{2}{3}$ 0.2 $\frac{1}{2}$ $\frac{5}{6}$

:

___ ___ ___ ___ ___   ___ ___ ___
$\frac{2}{3}$ $\frac{1}{5}$ $\frac{0}{2}$ 1.0 $\frac{4}{6}$;   0.2   0.5 $\frac{5}{6}$

___ ___ ___ ___ ___   ___ ___ ___ ___ ___
0   $\frac{1}{5}$ $\frac{1}{2}$ $\frac{5}{6}$ $\frac{4}{5}$ $\frac{4}{6}$ $\frac{1}{5}$ $\frac{0}{2}$ 1 $\frac{2}{3}$

___ ___ ___   ___ ___ ___ ___
0.2 $\frac{1}{2}$ $\frac{5}{6}$ $\frac{1}{6}$ 0 $\frac{4}{6}$ $\frac{5}{6}$

Compute theoretical probabilities for simple chance events

Probability

Determine the probability of each event.

When rolling a standard six-sided die, what is the probability of getting...?

1. a 3 _____

2. a 2 _____

3. a 4 or a 5 _____

4. an odd number _____

5. an even number _____

6. a 7 _____

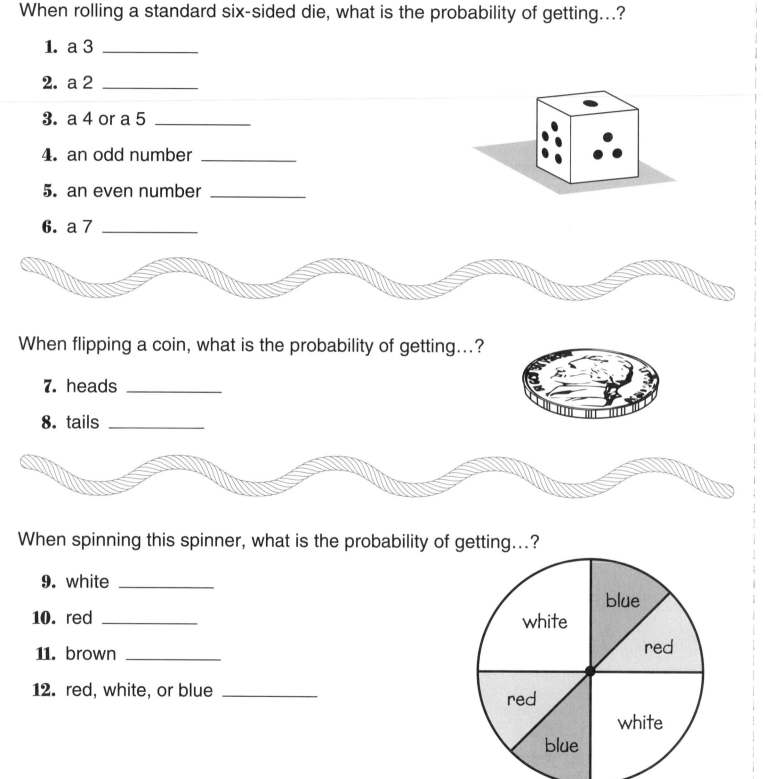

When flipping a coin, what is the probability of getting...?

7. heads _____

8. tails _____

When spinning this spinner, what is the probability of getting...?

9. white _____

10. red _____

11. brown _____

12. red, white, or blue _____

Compute theoretical probabilities for simple chance events

EMC 3019 • Basic Math Skills, Grade 6 • ©2003 by Evan-Moor Corp.

Bags of Probability

Name _____

There is a bag with 18 colored marbles inside. There are 6 white marbles, 2 green marbles, 1 red marble, and 9 blue marbles inside the bag. If one marble is selected at random, what is the probability that it will be…?

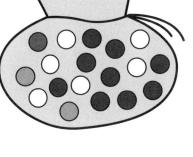

1. green _____

2. white _____

3. blue _____

4. red _____

There is a bag with 9 tiles. The tiles have the following letters, one letter on each tile: A, B, C, E, G, H, I, L, and O. If one tile is selected at random, what is the probability that it will be…?

5. the letter B _____

6. the letter H _____

7. a vowel _____

8. a consonant _____

There is a bag with 8 colored tiles. The tiles include 2 red, 3 orange, 2 blue, and 1 green. If one colored tile is selected at random, what is the probability that it will be…?

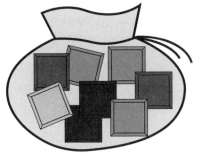

9. green _____

10. red or blue _____

11. purple _____

12. orange, blue, green, or red _____

Compute theoretical probabilities for simple chance events

Data Analysis & Probability

Spinners

Use the following clues to determine what spinner is being described. Draw the spinner for each set of clues.

1. The first spinner has the following facts: $P(1) = \frac{1}{2}$ $P(2) = \frac{1}{4}$ $P(3) = \frac{1}{4}$	
2. The second spinner has the following facts: $P(\text{red}) = \frac{1}{3}$ $P(\text{red, blue, or green}) = 1$ $P(\text{red or blue}) = \frac{2}{3}$	
3. The third spinner has the following facts: $P(\text{A, B, or C}) = 1$ $P(\text{B}) = P(\text{C}) = \frac{2}{5}$	
4. The fourth spinner has the following facts: $P(\text{white}) = \frac{1}{2}$ $P(\text{red}) = \frac{1}{4}$ $P(\text{blue or green}) = \frac{1}{4}$ $P(\text{blue}) = P(\text{green})$	
5. The fifth spinner has the following facts: $P(1, 2, 3, 4, \text{or } 5) = 1$ $P(2) = P(3) = P(4)$ $P(2) = P(1) + P(5)$ $P(1) = \frac{1}{8}$ $P(1) = P(5)$	

Compute theoretical probabilities for simple chance events

Dice

Name _____

Each of the following scenarios describes a six-sided die. Your task is to tell what is on each of the six sides, listing the six numbers in order from smallest to largest.

1. The first six-sided die has the following facts:

$P(\text{even number}) = \frac{1}{3}$

$P(\text{odd number}) = \frac{2}{3}$

$P(7) = \frac{1}{3}$

$P(3) = \frac{1}{3}$

$P(4) = \frac{1}{3}$

2. The second six-sided die has the following facts:

$P(\text{even number}) = 1$

$P(\text{number less than 25}) = 1$

$P(10) = P(20) = P(2) = P(16) = \frac{1}{6}$

The sum of six sides is 68.

$P(\text{number greater than 12}) = \frac{1}{3}$

Each side has a different number.

3. The third six-sided die has the following facts:

$P(\text{odd number}) = \frac{1}{2}$

$P(6) = \frac{1}{2}$

Three numbers are consecutive odd numbers.

The sum of all six sides is 27.

4. The fourth six-sided die has the following facts:

$P(\text{odd number}) = \frac{1}{2}$

$P(\text{number larger than 4}) = 1$

$P(\text{number smaller than 16}) = 1$

The sum of all six sides is 65.

$P(10) = \frac{1}{3}$

One side is twice another side.

One side is three times another side.

$P(12) = P(13) = \frac{1}{6}$

Compute theoretical probabilities for simple chance events

Math Test

Name_____

Fill in the circle next to the correct answer.

For Numbers 1 through 4, use this spinner.

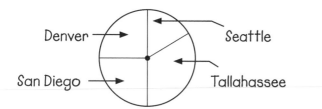

1. What is the probability of landing on Denver when you spin the spinner?

(A) $\frac{1}{2}$ (B) $\frac{1}{4}$ (C) $\frac{1}{3}$ (D) $\frac{1}{6}$

2. What is the probability of landing on Tallahassee when you spin the spinner?

(A) $\frac{1}{2}$ (B) $\frac{1}{4}$ (C) $\frac{1}{3}$ (D) $\frac{1}{6}$

3. What is the probability of landing on Denver or San Diego when you spin the spinner?

(A) $\frac{1}{2}$ (B) $\frac{1}{4}$ (C) $\frac{1}{3}$ (D) 0

4. What is the probability of landing on New York when you spin the spinner?

(A) $\frac{1}{2}$ (B) $\frac{1}{4}$ (C) $\frac{1}{3}$ (D) 0

For Numbers 5 and 6, use this bag of marbles.

5. What is the probability of drawing a white marble at random from the bag?

(A) $\frac{1}{2}$ (B) $\frac{1}{3}$ (C) $\frac{2}{7}$ (D) $\frac{2}{9}$

6. What is the probability of drawing a black marble at random from the bag?

(A) $\frac{1}{2}$ (B) $\frac{1}{3}$ (C) $\frac{3}{6}$ (D) $\frac{3}{4}$

For Numbers 7 and 8, use this die.

7. What is the probability of getting a 3 when you roll the die?

(A) $\frac{1}{3}$ (B) $\frac{1}{5}$ (C) $\frac{3}{5}$ (D) $\frac{1}{6}$

8. What is the probability of getting an even number when you roll the die?

(A) 1   (B) $\frac{2}{3}$ (C) $\frac{1}{2}$ (D) $\frac{1}{3}$

9. Draw a spinner where $P(A) = \frac{1}{2}$, $P(B) = \frac{1}{4}$, and $P(C) = \frac{1}{4}$.

10. On the spinner you drew in Number 9, what is $P(A$ or $B)$?

_____

Compute theoretical probabilities for simple chance events

Data Analysis & Probability   EMC 3019 • Basic Math Skills, Grade 6 • ©2003 by Evan-Moor Corp.

Riddle

Name _____

What is the difference between an umbrella and a chatterbox?

Find the number of combinations that can be made with the items listed. Then write the corresponding letter on the line above the correct number. The letters will spell out the answer to the riddle.

A 2 different turkeys and 2 different types of stuffing = _____

B 3 different colors of sheets in 2 different patterns = _____

C 2 different cups with 2 different saucers with 2 different plates = _____

E 3 colors of thread with 3 different patches = _____

H 5 different colors of carpet with 2 different colors of paint = _____

L 3 different colored pants and 4 different shirts = _____

M 7 different types of meat and 2 different types of bread = _____

N 5 different colors of paper with 3 different colors of glitter = _____

O 8 different types of sandwiches and 2 different drinks = _____

P 9 types of plates and 2 different colors = _____

R 5 types of cars and 4 different colors = _____

S 7 different types of cheese and 3 different kinds of crackers = _____

T 3 different kinds of bread, 4 different kinds of meat, and 2 different types of cheeses = _____

U 9 different kinds of shovels with 3 different-sized handles = _____

Y 4 types of ice-cream cones and 7 ice-cream flavors = _____

___ ___ ___   ___ ___ ___
28   16   27   8   4   15

___ ___ ___ ___   ___ ___
21   10   27   24   4   15

___ ___ ___ ___ ___ ___ ___ ___   ___ ___
27   14   6   20   9   12   12   4   27   18

Utilize counting techniques, tree charts, and organized lists to determine all possible combinations

What Did the Puddle Say to the Rain?

Name _____

On the line at the end of each list, write the number of combinations that can be made with the items listed. Then write the corresponding letter on the line in front of the list. The letters will spell out the answer to the riddle when read from **the bottom up**.

_____ 6 types of plates and 2 different colors _____

_____ 4 different colors of lights and 4 different wattages _____

_____ 5 different colors of paper with 3 different colors of glitter _____

_____ 2 different types of cones, 4 different flavors of ice cream, with 4 different sizes _____

_____ 6 different styles of umbrellas and 2 different colors _____

_____ 2 different colored pants, 4 different shirts, and 2 different types of shoes _____

_____ 3 colors of thread with 6 different patches _____

_____ 5 different colors of carpet with 2 different colors of paint and 3 different styles of trim _____

_____ 17 different colors of sheets in only 1 pattern _____

_____ 5 different types of meat and 3 different types of bread _____

_____ 5 different colors of cars, 2 different styles, and 2 different makes _____

_____ 3 different colors of sheets with 3 different sizes in 2 different patterns _____

_____ 2 different cups with 4 different saucers with 3 different plates _____

_____ 5 different computers and 2 different sizes of monitors _____

| 10 **D** | 15 **I** | 17 **N** | 20 **P** | 30 **S** |
| 12 **E** | 16 **M** | 18 **O** | 24 **R** | 32 **T** |

Utilize counting techniques, tree charts, and organized lists to determine all possible combinations

Data Analysis & Probability   EMC 3019 • Basic Math Skills, Grade 6 • ©2003 by Evan-Moor Corp.

Trees

Name_____

Tree diagrams are very useful in showing combinations of items. The tree diagram below shows the number of different combinations of cars that can be created from two colors of paint (red and green) and two colors of interior (white and black). Each "branch" lists one possible combination. For example, the top branch shows the car with red paint and white interior. There are a total of four different combinations on this tree diagram.

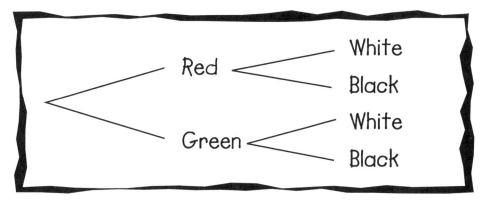

Draw a tree diagram for each of the following situations and tell how many combinations there are for each. You may need to use another sheet of paper.

1. Four colors of shirts (green, blue, red, and white) and two pairs of pants (blue and black)

_____ combinations

2. Two colors of paper (white and yellow), two colors of glitter (silver and gold), and two different stamps (a bear and a horse)

_____ combinations

Utilize counting techniques, tree charts, and organized lists to determine all possible combinations

Organized Lists

Name_____

Organized lists are very useful in showing combinations of items. This organized list demonstrates the number of different cars that can be created from two colors of paint (red and green) and two colors of interior (white and black). Each row lists one possible combination of car. For example, the top row shows the car with red paint and white interior. There are a total of four different combinations in this list.

Color of Paint	Color of Interior
Red	White
Red	Black
Green	White
Green	Black

Make an organized list for each of the following situations and tell how many combinations there are for each. You may need to use another sheet of paper.

1. Three colors of shirts (denim, white, and red) and two types of pants (blue jeans and white slacks)

_____ combinations

2. Two types of tacos (chicken and beef), two types of salsa (mild and hot), and three sizes of drinks (small, medium, and large)

_____ combinations

Utilize counting techniques, tree charts, and organized lists to determine all possible combinations

EMC 3019 • Basic Math Skills, Grade 6 • ©2003 by Evan-Moor Corp.

Counting Principle

One way to determine the number of combinations is known as the counting principle. This principle is a method of multiplying the number of possibilities of particular events to find out how many different ways the events can happen together. For example, if there are 5 shirts and 3 pairs of pants, we can make 15 different outfits since 5 times 3 equals 15.

Use this same method to determine the number of combinations for each of the following situations:

1. 5 ice-cream flavors and 3 kinds of cones _____

2. 6 colors of shirts and 2 different styles _____

3. 4 colors of paper and 3 colors of markers _____

4. 6 colors of paint and 4 kinds of paper _____

5. 7 kinds of meat, 3 kinds of cheese, and 2 kinds of bread _____

6. 8 colors of sports jerseys, 9 numbers, and 2 lengths of sleeves _____

7. Choose one of the above situations and show the number _____
   of combinations another way (for example, an organized
   list or a tree diagram).

Utilize counting techniques, tree charts, and organized lists to determine all possible combinations

Basketball Jerseys

Name_____

Ian and Brandon are playing on a basketball team. They are on one of four different teams. There are eight players on each team, and each player has been assigned a number from one to eight.

1. How many different jerseys are needed in all? Are they all different?

_____

2. In the space below, draw a tree diagram to show the different combinations of jerseys.

3. On the back of this sheet of paper, show the same set of jerseys in an organized list.

4. Which method do you prefer to display the set of jerseys? Why?

Utilize counting techniques, tree charts, and organized lists to determine all possible combinations

Data Analysis & Probability   EMC 3019 • Basic Math Skills, Grade 6 • ©2003 by Evan-Moor Corp.

Math Test

Fill in the circle next to the correct answer.

On a piece of paper, write an organized list to show all the possible combinations of three shirts (red, blue, and green), two pants (blue and black), and two pairs of shoes (tennis shoes and cowboy boots). Use this list to answer Numbers 1 through 4.

1. How many times do black pants appear on the list?

- Ⓐ 1
- Ⓑ 2
- Ⓒ 3
- Ⓓ 6

2. How many times does the outfit with the red shirt, black pants, and tennis shoes appear on the list?

- Ⓐ 1
- Ⓑ 2
- Ⓒ 3
- Ⓓ 6

3. How many combinations are there in all?

- Ⓐ 2
- Ⓑ 3
- Ⓒ 6
- Ⓓ 12

4. If you added one more pair of shoes to the list, how many additional combinations would that create?

- Ⓐ 1
- Ⓑ 6
- Ⓒ 12
- Ⓓ 15

5. How many different single-scoop ice-cream cones can be made with two different cones and three different flavors of ice cream?

- Ⓐ 1
- Ⓑ 2
- Ⓒ 3
- Ⓓ 6

6. How many different sandwiches can be made with three different meats, three different cheeses, and two different breads?

- Ⓐ 3
- Ⓑ 6
- Ⓒ 9
- Ⓓ 18

7. How many different posters can be made with three different colors of paper, four different colors of markers, and three different kinds of stickers?

- Ⓐ 36
- Ⓑ 12
- Ⓒ 48
- Ⓓ 9

8. How many different pillows can be made with nine different fabrics, three different colors of lace trim, and only one kind of thread?

- Ⓐ 9
- Ⓑ 27
- Ⓒ 1
- Ⓓ 54

9. Draw a tree diagram to represent the number of combinations of 2 colors of paint (yellow and blue) and three colors of paper (white, black, and red).

10. Make an organized list for Number 9's problem.

Utilize counting techniques, tree charts, and organized lists to determine all possible combinations

Resources

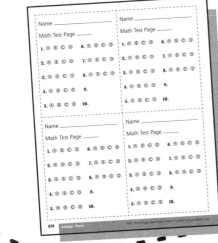

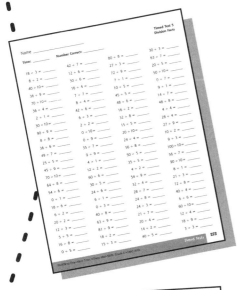

Name _____

Time: _____   Number Correct: _____

6 − 6 = _____	7 + 8 = _____	1 + 5 = _____	2 − 1 = _____
11 − 3 = _____	2 + 3 = _____	8 − 3 = _____	9 + 0 = _____
7 + 3 = _____	7 − 7 = _____	7 + 5 = _____	8 − 2 = _____
3 + 8 = _____	16 − 7 = _____	8 − 0 = _____	16 − 9 = _____
10 + 1 = _____	10 − 9 = _____	14 − 5 = _____	5 + 7 = _____
9 + 8 = _____	2 + 7 = _____	10 + 3 = _____	14 − 10 = _____
12 − 2 = _____	6 − 3 = _____	12 − 7 = _____	3 + 10 = _____
0 + 7 = _____	13 − 6 = _____	9 + 5 = _____	14 − 8 = _____
13 − 10 = _____	4 + 1 = _____	18 − 10 = _____	3 + 1 = _____
3 + 6 = _____	6 + 6 = _____	3 + 9 = _____	10 − 1 = _____
10 + 10 = _____	12 − 4 = _____	7 + 9 = _____	9 − 4 = _____
8 − 1 = _____	4 + 3 = _____	5 − 3 = _____	10 + 4 = _____
4 + 5 = _____	6 − 4 = _____	10 − 5 = _____	6 + 5 = _____
9 − 9 = _____	0 + 0 = _____	2 + 6 = _____	12 − 9 = _____
2 + 2 = _____	10 − 7 = _____	1 + 10 = _____	3 + 2 = _____
7 − 4 = _____	17 − 8 = _____	19 − 10 = _____	8 + 1 = _____
12 − 3 = _____	6 + 4 = _____	8 + 8 = _____	10 − 6 = _____
15 − 9 = _____	8 + 3 = _____	1 + 2 = _____	1 + 0 = _____
5 + 8 = _____	9 − 2 = _____	5 + 5 = _____	1 − 0 = _____
10 + 0 = _____	8 + 2 = _____	10 + 6 = _____	6 − 1 = _____
7 − 6 = _____	9 + 3 = _____	4 + 9 = _____	10 − 3 = _____
10 − 10 = _____	2 + 9 = _____	5 + 9 = _____	6 + 2 = _____
5 + 6 = _____	11 − 5 = _____	7 − 2 = _____	2 − 2 = _____
0 + 8 = _____	14 − 4 = _____	9 − 8 = _____	9 − 6 = _____
4 − 2 = _____	18 − 9 = _____	18 − 8 = _____	11 − 10 = _____

Name _____

Time: _____   Number Correct: _____

17 − 9 = _____	4 − 4 = _____	2 + 10 = _____	5 − 4 = _____
11 − 1 = _____	5 + 3 = _____	6 − 5 = _____	15 − 6 = _____
6 + 7 = _____	6 + 10 = _____	0 + 6 = _____	11 − 4 = _____
3 + 0 = _____	3 + 4 = _____	13 − 7 = _____	5 + 0 = _____
9 − 7 = _____	0 + 10 = _____	17 − 10 = _____	7 + 0 = _____
1 + 9 = _____	0 + 9 = _____	6 + 8 = _____	1 + 7 = _____
3 − 3 = _____	4 − 3 = _____	8 + 10 = _____	1 + 6 = _____
9 + 10 = _____	6 − 2 = _____	0 + 5 = _____	4 − 1 = _____
5 − 1 = _____	6 + 9 = _____	2 + 8 = _____	5 − 0 = _____
11 − 6 = _____	10 − 4 = _____	5 + 4 = _____	4 + 8 = _____
7 − 5 = _____	10 + 5 = _____	4 + 4 = _____	10 − 0 = _____
15 − 8 = _____	7 + 6 = _____	15 − 5 = _____	9 − 5 = _____
0 + 4 = _____	10 − 2 = _____	1 + 4 = _____	5 + 10 = _____
3 − 2 = _____	8 − 5 = _____	4 + 10 = _____	3 − 0 = _____
3 + 7 = _____	2 + 1 = _____	10 − 8 = _____	9 + 9 = _____
15 − 7 = _____	6 + 0 = _____	16 − 10 = _____	9 + 7 = _____
14 − 6 = _____	7 + 2 = _____	13 − 3 = _____	5 + 2 = _____
19 − 9 = _____	3 + 5 = _____	7 + 10 = _____	7 − 1 = _____
0 + 1 = _____	8 + 4 = _____	6 − 0 = _____	2 + 4 = _____
8 + 6 = _____	9 + 2 = _____	0 − 0 = _____	11 − 7 = _____
7 − 3 = _____	15 − 10 = _____	9 + 4 = _____	12 − 5 = _____
7 + 7 = _____	10 + 8 = _____	14 − 9 = _____	9 − 3 = _____
5 − 2 = _____	9 − 1 = _____	13 − 5 = _____	1 + 8 = _____
8 − 4 = _____	16 − 6 = _____	2 + 0 = _____	12 − 8 = _____
11 − 9 = _____	4 + 6 = _____	13 − 9 = _____	3 − 1 = _____

Name _____

Time: _____ **Number Correct:** _____

5 × 4 = _____	3 × 7 = _____	4 × 5 = _____	7 × 6 = _____
1 × 6 = _____	5 × 10 = _____	4 × 4 = _____	2 × 9 = _____
5 × 1 = _____	7 × 4 = _____	0 × 10 = _____	10 × 0 = _____
9 × 8 = _____	6 × 5 = _____	10 × 2 = _____	3 × 10 = _____
2 × 8 = _____	9 × 3 = _____	6 × 4 = _____	3 × 3 = _____
1 × 9 = _____	8 × 6 = _____	0 × 6 = _____	7 × 7 = _____
10 × 6 = _____	2 × 7 = _____	0 × 8 = _____	8 × 4 = _____
3 × 5 = _____	7 × 10 = _____	6 × 1 = _____	0 × 9 = _____
2 × 3 = _____	1 × 0 = _____	3 × 0 = _____	6 × 3 = _____
10 × 8 = _____	4 × 3 = _____	4 × 6 = _____	2 × 2 = _____
5 × 7 = _____	6 × 8 = _____	5 × 2 = _____	0 × 4 = _____
9 × 6 = _____	7 × 3 = _____	2 × 10 = _____	7 × 0 = _____
8 × 1 = _____	3 × 2 = _____	9 × 1 = _____	6 × 6 = _____
7 × 2 = _____	5 × 8 = _____	6 × 10 = _____	9 × 7 = _____
3 × 4 = _____	2 × 5 = _____	8 × 7 = _____	8 × 10 = _____
0 × 1 = _____	8 × 5 = _____	7 × 1 = _____	5 × 6 = _____
4 × 0 = _____	7 × 5 = _____	9 × 4 = _____	9 × 0 = _____
10 × 5 = _____	4 × 2 = _____	8 × 8 = _____	3 × 9 = _____
1 × 2 = _____	2 × 6 = _____	2 × 4 = _____	6 × 7 = _____
3 × 6 = _____	7 × 8 = _____	4 × 1 = _____	9 × 5 = _____
4 × 10 = _____	10 × 10 = _____	5 × 5 = _____	3 × 8 = _____
1 × 4 = _____	8 × 3 = _____	7 × 9 = _____	6 × 2 = _____
4 × 8 = _____	5 × 9 = _____	10 × 4 = _____	9 × 9 = _____
8 × 9 = _____	2 × 1 = _____	6 × 9 = _____	0 × 2 = _____
6 × 0 = _____	0 × 5 = _____	2 × 0 = _____	1 × 3 = _____

Name _____

Time: _____   Number Correct: _____

$4 \times 8 =$ _____	$9 \times 2 =$ _____	$5 \times 1 =$ _____	$7 \times 1 =$ _____
$4 \times 10 =$ _____	$8 \times 0 =$ _____	$1 \times 5 =$ _____	$6 \times 10 =$ _____
$3 \times 3 =$ _____	$9 \times 5 =$ _____	$3 \times 9 =$ _____	$8 \times 7 =$ _____
$10 \times 6 =$ _____	$9 \times 8 =$ _____	$10 \times 1 =$ _____	$9 \times 9 =$ _____
$6 \times 4 =$ _____	$5 \times 6 =$ _____	$6 \times 7 =$ _____	$10 \times 2 =$ _____
$2 \times 1 =$ _____	$3 \times 8 =$ _____	$7 \times 5 =$ _____	$0 \times 5 =$ _____
$6 \times 8 =$ _____	$10 \times 0 =$ _____	$10 \times 4 =$ _____	$1 \times 6 =$ _____
$8 \times 3 =$ _____	$10 \times 5 =$ _____	$6 \times 2 =$ _____	$10 \times 10 =$ _____
$3 \times 5 =$ _____	$6 \times 9 =$ _____	$5 \times 8 =$ _____	$0 \times 9 =$ _____
$4 \times 2 =$ _____	$7 \times 6 =$ _____	$7 \times 4 =$ _____	$4 \times 5 =$ _____
$1 \times 7 =$ _____	$2 \times 10 =$ _____	$1 \times 9 =$ _____	$9 \times 7 =$ _____
$0 \times 3 =$ _____	$8 \times 4 =$ _____	$7 \times 10 =$ _____	$5 \times 2 =$ _____
$5 \times 3 =$ _____	$4 \times 6 =$ _____	$4 \times 4 =$ _____	$6 \times 5 =$ _____
$8 \times 2 =$ _____	$4 \times 1 =$ _____	$5 \times 7 =$ _____	$3 \times 2 =$ _____
$9 \times 10 =$ _____	$7 \times 3 =$ _____	$9 \times 4 =$ _____	$6 \times 6 =$ _____
$3 \times 1 =$ _____	$7 \times 2 =$ _____	$10 \times 8 =$ _____	$8 \times 6 =$ _____
$2 \times 4 =$ _____	$8 \times 9 =$ _____	$2 \times 3 =$ _____	$9 \times 1 =$ _____
$6 \times 0 =$ _____	$3 \times 10 =$ _____	$1 \times 3 =$ _____	$4 \times 3 =$ _____
$2 \times 7 =$ _____	$4 \times 7 =$ _____	$4 \times 0 =$ _____	$8 \times 5 =$ _____
$8 \times 1 =$ _____	$9 \times 6 =$ _____	$2 \times 6 =$ _____	$7 \times 7 =$ _____
$5 \times 4 =$ _____	$3 \times 6 =$ _____	$2 \times 5 =$ _____	$6 \times 3 =$ _____
$2 \times 2 =$ _____	$2 \times 9 =$ _____	$1 \times 8 =$ _____	$2 \times 8 =$ _____
$0 \times 0 =$ _____	$1 \times 10 =$ _____	$0 \times 10 =$ _____	$1 \times 0 =$ _____
$1 \times 1 =$ _____	$9 \times 0 =$ _____	$5 \times 5 =$ _____	$10 \times 3 =$ _____
$2 \times 0 =$ _____	$5 \times 9 =$ _____	$0 \times 7 =$ _____	$1 \times 4 =$ _____

Name _____

Time: _____   Number Correct: _____

18 ÷ 3 = _____	42 ÷ 7 = _____	80 ÷ 8 = _____	30 ÷ 3 = _____
8 ÷ 2 = _____	12 ÷ 6 = _____	27 ÷ 3 = _____	63 ÷ 7 = _____
40 ÷ 10 = _____	30 ÷ 6 = _____	72 ÷ 9 = _____	20 ÷ 5 = _____
36 ÷ 9 = _____	16 ÷ 4 = _____	7 ÷ 1 = _____	50 ÷ 10 = _____
70 ÷ 10 = _____	7 ÷ 7 = _____	10 ÷ 5 = _____	0 ÷ 7 = _____
36 ÷ 4 = _____	8 ÷ 4 = _____	45 ÷ 5 = _____	9 ÷ 1 = _____
2 ÷ 1 = _____	42 ÷ 6 = _____	48 ÷ 6 = _____	14 ÷ 7 = _____
30 ÷ 10 = _____	6 ÷ 3 = _____	16 ÷ 2 = _____	48 ÷ 8 = _____
90 ÷ 9 = _____	2 ÷ 2 = _____	32 ÷ 8 = _____	4 ÷ 4 = _____
8 ÷ 8 = _____	0 ÷ 10 = _____	15 ÷ 5 = _____	28 ÷ 4 = _____
36 ÷ 6 = _____	0 ÷ 9 = _____	20 ÷ 10 = _____	27 ÷ 9 = _____
49 ÷ 7 = _____	35 ÷ 7 = _____	24 ÷ 4 = _____	10 ÷ 2 = _____
25 ÷ 5 = _____	9 ÷ 9 = _____	56 ÷ 8 = _____	9 ÷ 3 = _____
45 ÷ 9 = _____	4 ÷ 1 = _____	50 ÷ 5 = _____	100 ÷ 10 = _____
70 ÷ 10 = _____	12 ÷ 2 = _____	35 ÷ 5 = _____	56 ÷ 7 = _____
64 ÷ 8 = _____	60 ÷ 6 = _____	4 ÷ 2 = _____	90 ÷ 10 = _____
54 ÷ 6 = _____	30 ÷ 5 = _____	54 ÷ 9 = _____	8 ÷ 1 = _____
0 ÷ 1 = _____	24 ÷ 6 = _____	32 ÷ 4 = _____	21 ÷ 3 = _____
18 ÷ 6 = _____	6 ÷ 1 = _____	28 ÷ 7 = _____	72 ÷ 8 = _____
6 ÷ 2 = _____	0 ÷ 3 = _____	24 ÷ 8 = _____	40 ÷ 4 = _____
20 ÷ 2 = _____	40 ÷ 8 = _____	24 ÷ 3 = _____	6 ÷ 6 = _____
12 ÷ 3 = _____	63 ÷ 9 = _____	21 ÷ 7 = _____	60 ÷ 10 = _____
5 ÷ 5 = _____	81 ÷ 9 = _____	20 ÷ 4 = _____	12 ÷ 4 = _____
16 ÷ 8 = _____	18 ÷ 2 = _____	14 ÷ 2 = _____	18 ÷ 9 = _____
0 ÷ 5 = _____	15 ÷ 3 = _____	40 ÷ 5 = _____	3 ÷ 3 = _____

Name _____

Time: _____   Number Correct: _____

$24 \div 8 =$ _____	$64 \div 8 =$ _____	$10 \div 2 =$ _____	$10 \div 1 =$ _____
$36 \div 9 =$ _____	$30 \div 10 =$ _____	$32 \div 4 =$ _____	$25 \div 5 =$ _____
$24 \div 3 =$ _____	$0 \div 8 =$ _____	$9 \div 1 =$ _____	$20 \div 4 =$ _____
$42 \div 7 =$ _____	$4 \div 1 =$ _____	$30 \div 3 =$ _____	$36 \div 4 =$ _____
$36 \div 6 =$ _____	$40 \div 8 =$ _____	$35 \div 5 =$ _____	$24 \div 4 =$ _____
$56 \div 8 =$ _____	$20 \div 5 =$ _____	$56 \div 7 =$ _____	$50 \div 5 =$ _____
$80 \div 10 =$ _____	$5 \div 1 =$ _____	$40 \div 10 =$ _____	$0 \div 1 =$ _____
$28 \div 4 =$ _____	$12 \div 3 =$ _____	$40 \div 5 =$ _____	$6 \div 2 =$ _____
$2 \div 2 =$ _____	$8 \div 4 =$ _____	$16 \div 8 =$ _____	$16 \div 4 =$ _____
$10 \div 5 =$ _____	$8 \div 8 =$ _____	$9 \div 3 =$ _____	$12 \div 2 =$ _____
$72 \div 8 =$ _____	$0 \div 6 =$ _____	$12 \div 4 =$ _____	$20 \div 2 =$ _____
$35 \div 7 =$ _____	$18 \div 2 =$ _____	$21 \div 7 =$ _____	$70 \div 10 =$ _____
$18 \div 6 =$ _____	$49 \div 7 =$ _____	$9 \div 9 =$ _____	$81 \div 9 =$ _____
$32 \div 8 =$ _____	$60 \div 6 =$ _____	$30 \div 5 =$ _____	$54 \div 6 =$ _____
$8 \div 2 =$ _____	$54 \div 9 =$ _____	$6 \div 3 =$ _____	$27 \div 3 =$ _____
$6 \div 1 =$ _____	$7 \div 7 =$ _____	$14 \div 2 =$ _____	$12 \div 6 =$ _____
$90 \div 10 =$ _____	$7 \div 1 =$ _____	$48 \div 6 =$ _____	$27 \div 9 =$ _____
$5 \div 5 =$ _____	$70 \div 7 =$ _____	$21 \div 3 =$ _____	$20 \div 10 =$ _____
$63 \div 9 =$ _____	$30 \div 6 =$ _____	$48 \div 8 =$ _____	$0 \div 4 =$ _____
$15 \div 5 =$ _____	$72 \div 9 =$ _____	$2 \div 1 =$ _____	$45 \div 9 =$ _____
$42 \div 6 =$ _____	$45 \div 5 =$ _____	$0 \div 10 =$ _____	$18 \div 3 =$ _____
$6 \div 6 =$ _____	$50 \div 10 =$ _____	$100 \div 10 =$ _____	$63 \div 7 =$ _____
$40 \div 8 =$ _____	$0 \div 3 =$ _____	$40 \div 4 =$ _____	$4 \div 4 =$ _____
$14 \div 7 =$ _____	$18 \div 9 =$ _____	$16 \div 2 =$ _____	$80 \div 8 =$ _____
$15 \div 3 =$ _____	$24 \div 6 =$ _____	$0 \div 5 =$ _____	$28 \div 7 =$ _____

Name _____

Time: _____   Number Correct: _____

9 × 7 = _____	10 × 6 = _____	3 × 1 = _____	8 × 3 = _____
5 × 5 = _____	8 × 11 = _____	2 × 8 = _____	9 × 6 = _____
4 × 7 = _____	5 × 2 = _____	7 × 10 = _____	5 × 11 = _____
1 × 6 = _____	10 × 10 = _____	2 × 4 = _____	9 × 8 = _____
11 × 4 = _____	4 × 10 = _____	4 × 9 = _____	9 × 9 = _____
2 × 10 = _____	11 × 8 = _____	7 × 8 = _____	5 × 7 = _____
1 × 3 = _____	10 × 9 = _____	9 × 2 = _____	2 × 11 = _____
1 × 11 = _____	6 × 11 = _____	7 × 2 = _____	7 × 3 = _____
5 × 10 = _____	2 × 1 = _____	7 × 4 = _____	5 × 6 = _____
6 × 5 = _____	3 × 9 = _____	8 × 5 = _____	10 × 8 = _____
11 × 6 = _____	3 × 11 = _____	5 × 9 = _____	8 × 10 = _____
2 × 3 = _____	11 × 5 = _____	6 × 4 = _____	7 × 7 = _____
7 × 11 = _____	9 × 4 = _____	11 × 3 = _____	11 × 11 = _____
5 × 3 = _____	2 × 6 = _____	4 × 6 = _____	1 × 5 = _____
4 × 8 = _____	4 × 3 = _____	11 × 1 = _____	6 × 10 = _____
1 × 9 = _____	8 × 1 = _____	2 × 5 = _____	6 × 2 = _____
6 × 7 = _____	10 × 4 = _____	1 × 8 = _____	8 × 8 = _____
3 × 4 = _____	3 × 2 = _____	1 × 4 = _____	5 × 1 = _____
3 × 6 = _____	5 × 8 = _____	7 × 5 = _____	4 × 11 = _____
8 × 9 = _____	11 × 9 = _____	10 × 11 = _____	9 × 1 = _____
10 × 3 = _____	4 × 1 = _____	11 × 2 = _____	6 × 6 = _____
1 × 7 = _____	9 × 10 = _____	6 × 9 = _____	3 × 7 = _____
4 × 4 = _____	3 × 10 = _____	1 × 2 = _____	5 × 4 = _____
3 × 3 = _____	6 × 1 = _____	7 × 9 = _____	3 × 5 = _____
11 × 7 = _____	11 × 10 = _____	9 × 11 = _____	6 × 3 = _____

Name _____

Time: _____   Number Correct: _____

4 × 7 = _____	8 × 12 = _____	3 × 4 = _____	3 × 6 = _____
5 × 6 = _____	9 × 5 = _____	2 × 8 = _____	9 × 11 = _____
7 × 8 = _____	4 × 11 = _____	9 × 2 = _____	4 × 12 = _____
3 × 3 = _____	2 × 6 = _____	6 × 2 = _____	11 × 10 = _____
8 × 10 = _____	2 × 12 = _____	3 × 11 = _____	1 × 8 = _____
12 × 9 = _____	8 × 4 = _____	9 × 6 = _____	7 × 11 = _____
3 × 8 = _____	3 × 10 = _____	2 × 9 = _____	4 × 10 = _____
9 × 9 = _____	12 × 8 = _____	2 × 11 = _____	6 × 1 = _____
1 × 10 = _____	8 × 3 = _____	1 × 11 = _____	5 × 3 = _____
4 × 9 = _____	9 × 8 = _____	8 × 9 = _____	12 × 11 = _____
6 × 3 = _____	3 × 5 = _____	12 × 2 = _____	7 × 4 = _____
8 × 2 = _____	2 × 2 = _____	11 × 1 = _____	9 × 3 = _____
5 × 10 = _____	1 × 12 = _____	3 × 2 = _____	10 × 9 = _____
11 × 12 = _____	5 × 8 = _____	6 × 8 = _____	12 × 10 = _____
10 × 2 = _____	11 × 11 = _____	10 × 7 = _____	2 × 5 = _____
11 × 8 = _____	7 × 9 = _____	11 × 9 = _____	7 × 3 = _____
6 × 10 = _____	7 × 12 = _____	8 × 7 = _____	7 × 10 = _____
2 × 10 = _____	9 × 7 = _____	3 × 9 = _____	11 × 6 = _____
11 × 7 = _____	3 × 7 = _____	6 × 6 = _____	10 × 5 = _____
8 × 5 = _____	2 × 4 = _____	12 × 7 = _____	5 × 4 = _____
11 × 5 = _____	12 × 6 = _____	7 × 6 = _____	10 × 10 = _____
6 × 5 = _____	11 × 2 = _____	12 × 12 = _____	11 × 3 = _____
1 × 9 = _____	2 × 7 = _____	8 × 6 = _____	4 × 8 = _____
1 × 4 = _____	11 × 4 = _____	4 × 5 = _____	1 × 3 = _____
9 × 1 = _____	4 × 2 = _____	4 × 1 = _____	1 × 1 = _____

Math Timed Tests–Class Record Sheet

Student Names	Test 1 +/− Facts	Test 2 +/− Facts	Test 3 × Facts Through 10s	Test 4 × Facts Through 10s	Test 5 ÷ Facts	Test 6 ÷ Facts	Test 7 × Facts Through 11s	Test 8 × Facts Through 12s

Name _____

Math Test Page _____

1. Ⓐ Ⓑ Ⓒ Ⓓ   5. Ⓐ Ⓑ Ⓒ Ⓓ
2. Ⓐ Ⓑ Ⓒ Ⓓ   6. Ⓐ Ⓑ Ⓒ Ⓓ
3. Ⓐ Ⓑ Ⓒ Ⓓ   7. Ⓐ Ⓑ Ⓒ Ⓓ
4. Ⓐ Ⓑ Ⓒ Ⓓ   8. Ⓐ Ⓑ Ⓒ Ⓓ

9.   10.

Name _____

Math Test Page _____

1. Ⓐ Ⓑ Ⓒ Ⓓ   5. Ⓐ Ⓑ Ⓒ Ⓓ
2. Ⓐ Ⓑ Ⓒ Ⓓ   6. Ⓐ Ⓑ Ⓒ Ⓓ
3. Ⓐ Ⓑ Ⓒ Ⓓ   7. Ⓐ Ⓑ Ⓒ Ⓓ
4. Ⓐ Ⓑ Ⓒ Ⓓ   8. Ⓐ Ⓑ Ⓒ Ⓓ

9.   10.

Name _____

Math Test Page _____

1. Ⓐ Ⓑ Ⓒ Ⓓ   5. Ⓐ Ⓑ Ⓒ Ⓓ
2. Ⓐ Ⓑ Ⓒ Ⓓ   6. Ⓐ Ⓑ Ⓒ Ⓓ
3. Ⓐ Ⓑ Ⓒ Ⓓ   7. Ⓐ Ⓑ Ⓒ Ⓓ
4. Ⓐ Ⓑ Ⓒ Ⓓ   8. Ⓐ Ⓑ Ⓒ Ⓓ

9.   10.

Name _____

Math Test Page _____

1. Ⓐ Ⓑ Ⓒ Ⓓ   5. Ⓐ Ⓑ Ⓒ Ⓓ
2. Ⓐ Ⓑ Ⓒ Ⓓ   6. Ⓐ Ⓑ Ⓒ Ⓓ
3. Ⓐ Ⓑ Ⓒ Ⓓ   7. Ⓐ Ⓑ Ⓒ Ⓓ
4. Ⓐ Ⓑ Ⓒ Ⓓ   8. Ⓐ Ⓑ Ⓒ Ⓓ

9.   10.

EMC 3019 • Basic Math Skills, Grade 6 • ©2003 by Evan-Moor Corp.

Awards

You're a STⓈR

You're doing GREAT!
Keep up the good work!

MATH Genius

#1 in MATH

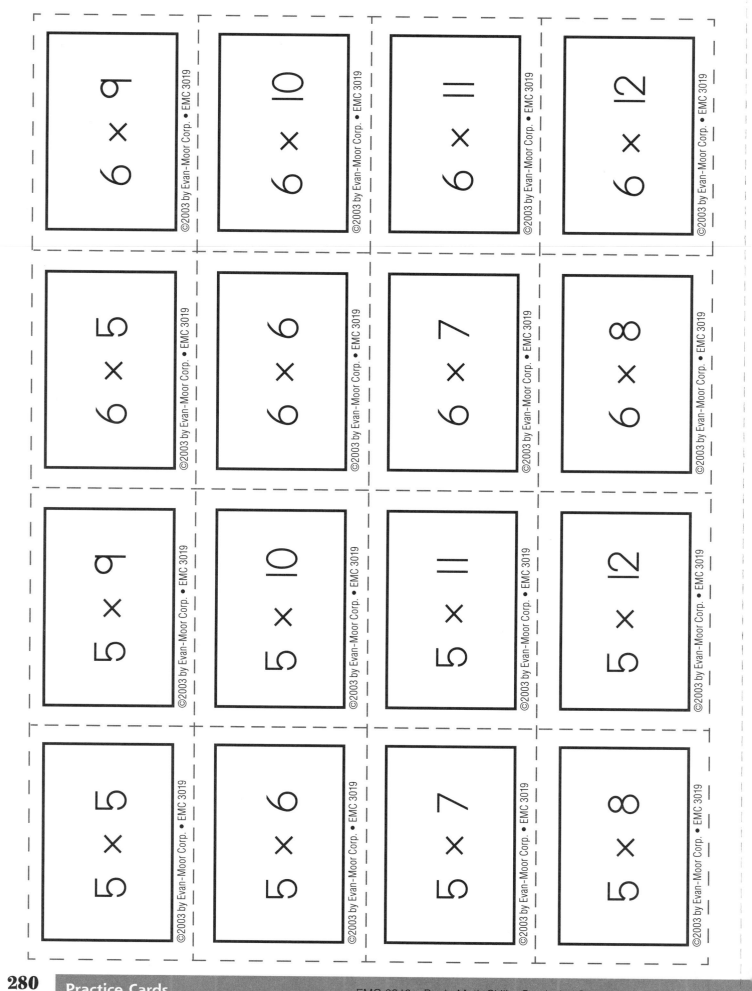

6 × 9   ©2003 by Evan-Moor Corp. • EMC 3019

6 × 10   ©2003 by Evan-Moor Corp. • EMC 3019

6 × 11   ©2003 by Evan-Moor Corp. • EMC 3019

6 × 12   ©2003 by Evan-Moor Corp. • EMC 3019

6 × 5   ©2003 by Evan-Moor Corp. • EMC 3019

6 × 6   ©2003 by Evan-Moor Corp. • EMC 3019

6 × 7   ©2003 by Evan-Moor Corp. • EMC 3019

6 × 8   ©2003 by Evan-Moor Corp. • EMC 3019

5 × 9   ©2003 by Evan-Moor Corp. • EMC 3019

5 × 10   ©2003 by Evan-Moor Corp. • EMC 3019

5 × 11   ©2003 by Evan-Moor Corp. • EMC 3019

5 × 12   ©2003 by Evan-Moor Corp. • EMC 3019

5 × 5   ©2003 by Evan-Moor Corp. • EMC 3019

5 × 6   ©2003 by Evan-Moor Corp. • EMC 3019

5 × 7   ©2003 by Evan-Moor Corp. • EMC 3019

5 × 8   ©2003 by Evan-Moor Corp. • EMC 3019

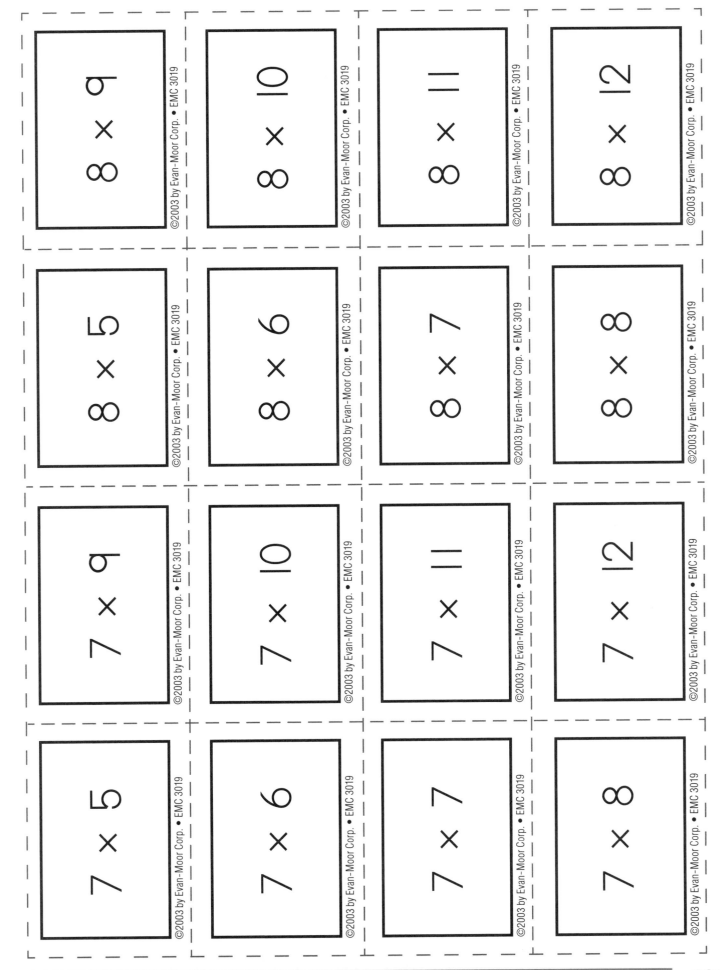

8 × 9	8 × 10	8 × 11	8 × 12
8 × 5	8 × 6	8 × 7	8 × 8
7 × 9	7 × 10	7 × 11	7 × 12
7 × 5	7 × 6	7 × 7	7 × 8

©2003 by Evan-Moor Corp. • EMC 3019

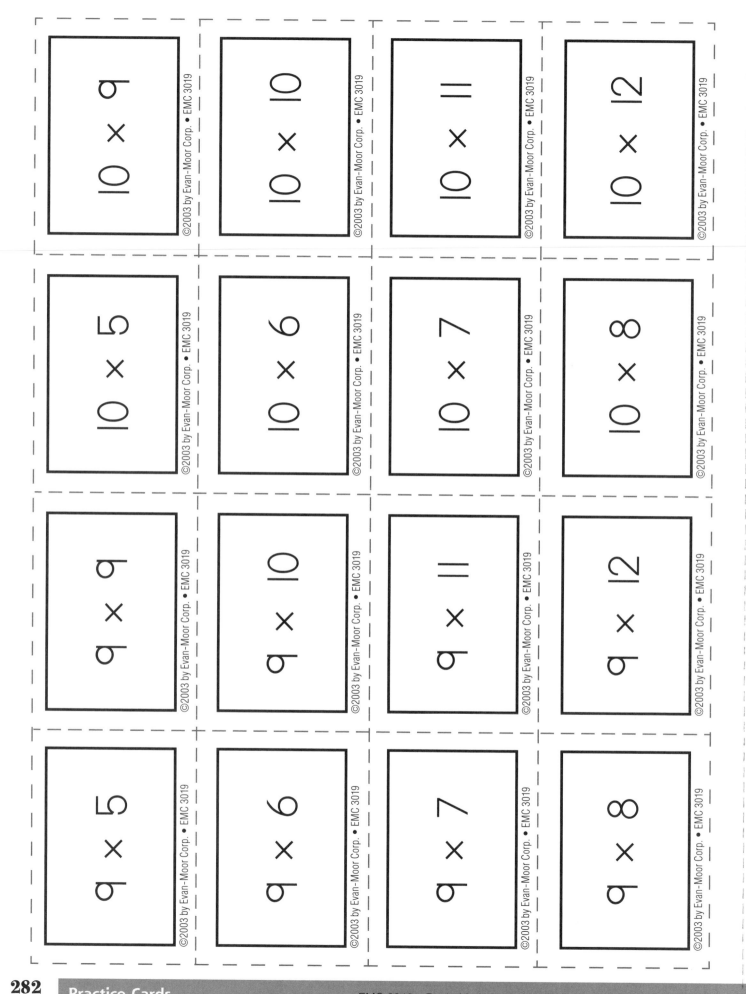

10×9	10×10	10×11	10×12
10×5	10×6	10×7	10×8
9×9	9×10	9×11	9×12
9×5	9×6	9×7	9×8

©2003 by Evan-Moor Corp. • EMC 3019

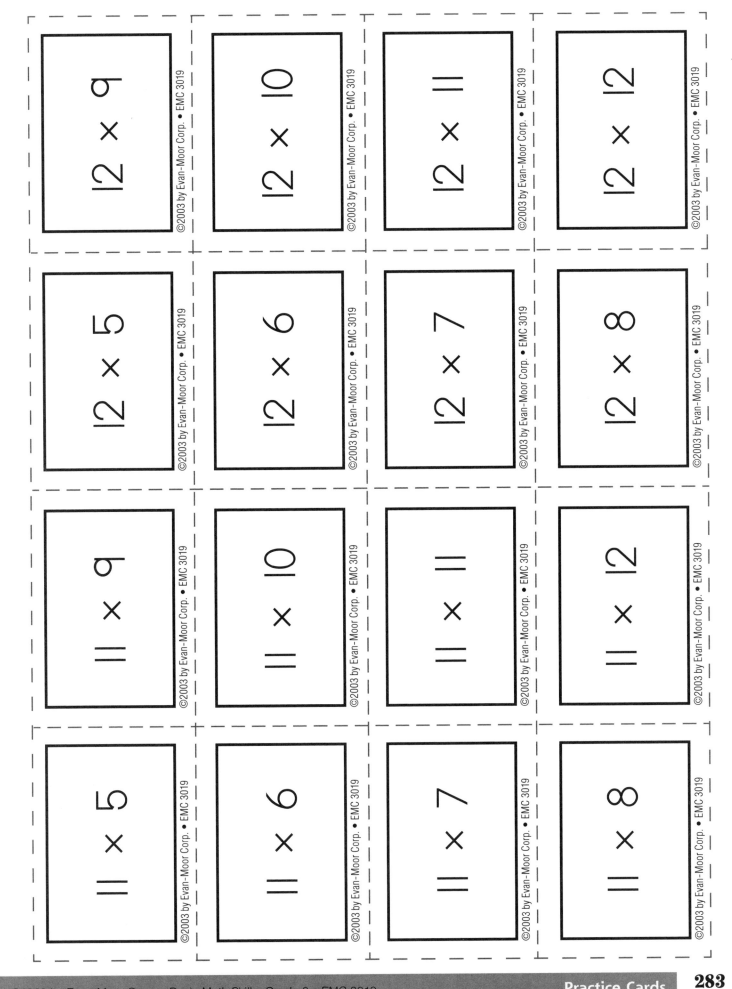

12 × 9

©2003 by Evan-Moor Corp. • EMC 3019

12 × 10

©2003 by Evan-Moor Corp. • EMC 3019

12 × 11

©2003 by Evan-Moor Corp. • EMC 3019

12 × 12

©2003 by Evan-Moor Corp. • EMC 3019

12 × 5

©2003 by Evan-Moor Corp. • EMC 3019

12 × 6

©2003 by Evan-Moor Corp. • EMC 3019

12 × 7

©2003 by Evan-Moor Corp. • EMC 3019

12 × 8

©2003 by Evan-Moor Corp. • EMC 3019

11 × 9

©2003 by Evan-Moor Corp. • EMC 3019

11 × 10

©2003 by Evan-Moor Corp. • EMC 3019

11 × 11

©2003 by Evan-Moor Corp. • EMC 3019

11 × 12

©2003 by Evan-Moor Corp. • EMC 3019

11 × 5

©2003 by Evan-Moor Corp. • EMC 3019

11 × 6

©2003 by Evan-Moor Corp. • EMC 3019

11 × 7

©2003 by Evan-Moor Corp. • EMC 3019

11 × 8

©2003 by Evan-Moor Corp. • EMC 3019

$9\overline{)63}$ ©2003 by Evan-Moor Corp. • EMC 3019

$9\overline{)54}$ ©2003 by Evan-Moor Corp. • EMC 3019

$9\overline{)45}$ ©2003 by Evan-Moor Corp. • EMC 3019

$9\overline{)36}$ ©2003 by Evan-Moor Corp. • EMC 3019

$10\overline{)10}$ ©2003 by Evan-Moor Corp. • EMC 3019

$10\overline{)0}$ ©2003 by Evan-Moor Corp. • EMC 3019

$9\overline{)18}$ ©2003 by Evan-Moor Corp. • EMC 3019

$9\overline{)72}$ ©2003 by Evan-Moor Corp. • EMC 3019

$10\overline{)50}$ ©2003 by Evan-Moor Corp. • EMC 3019

$10\overline{)40}$ ©2003 by Evan-Moor Corp. • EMC 3019

$10\overline{)30}$ ©2003 by Evan-Moor Corp. • EMC 3019

$10\overline{)20}$ ©2003 by Evan-Moor Corp. • EMC 3019

$10\overline{)90}$ ©2003 by Evan-Moor Corp. • EMC 3019

$10\overline{)80}$ ©2003 by Evan-Moor Corp. • EMC 3019

$10\overline{)70}$ ©2003 by Evan-Moor Corp. • EMC 3019

$10\overline{)60}$ ©2003 by Evan-Moor Corp. • EMC 3019

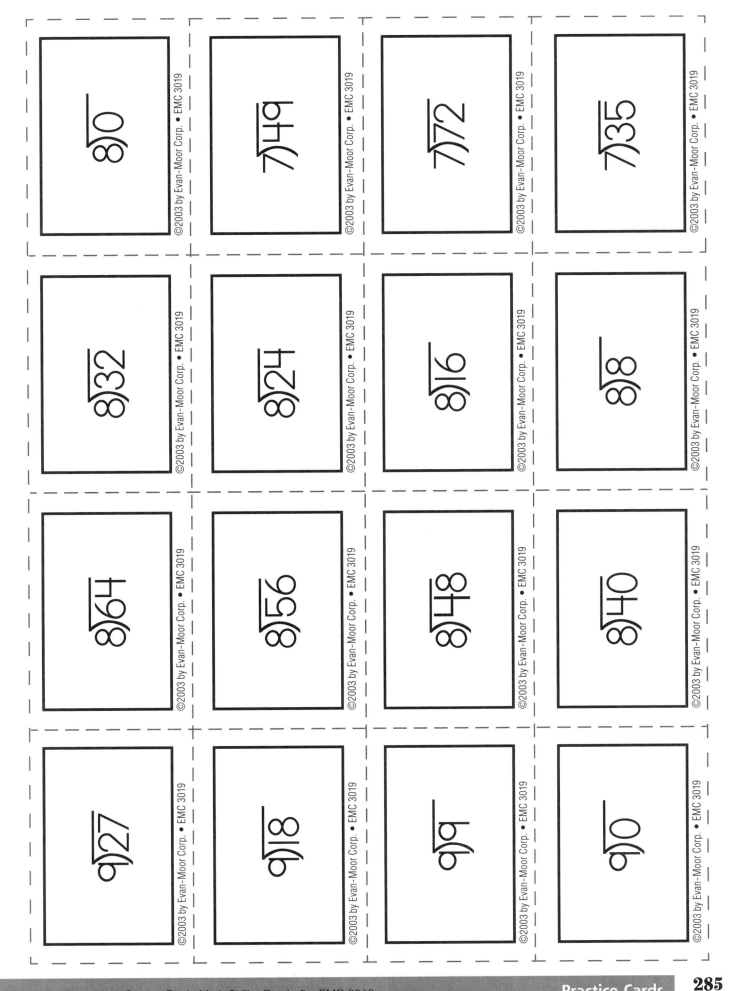

Each card displays a division problem (cards oriented sideways):

$8\overline{)0}$ $7\overline{)49}$ $7\overline{)72}$ $7\overline{)35}$

$8\overline{)32}$ $8\overline{)24}$ $8\overline{)16}$ $8\overline{)8}$

$8\overline{)64}$ $8\overline{)56}$ $8\overline{)48}$ $8\overline{)40}$

$9\overline{)27}$ $9\overline{)18}$ $9\overline{)9}$ $9\overline{)0}$

Answer Key

Page 5: Bluebirds in blue birdbaths

Page 6: A carpet slipper

Page 7	**Page 8**
1. 1,600	1. 1,140
2. 3,948	2. 2,928
3. 517	3. 14,444
4. 5,248	4. 17,892
5. 1,728	5. 36,849
6. 4,794	6. 77,420
7. 3,168	7. 32,000
8. 2,368	8. 47,940
9. 546	9. 44,268
10. 1,653	10. 54,318

Page 9

1. 840 chairs
2. $15,960
3. 384 years
4. 594 students
5. $4,158

Page 10

1. 768 sodas
2. 360 cupcakes
3. 1,620 pieces of candy
4. 840 cups and plates
5. Julie

Page 11

1. D
2. B
3. C
4. A
5. A
6. C
7. A
8. D
9. 2,304 pens
10. Answers will vary, but should require students to multiply 12 x 26.

Page 12: Luke likes licorice

Page 13: With hogs and kisses

Page 14

1. 25
2. 16
3. 47
4. 42
5. 72
6. 41
7. 800
8. 48
9. 70
10. 806

Page 15

1. 50
2. 52
3. 80
4. 10
5. 952
6. 43
7. 215
8. 420
9. 49
10. 419

Page 16

1. 32
2. 100
3. 525
4. 318 and 477; Answers will vary.

Page 17

1. 20 bags
2. 13 shelves
3. 21 pages
4. 209 sheets
5. 31 pieces

Page 18

1. B
2. B
3. C
4. D
5. B
6. C
7. C
8. A
9. 141 pages
10. 9 buses

Page 19: Flat feet

Page 20: Hot, because you can catch a cold

Page 21

1. 7
2. $7\frac{5}{8}$
3. $7\frac{1}{7}$
4. $7\frac{1}{3}$
5. $7\frac{2}{5}$
6. $\frac{7}{12}$
7. $\frac{29}{35}$
8. $\frac{5}{9}$
9. $4\frac{2}{15}$
10. $11\frac{7}{15}$

Page 22

1. $\frac{3}{7}$
2. $\frac{3}{8}$
3. $\frac{5}{14}$
4. $\frac{1}{9}$
5. $\frac{3}{10}$
6. $1\frac{1}{6}$
7. $5\frac{3}{5}$
8. $3\frac{1}{6}$
9. $5\frac{5}{12}$
10. $4\frac{5}{6}$

EMC 3019 • Basic Math Skills, Grade 6 • ©2003 by Evan-Moor Corp.

Page 23

1. $1\frac{1}{4}$ cups
2. $6\frac{5}{12}$ cups
3. $7\frac{1}{2}$ cups left; 72 cookies
4. $1\frac{3}{4}$ cups
5. $\frac{7}{12}$ cup

Page 24

1. Yes, $4\frac{1}{12}$ yards
2. No, $5\frac{7}{12}$ yards
3. Yes, $9\frac{5}{12}$ yards
4. Yes; $1\frac{5}{12}$ spools of thread
5. No, needs $5\frac{1}{4}$ yards

Page 25

1. C
2. A
3. B
4. D
5. A
6. B
7. D
8. C
9. Yes, $24\frac{5}{8}$ inches
10. $18\frac{7}{12}$ feet

Page 26: A piano; it has eighty-eight keys

Page 27: Spicy fish sauce

Page 28

1. $\frac{2}{15}$
2. $\frac{3}{28}$
3. $\frac{3}{16}$
4. $\frac{6}{35}$
5. $\frac{9}{28}$
6. $\frac{5}{27}$
7. $\frac{3}{10}$
8. $\frac{5}{18}$
9. $\frac{16}{27}$
10. $\frac{5}{24}$
11. $1\frac{1}{5}$
12. $\frac{2}{9}$
13. $1\frac{3}{7}$
14. 1
15. $\frac{3}{7}$
16. $\frac{1}{4}$
17. $\frac{1}{5}$
18. $\frac{2}{3}$
19. $\frac{1}{2}$
20. $\frac{2}{3}$

Page 29

1. $5\frac{1}{4}$
2. $8\frac{1}{2}$
3. $2\frac{1}{7}$
4. $10\frac{2}{7}$
5. $3\frac{17}{20}$
6. $15\frac{3}{4}$
7. $9\frac{3}{4}$
8. $10\frac{1}{2}$
9. $19\frac{1}{4}$
10. 7

Page 30

1. $1\frac{1}{2}$
2. $3\frac{2}{5}$
3. $4\frac{1}{5}$
4. $\frac{4}{8}$

Page 31

1. $18\frac{3}{4}$ square feet
2. 25 square feet
3. 290 square inches
4. 4 square feet
5. 144 square feet

Page 32

1. A
2. C
3. B
4. D
5. B
6. A
7. C
8. D
9. $\frac{15}{4} \times \frac{3}{1} = \frac{45}{4} = 11\frac{1}{4}$
10. $114\frac{1}{3}$ square inches

Page 33: A nightmare

Page 34: Attention

Page 35

1. $1\frac{1}{2}$
2. $\frac{8}{9}$
3. $\frac{4}{5}$
4. $1\frac{1}{5}$
5. 3
6. $1\frac{1}{3}$
7. $\frac{3}{5}$
8. 4
9. $3\frac{1}{3}$
10. $\frac{4}{9}$
11. $\frac{12}{35}$
12. $\frac{2}{3}$
13. $1\frac{3}{7}$
14. $\frac{9}{32}$
15. $\frac{3}{40}$

Page 36

1. $1\frac{7}{15}$
2. $2\frac{13}{16}$
3. 2
4. 3
5. $\frac{8}{13}$
6. $\frac{13}{20}$
7. $\frac{7}{9}$
8. $\frac{15}{16}$
9. 2
10. $\frac{5}{27}$
11. 3
12. $2\frac{1}{42}$
13. $1\frac{17}{32}$
14. $1\frac{3}{19}$
15. 2

Page 37

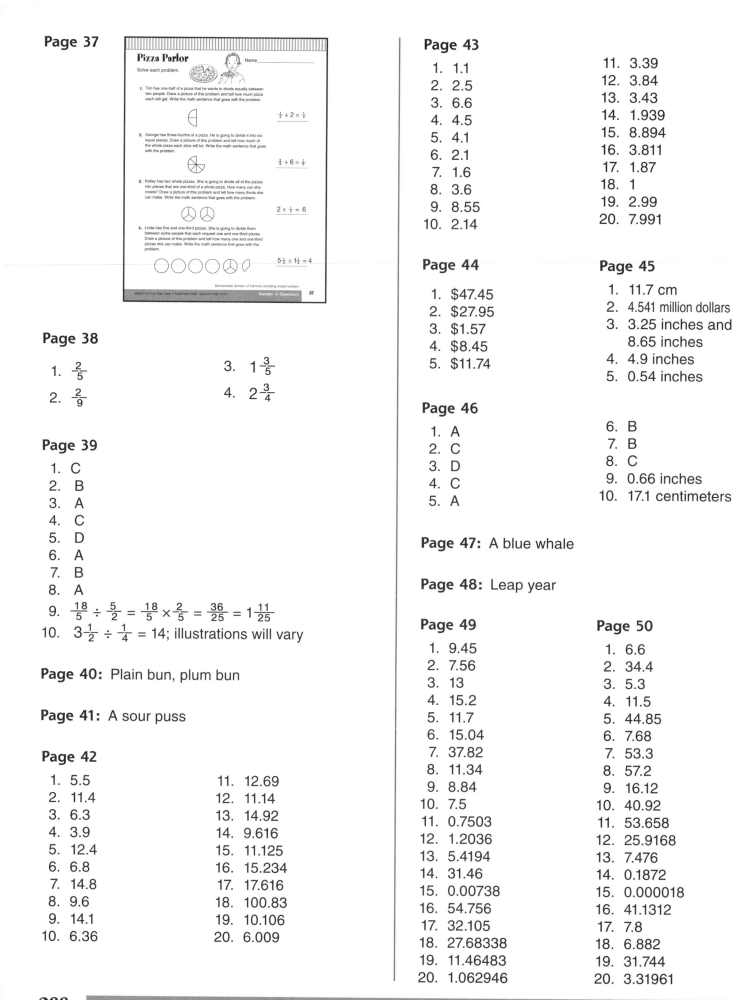

Page 38

1. $\frac{2}{5}$
2. $\frac{2}{9}$
3. $1\frac{3}{5}$
4. $2\frac{3}{4}$

Page 39

1. C
2. B
3. A
4. C
5. D
6. A
7. B
8. A
9. $\frac{18}{5} \div \frac{5}{2} = \frac{18}{5} \times \frac{2}{5} = \frac{36}{25} = 1\frac{11}{25}$
10. $3\frac{1}{2} \div \frac{1}{4} = 14$; illustrations will vary

Page 40: Plain bun, plum bun

Page 41: A sour puss

Page 42

1. 5.5
2. 11.4
3. 6.3
4. 3.9
5. 12.4
6. 6.8
7. 14.8
8. 9.6
9. 14.1
10. 6.36
11. 12.69
12. 11.14
13. 14.92
14. 9.616
15. 11.125
16. 15.234
17. 17.616
18. 100.83
19. 10.106
20. 6.009

Page 43

1. 1.1
2. 2.5
3. 6.6
4. 4.5
5. 4.1
6. 2.1
7. 1.6
8. 3.6
9. 8.55
10. 2.14
11. 3.39
12. 3.84
13. 3.43
14. 1.939
15. 8.894
16. 3.811
17. 1.87
18. 1
19. 2.99
20. 7.991

Page 44

1. $47.45
2. $27.95
3. $1.57
4. $8.45
5. $11.74

Page 46

1. A
2. C
3. D
4. C
5. A

Page 47: A blue whale

Page 48: Leap year

Page 49

1. 9.45
2. 7.56
3. 13
4. 15.2
5. 11.7
6. 15.04
7. 37.82
8. 11.34
9. 8.84
10. 7.5
11. 0.7503
12. 1.2036
13. 5.4194
14. 31.46
15. 0.00738
16. 54.756
17. 32.105
18. 27.68338
19. 11.46483
20. 1.062946

Page 45

1. 11.7 cm
2. 4.541 million dollars
3. 3.25 inches and 8.65 inches
4. 4.9 inches
5. 0.54 inches
6. B
7. B
8. C
9. 0.66 inches
10. 17.1 centimeters

Page 50

1. 6.6
2. 34.4
3. 5.3
4. 11.5
5. 44.85
6. 7.68
7. 53.3
8. 57.2
9. 16.12
10. 40.92
11. 53.658
12. 25.9168
13. 7.476
14. 0.1872
15. 0.000018
16. 41.1312
17. 7.8
18. 6.882
19. 31.744
20. 3.31961

Page 51

1. 5.73
2. 2.61
3. 4.374
4. 76.245

Page 52

1. $356.25
2. $100 ($100.24)
3. No, the total is $67
4. $49.80
5. $343.85

Page 53

1. B
2. B
3. A
4. C
5. D
6. D
7. C
8. A
9. $74.75
10. 7.8645

Page 54: Moo York

Page 55: Red leather, yellow leather

Page 56

1. 4
2. 0.6
3. 1.3
4. 2.9
5. 5.1
6. 5.12
7. 3.4
8. 4.08
9. 6.72
10. 4.19

Page 57

1. 3.2
2. 4.6
3. 5.2
4. 6.54
5. 2.2
6. 0.23
7. 0.11
8. 200
9. 3.5
10. 5.2

Page 58

1. 35¢, 15¢ profit
2. 34¢, 16¢ profit
3. by the case; 24¢

Page 59

1. 12.6
2. 3.75
3. 14.6
4. 13.35

Page 60

1. D
2. C
3. A
4. A
5. C
6. B
7. D
8. D
9. 4.125 ounces
10. 37¢

Page 61: Time to get a new clock

Page 62: It improves his service

Page 63

1. 25
2. 6
3. 12
4. 35
5. 24
6. 36
7. 7
8. 16
9. 22
10. 16
11. 42
12. 5
13. 63
14. 27
15. 5
16. 7
17. 24
18. 63
19. 12
20. 41

Page 64

1. 3
2. 25
3. 14
4. 150
5. 2
6. 12
7. 4
8. 30
9. 2
10. 38
11. 32
12. 44
13. 6
14. 51
15. 18
16. 150

Page 65

1. $72
2. $38
3. $15
4. $18
5. $22.50 each

Page 66

1. $5,300
2. $3,375
3. $6,300
4. $2,400 and $9,600
5. $162.50 and $86.67

Page 67

1. A
2. C
3. C
4. D
5. B
6. B
7. A
8. D
9. $33.75
10. $7.20

Page 68: Three blind mice blew bugles

Page 69: A box of matches

Page 70

1. 25%
2. $\frac{1}{2}$
3. 0.7, 70%
4. $\frac{3}{4}$, 0.75
5. $\frac{4}{5}$, 80%
6. 0.4, 40%
7. 0.125, 12.5%
8. $\frac{3}{8}$, 0.375
9. $\frac{9}{10}$, 90%
10. $\frac{5}{8}$, 62.5%

Page 71

1. $\frac{1}{2}$, 0.5
2. 0.125, 12.5%
3. $\frac{7}{8}$, 87.5%
4. 0.25, 25%
5. $\frac{5}{8}$, 0.625
6. 0.7, 70%
7. $\frac{3}{10}$, 30%
8. $\frac{3}{4}$, 75%
9. $\frac{9}{10}$, 0.9
10. $\frac{3}{8}$, 37.5%

Page 72

1. 0.4
2. $\frac{1}{5}$ off
3. 0.065
4. 41%
5. Need the original prices for each store; if they were the same prices, then the sales prices would also be the same.

Page 73

1. 95%
2. 40%
3. 85%
4. 76%
5. 4%
6. $\frac{2}{5}$
7. $\frac{1}{2}$
8. $\frac{1}{4}$

Page 74

1. B
2. C
3. C
4. D
5. A
6. C
7. A
8. B
9. $\frac{1}{4}$ and 0.25
10. Answers will vary, for example, move the decimal point two places to the right.

Page 75: Floodlights

Page 76: Stepfarther

Page 77

1. True
2. True
3. False
4. False
5. True
6. False
7. True
8. True
9. False
10. True
11. False
12. True
13. False
14. True
15. False
16. False
17. True
18. False
19. True
20. False

Page 78

1. >
2. <
3. >
4. =
5. >
6. <
7. <
8. <
9. <
10. =
11. =
12. >
13. <
14. <
15. <
16. <
17. =
18. <
19. >
20. <

Page 79

1. Answers will vary.
2. Answers will vary: Mary is incorrect; she could compare 614 to 620.
3. $\leq$, $\geq$, and =
4. Luke is correct

Page 80

1. $56.25 < $63
2. $18 < $24
3. $40.50 < $52.50
4. $39.20 < $41.33
5. $67.50 < $68 < $72

Page 81

1. A
2. C
3. D
4. C
5. D
6. A
7. B
8. C
9. 3.51 > 3.5
10. 15.82 < 15.8201

Page 82: It was toad away

Page 83: Three pairs of pants

Page 84

1. 5×5
2. $2 \times 2 \times 2 \times 2 \times 2$
3. $2 \times 2 \times 2 \times 2 \times 2 \times 2$
4. $2 \times 5 \times 5$
5. $2 \times 2 \times 2 \times 2 \times 3$
6. 7×7
7. $2 \times 2 \times 2 \times 3$
8. $2 \times 2 \times 2 \times 2$
9. $2 \times 2 \times 2 \times 3 \times 3$
10. $2 \times 2 \times 17$
11. $2 \times 3 \times 5$
12. $2 \times 2 \times 2$
13. $2 \times 2 \times 3$
14. $2 \times 2 \times 19$
15. $2 \times 2 \times 2 \times 2 \times 5$
16. 3×3
17. 2×5
18. $2 \times 2 \times 3 \times 3$
19. $3 \times 3 \times 3$
20. $3 \times 3 \times 3 \times 3$

Page 85

1. $2 \times 2 \times 2 \times 5 \times 5$
2. $2 \times 3 \times 3 \times 11$
3. $3 \times 5 \times 7$
4. $2 \times 2 \times 3 \times 3 \times 5$
5. $2 \times 2 \times 2 \times 3 \times 7$
6. $2 \times 3 \times 17$
7. $2 \times 2 \times 2 \times 2 \times 2 \times 5$
8. $2 \times 2 \times 2 \times 23$
9. $2 \times 2 \times 3 \times 3 \times 3$
10. $2 \times 2 \times 3 \times 11$
11. $2 \times 2 \times 3 \times 17$
12. $2 \times 2 \times 2 \times 3 \times 5$
13. $2 \times 3 \times 5 \times 7$
14. $5 \times 5 \times 7$
15. $2 \times 2 \times 2 \times 2 \times 3 \times 3$
16. $3 \times 7 \times 7$
17. $3 \times 3 \times 5 \times 5$
18. 11×11
19. $2 \times 2 \times 3 \times 13$
20. 5×43

Page 86

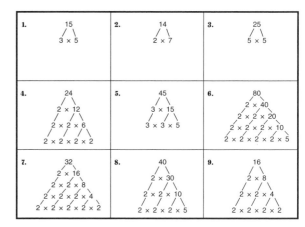

Page 87

1. $2 \underline{|18}$ $3 \underline{|9}$ 3	2. $2 \underline{|20}$ $2 \underline{|10}$ 5	3. $2 \underline{|24}$ $2 \underline{|12}$ $2 \underline{|6}$ 3
4. $3 \underline{|15}$ 5	5. $2 \underline{|30}$ $3 \underline{|15}$ 5	6. $2 \underline{|22}$ 11
7. $3 \underline{|27}$ $3 \underline{|9}$ 3	8. $2 \underline{|60}$ $2 \underline{|30}$ $3 \underline{|15}$ 5	9. $2 \underline{|48}$ $2 \underline{|24}$ $2 \underline{|12}$ $2 \underline{|6}$ 3

Page 88

1. A
2. C
3. B
4. D
5. B
6. C
7. A
8. A
9. (factor tree)
   20 → 2, 10; 10 → 2, 5; 2 → 2, 2
10. $2 \underline{|30}$ $3 \underline{|15}$ 5

Page 89: Fleas fly from flies

Page 9: A tennis ball

Page 91

1. 2
2. 3
3. 5
4. 4
5. 2
6. 2
7. 1
8. 2
9. 1
10. 1
11. 3
12. 5
13. 4
14. 4
15. 20
16. 10
17. 25
18. 9
19. 6
20. 1

Page 92
1. 5
2. 2
3. 12
4. 9
5. 30
6. 5
7. 1
8. 23
9. 16
10. 4

Page 93
1. 8
2. C
3. C
4. C
5. 1
6. C
7. 1
8. 15
9. 14
10. C

Page 94
1. $\frac{1}{3}$
2. $\frac{1}{3}$
3. $\frac{1}{2}$
4. $\frac{3}{4}$
5. $\frac{4}{7}$
6. $\frac{1}{3}$
7. $\frac{4}{5}$
8. $\frac{5}{6}$
9. $\frac{1}{3}$
10. $\frac{6}{7}$

Page 95
1. D
2. B
3. C
4. A
5. D
6. A
7. C
8. B
9. 1, 2, 4, 8
10. 8

Page 96: Twenty-four thousand

Page 97: Tweatment

Page 98
1. 8
2. 28
3. 40
4. 30
5. 48
6. 120
7. 72
8. 91
9. 34
10. 330

Page 99
1. 12
2. 18
3. 28
4. 18
5. 30
6. 72
7. 60
8. 60
9. 120
10. 165

Page 100
1. 15
2. 35
3. 6
4. 20
5. 45
6. 60
7. 120
8. 45
9. 99
10. 144

Page 101

1. 2, 3

2. 3, 5

3. 2, 5

Page 102
1. C
2. A
3. B
4. D
5. A
6. B
7. A
8. D
9. 4, 8, 12, 16, 20, 24, 28 and 7, 14, 21, 28, 35, 42, 49
10. 28

Page 104: A fence

Page 105: Clean clams

Page 106
1. 28, 38, 43, 50
2. 10, 4, 0, ⁻2
3. 5, 16, 24, 35
4. 7, 11, 21, 33
5. 3, 9, 24, 20
6. 52, 15, 19, ⁻2
7. 24, 12, 5, ⁻3
8. 2, 3, 21, 11
9. 5, 4, 8, 10

Page 107
1. 5.45, 4.55, 6.61, 2.75
2. 1.75, 2.94, 4.15, 6.75
3. 3, 11, 17, 22
4. $11\frac{1}{2}$, $4\frac{1}{2}$, 8, 0
5. 5, 7, 8.5, 29
6. 8.74, 7.46, 11.3, 1.6
7. 8.41, 8.91, 10.41, 11
8. $1\frac{1}{4}$, $2\frac{1}{4}$, $3\frac{1}{4}$, 12
9. $4\frac{1}{2}$, 5, 7, 16

EMC 3019 • Basic Math Skills, Grade 6 • ©2003 by Evan-Moor Corp.

Page 108

Total Length of Path (Input)	Number of Gray Stones Rule = input ×2 +2	Number of White Stones Rule = input −2
11 stones (example)	24	9
15 stones	32	13
20 stones	42	18
45 stones	92	43
100 stones	202	98
240 stones	482	238
31	64	29
60	122	58
62	126	60
152	306	150

Page 109

Sheep (S)	Geese (G)	Total Number of Legs Rule is (4 × S) + (2 × G)
9	1	(9 × 4) + (2 × 1) = (36) + (2) = 38
8	2	36
7	3	34
6	4	32
5	5	30
4	6	28
3	7	26
2	8	24
1	9	22

Page 110

1. B
2. D
3. A
4. B
5. C
6. D
7. A
8. B
9. Answers will vary.
10. Answers will vary.

Page 111: Yell-oh

Page 112: Fry-day

Page 113

1. +1
2. −4
3. ×2 +1
4. ×3 −4
5. +1 ×2
6. ÷3 +1
7. ÷2 −1
8. ×3 +1
9. ×2 −2

Page 114

1. +5
2. −8
3. ×3 +1
4. ×5 −2
5. ÷2 +1
6. ÷3 −2
7. times 1 or plus zero
8. times zero or minus itself
9. × 11

Page 115

Answers will vary, for example:
1. ×4, ×3 +6, +18
2. −3, ÷2 +6, ÷3 +9
3. +8, ×2 −4, ÷2 +14
4. ÷4, −6, ×2 −14
5. −12, ÷2 −2, ÷5 ×2

Page 116

Total Length of the Path	Number of Gray Stones	Number of White Stones
(Input)	If the input is even, the rule is: ×3 ÷2 If the input is odd, the rule is: ×3 +1 ÷2	If the input is even, the rule is: ×3 ÷2 If the input is odd, the rule is: ×3 −1 ÷2
5 stones	8	7
8 stones	12	12
11 stones	17	16
100 stones	150	150

Page 117

1. C
2. B
3. A
4. B
5. B
6. A
7. A
8. D

9. Answers will vary, for example: ×2 +1, +3, ×3 −1
10. Answers will vary, for example: −3, ÷2 +2, ÷5 +5

Page 118: Free fruit flies

Page 119: A ham sandwich

Page 120

Page 121

Page 122

$3\frac{1}{4}$, $3\frac{1}{2}$, $4\frac{2}{3}$, $4\frac{3}{4}$, $5\frac{1}{4}$, $5\frac{1}{3}$, $5\frac{1}{2}$, $6\frac{1}{3}$, $6\frac{2}{3}$, $6\frac{3}{4}$

Page 123

3.8, 4.2, 4.7, 4.8, 4.9, 5.2, 5.5, 5.8, 6.2, 6.5

Page 124

1. B
2. A
3. D
4. C

5. B
6. D
7. C
8. A

9.

10.

Page 125

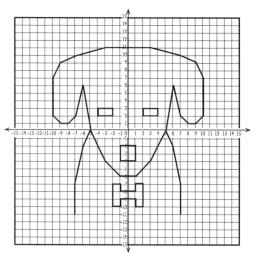

Page 126

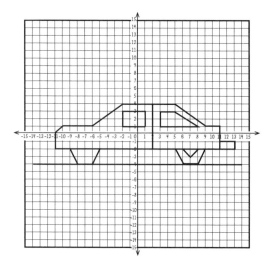

Page 127

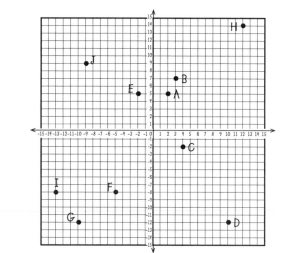

Page 128

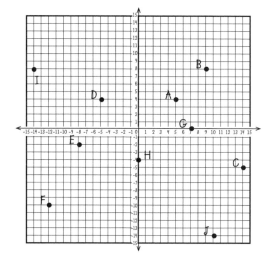

Page 129

1. (−5, 6)
2. City Bank is W, Town Food Court is Y
3. (6, −5)
4.

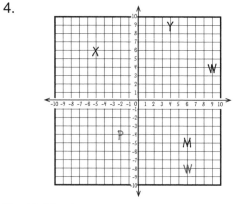

5. 12 blocks

1. (−4, −8)
2. City Market is Y and Town Bank is W

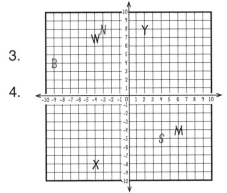

3.
4.

5. 22 blocks
6. Answers will vary.

Page 131

1. A
2. C
3. D
4. B
5. B
6. C
7. A
8. D

9. 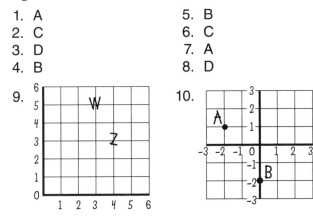 10.

Page 132: A flower with square roots

Page 133: A dinosnore

Page 134

1. 11
2. 36
3. 2
4. 49
5. 41
6. 6
7. 17
8. 18
9. 3
10. 7
11. 8
12. 12
13. 25
14. 17
15. 22
16. 18
17. 3
18. 2
19. 24
20. 14

Page 135

1. 72
2. 2
3. 10
4. 5
5. 23
6. 22
7. 14
8. 5
9. 55
10. 27
11. 15
12. 128
13. 14
14. 50
15. 10
16. 18
17. 55
18. 19
19. 78
20. 20

Page 136

1. Disagree; explanations will vary, for example, in problem a, you do the subtraction before the addition (left to right), but in b, you do the addition before the subtraction (because of the parentheses). The answer to a is 19 and the answer to b is 15.

2. Agree; explanations will vary, for example, with or without the parenthesis, you do the multiplication in this problem first. The answer is 14 for both problems.

3. Answers will vary, for example, do multiplication before addition, so start with the 4 x 3. The answer is 103.

Page 137

Trapezoid 1 = 15 square inches
Trapezoid 2 = 26 square inches
Trapezoid 3 = 75 square inches

Page 138

1. C
2. B
3. D
4. A
5. C
6. A
7. B
8. A
9. Answers will vary.
10. Answers will vary.

Page 139: Lots of broken telephone poles

Page 140: Elegant elephants

Page 141

1. 1
2. 4
3. 0
4. 9
5. 15
6. 3
7. 9
8. 4
9. 21
10. 13
11. 17
12. 11
13. 21
14. 17
15. 40
16. 30
17. 98
18. 10
19. 20
20. 73

Page 142

1. 4
2. 5
3. 4
4. 0
5. 5
6. 8
7. 12
8. 52
9. 9
10. 7
11. 24
12. 30
13. 75
14. 56
15. 77
16. 29
17. 66
18. 3
19. 9
20. 80

Page 143

2. is incorrect; he should have added 5 to each side.

8. is incorrect, he should have subtracted 18 from each side.

All others are correct.

Page 144

1. $x + 3 = 38$; $x = 35$
2. $x - 15 = 45$; $x = 60$
3. $18 + x = 30$; $x = 12$
4. $x - 36 = 85$; $x = 121$
5. $x + 62 = 130$; $x = 68$
6. $x - 49 = 15$; $x = 64$
7. $x - 22 = 54$; $x = 76$
8. $x + 55 = 108$; $x = 53$
9. $25 - x = 7$; $x = 18$
10. $653 + x = 1,637$; $x = 984$

Page 145

1. A
2. B
3. B
4. D
5. D
6. D
7. A
8. B
9. $x - 15 = 8$
10. $x = 23$

Page 146: A man with a splitting headache

Page 147: Picky pickpockets

Page 148

1. 3
2. 8
3. 6
4. 6
5. 3
6. 20
7. 48
8. 15
9. 25
10. 12
11. 7
12. 1
13. 125
14. 20
15. 15
16. 80
17. 16
18. 45
19. 7
20. 28
21. 9

Page 149

1. 4
2. 6
3. 6
4. 4
5. 11
6. 14
7. 27
8. 7
9. 48
10. 0
11. 5
12. 8
13. 72
14. 5
15. 8
16. 100
17. 7
18. 30
19. 40
20. 162
21. 1,000

Page 150

3. is incorrect, she should have multiplied by 6 on both sides.

7. is incorrect, she should have divided by 7 on both sides.

10. is incorrect, she should have multiplied by 4 on both sides.

All others are correct.

Page 151

1. $3x = 36$; $x = 12$
2. $x \div 8 = 3$; $x = 24$
3. $8x = 48$; $x = 6$
4. $30x = 90$; $x = 3$
5. $x \div 3 = 5$; $x = 15$
6. $12x = 108$; $x = 9$
7. $x \div 15 = 5$; $x = 75$
8. $15x = 345$; $x = 23$
9. $x \div 25 = 12$; $x = 300$
10. $8x = 208$; $x = 26$

EMC 3019 • Basic Math Skills, Grade 6 • ©2003 by Evan-Moor Corp.

Page 152

1. B
2. A
3. B
4. D
5. B

6. A
7. D
8. C
9. $5x = 80$
10. $x = 16$

Page 154: Do thick tinkers think?

Page 155: Mews at Ten

Page 156

1. rotated 90°
2. rotated 90° or reflected
3. rotated 90°
4. translated, rotated 180° or reflected
5. rotated 180° or reflected
6. rotated 90°

Page 157

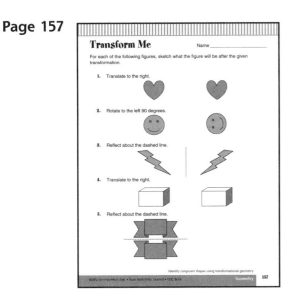

Page 158

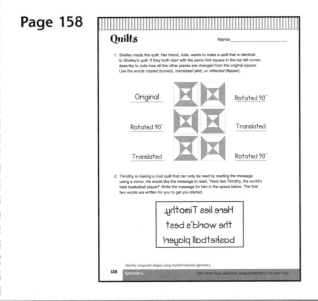

Page 159

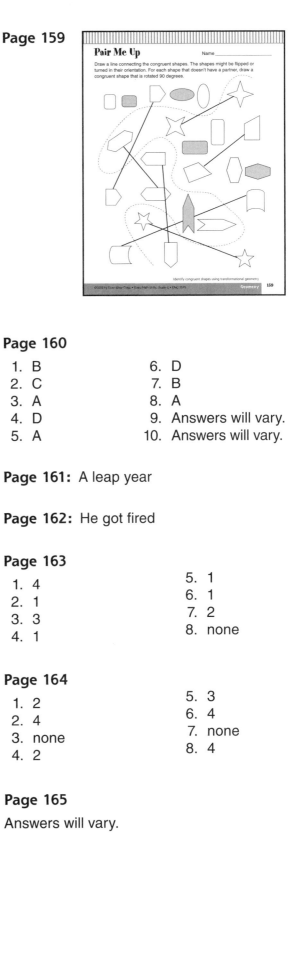

Page 160

1. B
2. C
3. A
4. D
5. A

6. D
7. B
8. A
9. Answers will vary.
10. Answers will vary.

Page 161: A leap year

Page 162: He got fired

Page 163

1. 4
2. 1
3. 3
4. 1

5. 1
6. 1
7. 2
8. none

Page 164

1. 2
2. 4
3. none
4. 2

5. 3
6. 4
7. none
8. 4

Page 165

Answers will vary.

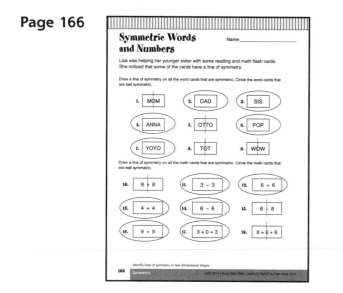

1. C
2. D
3. A
4. B
5. D

6. A
7. C
8. A
9. Answers will vary.
10. Answers will vary.

Page 168: Sleuth

Page 169: A frog horn

Page 170

1. obtuse
2. acute
3. obtuse
4. acute
5. acute
6. obtuse
7. right
8. obtuse

Page 171

1. acute
2. obtuse
3. obtuse
4. obtuse
5. obtuse
6. acute
7. right
8. acute

Page 172

Answers will vary.

Page 173

1. Answers will vary. For example, someone turning halfway around a circle; 180 degrees

2. Answers will vary. For example, someone turning all the way around in a circle; 360 degrees

3. Answers will vary; yes, it does matter which way you turn.

4. Answers will vary; No, it does not matter which way you turn.

5. 1,080 degrees

Page 174

1. A
2. B
3. C
4. B
5. C

6. B
7. A
8. A
9. Answers will vary.
10. Answers will vary.

Page 175: A wet sponge

Page 176: Mustard

Page 177

Figure	Number of Faces	Number of Edges	Number of Vertices
	6	12	8
	6	12	8
	5	9	6
	5	8	5
	7	12	7

Number of faces + vertices – number of edges = 2

Page 178

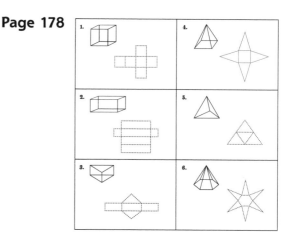

Page 179

	Tetrahedron	Octahedron
Number of faces	4	8
Shape of faces	equilateral triangle	equilateral triangle
Number of vertices	4	6
Number of faces that meet at each vertex	3	3

Page 180

1. Answers will vary.
2. 5 faces, 8 edges, and 5 vertices
3. 8 faces, 18 edges, and 12 vertices

Page 181

1. C
2. B
3. D
4. A
5. C
6. C
7. C
8. B
9. Answers will vary.
10. Answers will vary.

Page 183: A cheetah

Page 184: Your teeth

Page 185

1. $5\frac{1}{4}$ inches
2. $3\frac{3}{4}$ inches
3. 4 inches
4. $3\frac{1}{4}$ inches
5. $2\frac{3}{4}$ inches
6. $5\frac{3}{4}$ inches
7. $4\frac{1}{2}$ inches
8. $1\frac{1}{4}$ inches
9. $2\frac{1}{4}$ inches
10. 3 inches

Page 186

1. $5\frac{1}{2}$ centimeters
2. $13\frac{1}{2}$ centimeters
3. 4 centimeters
4. $9\frac{1}{2}$ centimeters
5. 12 centimeters
6. $8\frac{1}{2}$ centimeters
7. 6 centimeters
8. 10 centimeters
9. $7\frac{1}{2}$ centimeters
10. 11 centimeters

Page 187

Answers will vary.

Page 188

Answers will vary.

Page 189

1. C
2. D
3. B
4. A
5. C
6. C
7. D
8. D

9. 3 centimeters
10. Any rectangle that measures 6 centimeters by 3 centimeters.

Page 190: Tacky tractor trailer trucks

Page 191: A Cow-culator

Page 192

1. 12
2. 5,280
3. 2
4. 84
5. 7
6. 5,280
7. 180
8. 7,920
9. $2\frac{2}{3}$
10. 10,560

Page 193

1. 100
2. 2,000
3. 60
4. 1.5
5. 600
6. 80
7. 175
8. 50
9. 300,000
10. 52

Page 194

Answers will vary. Examples:

1. Timothy, because he went 300 feet in 21 seconds while it would have taken Juan 96 seconds to run the same 300 feet

2. Harold, because it would take him only 4 minutes 10 seconds to run one kilometer at his current rate, 5 seconds faster than Gerald

3. Darcy, because she walked 12 meters

4. 9,880 meters

5. 292 feet

Page 195

1. Yes, they have $10\frac{1}{2}$ feet
2. 8 packages
3. 4 packages
4. Answers will vary, but should be at least $1\frac{1}{2}$ meters.
5. 8.2 centimeters

Page 196

1. D
2. C
3. B
4. D
5. A
6. B
7. A
8. B

9. Answers will vary. (e.g., 1 yard, 3 feet)
10. Answers will vary. (e.g., 1 meter, 1,000 millimeters)

Page 197: A red car-nation

Page 198: A dead centipede

Page 199

1. 40 minutes
2. 45 minutes
3. 1 hour 5 minutes
4. 2 hours 25 minutes
5. 3 hours 52 minutes
6. 12 hours 45 minutes
7. 54 minutes
8. 6 hours 10 minutes
9. 4 hours 5 minutes
10. 16 hours 22 minutes

Page 200

1. 1 hour 45 minutes
2. 55 minutes
3. 4 hours 8 minutes
4. 8:05 A.M.
5. 9:50 P.M.
6. 11:09 A.M.
7. 5:12 P.M.
8. 7:28 A.M.
9. 15 hours 58 minutes
10. 5:33 A.M.

Page 201

1. 1 hour 30 minutes
2. 47 minutes
3. 6:24 A.M.
4. 5:02 P.M.
5. No, because it is only 28 minutes.
6. 6 hours 53 minutes
7. Yes, 22 minutes
8. 3 stars

Page 202

1. 5:11 P.M.
2. 6:27 P.M.
3. 24 minutes
4. 5:35 P.M.
5. 3:50 P.M.
6. 9:07 P.M.

Page 203

1. A
2. C
3. D
4. B
5. B
6. D
7. A
8. A
9. 6:33 P.M.
10. 6 hours 30 minutes

Page 204: A lunch break

Page 205: A right angle

Page 206

1. 90°
2. 135°
3. 75°
4. 125°
5. 45°
6. 145°
7. 55°
8. 140°

Page 207

1. 110°
2. 115°
3. 130°
4. 30°
5. 120°
6. 160°
7. 35°
8. 145°

Page 208

Answers will vary.

Page 209

Magnification should have all angles the same size as the original and all sides twice as long as the original.

Page 210

1. A
2. C
3. B
4. A
5. D
6. B
7. B
8. C
9. Any angle that measures 45.
10. Any angle that measures 120 degrees.

Page 211: Greece

Page 212: Bad black bran bread

Page 213

1. 16 units
2. 28 units
3. 40 units
4. 20 units
5. 20 units
6. 17 units
7. 22 units
8. 22 units
9. 48 units
10. 40 units

Page 214

1. 40 units
2. 24 units
3. 30 units
4. 20.4 units
5. 28 units
6. 21 units
7. 31.4 units
8. 27.1 units
9. $29\frac{1}{3}$ units
10. 32 units

Page 215: Answers will vary.

EMC 3019 • Basic Math Skills, Grade 6 • ©2003 by Evan-Moor Corp.

Page 216

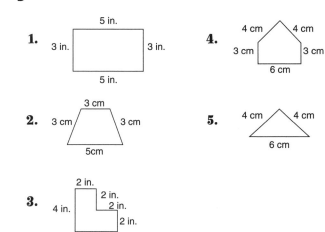

1. 5 in. / 3 in. / 3 in. / 5 in.
2. 3 cm / 3 cm / 3 cm / 5cm
3. 2 in. / 4 in. / 2 in. / 2 in. / 2 in. / 4 in
4. 4 cm / 4 cm / 3 cm / 3 cm / 6 cm
5. 4 cm / 4 cm / 6 cm

Page 217

1. B
2. D
3. C
4. A
5. B
6. C
7. D
8. D

9. Any figure with a perimeter of 20 units.
10. Any figure with a perimeter of 15 units.

Page 218: Ape cakes

Page 219: A centipede with athlete's foot

Page 220

1. 42 square units
2. 16 square units
3. 24 square units
4. 20 square units
5. 60 square units
6. 16 square units
7. 225 square units
8. 162 square units
9. 441 square units
10. 54 square units

Page 221

1. 30 square units
2. 100 square units
3. 54 square units
4. 12 square units
5. 63 square units
6. 112 square units
7. 144 square units
8. 78 square units
9. 12.25 square units
10. 38.5 square units

Page 222: 246 square feet with justification

Page 223: $34\frac{1}{2}$ square yards with justification

Page 224

1. B
2. D
3. C
4. A
5. D
6. C
7. D
8. A

9. Any figure with an area equal to 16 square units.
10. Any figure with an area equal to 15 square units.

Page 225: A flag

Page 226: Plenty of room

Page 227

1. 28.26 square inches
2. 50.24 square inches
3. 113.04 square centimeters
4. 153.86 square centimeters
5. 254.34 square inches
6. 314 square inches
7. 12.56 square centimeters
8. 78.5 square inches
9. 200.96 square centimeters
10. 63.585 square inches

Page 228

1. 6.28 centimeters
2. 12.56 centimeters
3. 37.68 inches
4. 25.12 centimeters
5. 56.52 inches
6. 43.96 inches
7. 18.84 centimeters
8. 62.8 inches
9. 50.24 centimeters
10. 31.4 inches

Page 229

1. 565.2 square inches
2. 62.8 inches
3. 301.44 cm
4. 75.36 cm
5. 2,307.9 square millimeters (or 23.079 square cm)

Page 230

1. Rectangle, because it is 128 square inches, while the other is 78.5 square inches.
2. No, he needs 50.24 and only has 36 inches.
3. 226.08 square inches
4. around $1\frac{5}{8}$ pounds

Page 231

1. B
2. C
3. D
4. C
5. C
6. A
7. D
8. B

9. 37.68 inches
10. 153.86 square inches

Page 232: It raises a stink

Page 233: Scrambled eggs

Page 234

1. 45 cubic centimeters
2. 40 cubic centimeters
3. 8 cubic centimeters
4. 420 cubic centimeters
5. 42 cubic centimeters
6. 216 cubic centimeters
7. 60 cubic centimeters
8. 756 cubic centimeters

Page 235

1. 72 cubic inches
2. 125 cubic inches
3. 192 cubic inches
4. 512 cubic inches
5. 360 cubic inches
6. 224 cubic inches
7. 180 cubic inches
8. 140 cubic inches

Page 236

1. 96
2. 8,640
3. Yes, it holds 560 cubic inches.
4. No, it only holds 512 cubic inches.

Page 237

1. $6 \times 6 \times 3$
2. $5 \times 7 \times 2$

3. triangle has a base of 12 inches and height of 6 inches; the height of the prism is 10 inches
4. triangle has a base of 15 inches and height of 10 inches; the height of the prism is 12 inches

Page 238

1. D
2. B
3. C
4. A
5. B
6. D
7. D
8. A
9. Any figure with a volume of 32 cubic inches.
10. Box 2 since it is 343 cubic inches compared to 315 cubic inches.

Page 240: Carpet

Page 241: A highway

Page 242

Circle graph should show the following: Cola 35%, Root Beer 25%, Lemon Lime 17%, Grape 8%, Orange 5%, Cherry 10%

Page 243

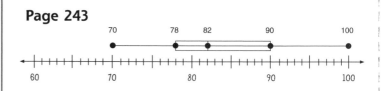

Page 244

Answers will vary, for example:

1. Turn on water and fill tub to $\frac{1}{3}$ full.
2. Turn water off and soak in tub.
3. Water too cold; add hot water.
4. Water too hot; add cold water.
5. Drain tub.

Page 245

1. Answers will vary, for example, the median in Sparkman's class is higher, or Johnson's range is much broader than Sparkmans class.

2. Answers will vary, for example, Richard's class has a smaller range, or scores are clustered closer together in Richard's class, or the upper score in Martinez's class is much higher.

3. Answers will vary.

EMC 3019 • Basic Math Skills, Grade 6 • ©2003 by Evan-Moor Corp.

Page 246

1. C	5. D
2. B	6. C
3. C	7. D
4. C	8. C

9.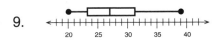

10.

Test Scores

Stem	Leaves
7	2 5
8	0 5 9
9	0 5 6 6 9 9

Page 247: The banana split

Page 248: Gooseberries

Page 249

1. 18	9. 6
2. 40	10. 7
3. 19	11. 19.5
4. 30	12. 27
5. 10	13. 32
6. 21	14. 19 and 21 (bimodal)
7. 32	15. no mode
8. 14	16. 24

Page 250

1. 11, 22.2, 23, 23
2. 8, 4.625, 4, 4
3. 0, 6, 6, 6
4. 18, 28, 26.5; none
5. 30, 55, 55; none

Page 251
Answers will vary

Page 252
1. 30

2. 10 (only one since 60 isn't a possible test score)

3. 38.35

4. No, it would have to be 73 and that isn't a possible test score.

5. 39

6. Any value between 0 and 50 except 39; 50 values can accomplish the goal.

Page 253

1. B	5. C
2. B	6. A
3. C	7. D
4. A	8. C

9. Any value greater than 44 will work; new median values will vary depending on value selected.
10. 54 with explanation

Page 254: Time to get a new car

Page 255: One know the stops,
the other stops the nose

Page 256

1. $\frac{1}{6}$
2. $\frac{1}{6}$
3. $\frac{1}{3}$
4. $\frac{1}{2}$
5. $\frac{1}{2}$
6. 0
7. $\frac{1}{2}$
8. $\frac{1}{2}$
9. $\frac{1}{2}$
10. $\frac{1}{4}$
11. 0
12. 1

Page 257

1. $\frac{1}{9}$
2. $\frac{1}{3}$
3. $\frac{1}{2}$
4. $\frac{1}{18}$
5. $\frac{1}{9}$
6. $\frac{1}{9}$
7. $\frac{4}{9}$
8. $\frac{5}{9}$
9. $\frac{1}{8}$
10. $\frac{1}{2}$
11. 0
12. 1

Page 258

1. Any circular spinner with $\frac{1}{2}$ labeled 1, $\frac{1}{4}$ labeled 2, and $\frac{1}{4}$ labeled 3.

2. Any circular spinner with $\frac{1}{3}$ labeled red, $\frac{1}{3}$ labeled blue, and $\frac{1}{3}$ labeled green.

3. Any circular spinner with $\frac{1}{5}$ labeled A, $\frac{2}{5}$ labeled B, and $\frac{2}{5}$ labeled C.

4. Any circular spinner with $\frac{1}{4}$ labeled red, $\frac{1}{2}$ labeled white, $\frac{1}{8}$ labeled blue, and $\frac{1}{8}$ labeled green.

5. Any circular spinner with $\frac{1}{4}$ labeled 2, $\frac{1}{4}$ labeled 3, $\frac{1}{4}$ labeled 4, $\frac{1}{8}$ labeled 1, and $\frac{1}{8}$ labeled 5.

Page 259

1. 3, 3, 4, 4, 7, 7
2. 2, 8, 10, 12, 16, 20
3. 1, 3, 5, 6, 6, 6
4. 5, 10, 10, 12, 13, 15

Page 260

1. B
2. C
3. A
4. D
5. D
6. B
7. D
8. C

9. Any spinner with $\frac{1}{2}$ A, $\frac{1}{4}$ B, and $\frac{1}{4}$ C.

10. P (A or B) = $\frac{3}{4}$

Page 261: You can shut an umbrella up

Page 262: Drop in sometime

Page 263

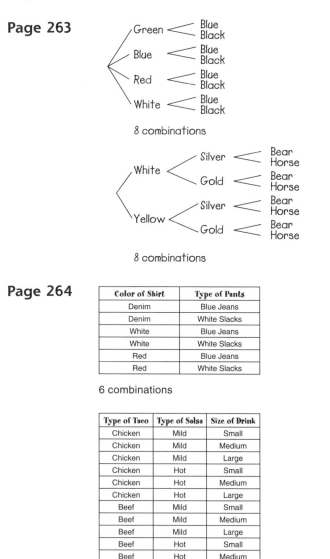

Page 264

Color of Shirt	Type of Pants
Denim	Blue Jeans
Denim	White Slacks
White	Blue Jeans
White	White Slacks
Red	Blue Jeans
Red	White Slacks

6 combinations

Type of Taco	Type of Salsa	Size of Drink
Chicken	Mild	Small
Chicken	Mild	Medium
Chicken	Mild	Large
Chicken	Hot	Small
Chicken	Hot	Medium
Chicken	Hot	Large
Beef	Mild	Small
Beef	Mild	Medium
Beef	Mild	Large
Beef	Hot	Small
Beef	Hot	Medium
Beef	Hot	Large

12 combinations

Page 265

1. 15
2. 12
3. 12
4. 24
5. 42
6. 144
7. Answers will vary.

Page 266

1. 32; Yes, they are all different.

2.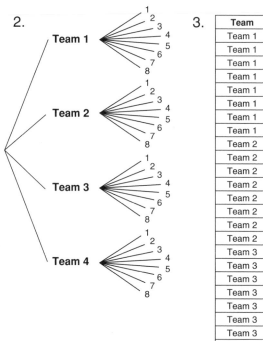

3.

Team	Player Number
Team 1	1
Team 1	2
Team 1	3
Team 1	4
Team 1	5
Team 1	6
Team 1	7
Team 1	8
Team 2	1
Team 2	2
Team 2	3
Team 2	4
Team 2	5
Team 2	6
Team 2	7
Team 2	8
Team 3	1
Team 3	2
Team 3	3
Team 3	4
Team 3	5
Team 3	6
Team 3	7
Team 3	8

4. Answers will vary.

Page 267

1. D
2. A
3. D
4. B
5. D
6. D
7. A
8. B

9.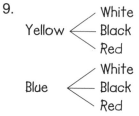

10.

Color of Paint	Color of Paper
Yellow	White
Yellow	Black
Yellow	Red
Blue	White
Blue	Black
Blue	Red

EMC 3019 • Basic Math Skills, Grade 6 • ©2003 by Evan-Moor Corp.